The Unfinished Business of 1776

The Unfinished Business of 1776

Why the American Revolution Never Ended

Thomas Richards Jr.

NEW YORK
LONDON

Map on page vii: Emma Willard, *A series of maps to Willard's History of the United States, or, Republic of America. Designed for Schools and Private Libraries* (New York: White, Gallaher, & White, 1828), courtesy of Library of Congress Geography and Map Division Washington, DC

Map on page 237: "Lesser United States" map from D.W. Meinig, *The Shaping of America: A Geographical Perspective on 500 Years of History: Volume 2: Continental America, 1800–1867*, volume 2 (New Haven, CT: Yale University Press, 1995), copyright Yale University Press

Published in the United States by The New Press, New York, 2026
Distributed by Two Rivers Distribution

ISBN 978-1-62097-924-2 (hc)
ISBN 978-1-62097-997-6 (ebook)

CIP data is available

The New Press publishes books that promote and enrich public discussion and understanding of the issues vital to our democracy and to a more equitable world. These books are made possible by the enthusiasm of our readers; the support of a committed group of donors, large and small; the collaboration of our many partners in the independent media and the not-for-profit sector; booksellers, who often hand-sell New Press books; librarians; and above all by our authors.

www.thenewpress.org

Composition by Westchester Publishing Services
This book was set in Adobe Caslon Pro

Printed in the United States of America

2 4 6 8 10 9 7 5 3

For Fran, Caleb, and Jo

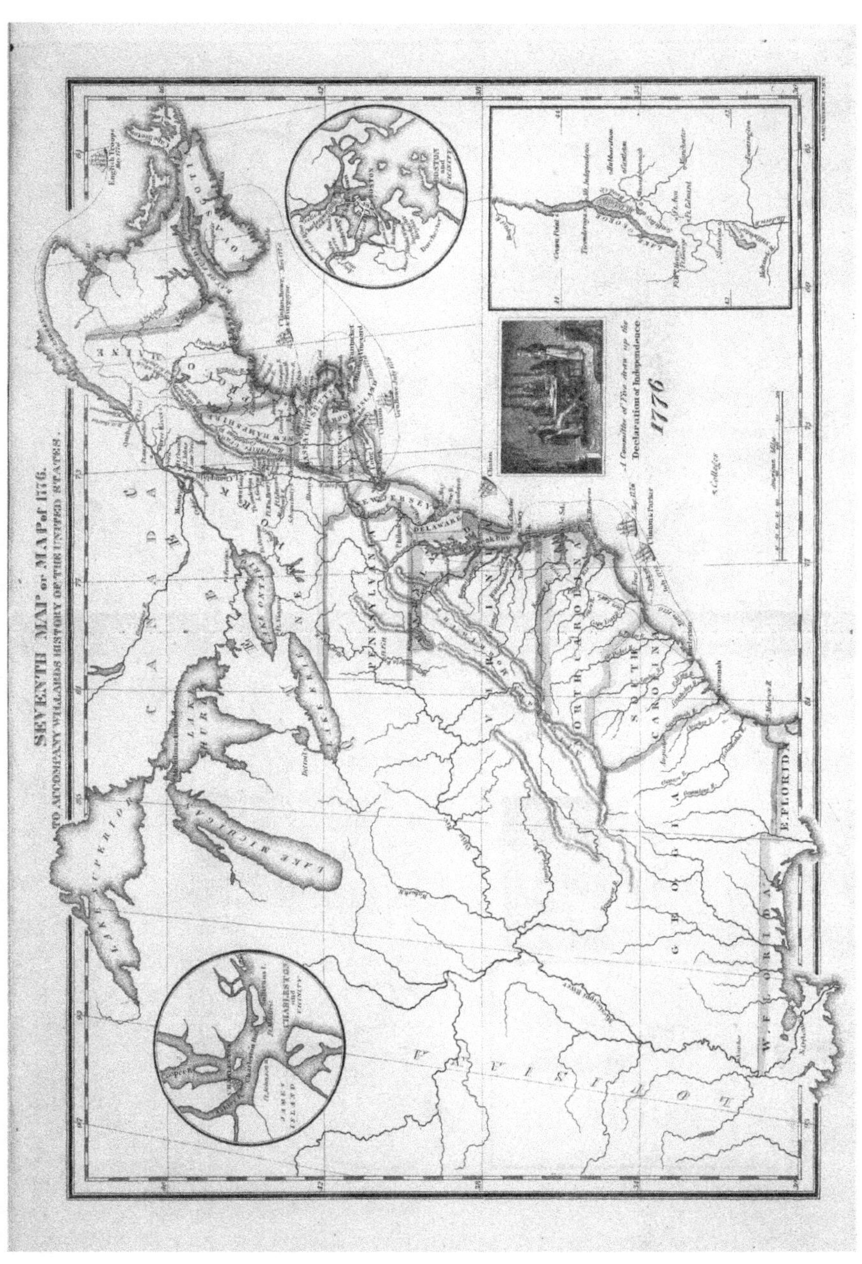

Produced in 1828 by Emma Willard, this map was part of the textbook *History of the United States, or Republic of America*. Visually, it reveals a very unfinished United States in 1776. Its production also reveals the unfinished American Revolution, as Willard spent much of her life advocating for increased female education.

Contents

The Unfinished Business of 1776

Introduction

The American Revolution was an inspirational and egalitarian fight for freedom. It challenged and overcame existing power structures, opening doors for thousands of Americans that would have remained forever closed under the hierarchical, stultifying rule of Great Britain. It made it possible for the non-elite—including women, black people, and the poor—to imagine a future where (paraphrasing the immortal words of Thomas Jefferson) they would be able to enjoy their own liberties and pursue their own happiness. In a harsh world of myriad divisions, the Revolution briefly united Americans around what they called a "common cause," and in doing so it shattered the injustices of the Old World while unveiling the promises of the New. Even after the Revolution ended, it continued—and continues—to inspire not just Americans, but millions around the world who long for their own freedom.

Or . . .

The American Revolution was a vicious, violent, and tragic struggle for power that pitted the local American elite—the so-called Founding Fathers—against a distant British Empire that was in fact quite benign, at least by the standards of the time. To co-opt the people they deemed the "lower sort," the Founding Fathers employed soaring rhetoric about liberty and equality, but they never meant what they said. On the contrary: After the Revolution, women remained subordinate to men, black people remained enslaved, Native people's independence was eroded and destroyed, and most poor white men—the supposed "winners" of the Revolution—still remained poor. The words of the Declaration of Independence were not inspirational but hypocritical, and this hypocrisy has continued to inform U.S. domestic and international policies ever since.

When many Americans cry freedom and equality, what they really mean is power and wealth.

For a quarter of a millennium, these two versions of the American Revolution—one triumphant, the other tragic—have lived side by side. Each version has leapfrogged the other in ascendancy, depending on the events and needs of the particular period. Neither version, however, has ever succeeded in erasing the other.[1]

Because both versions are true. The American Revolution was inspirational *and* tragic, profound *and* hypocritical, brilliant *and* brutal—ultimately, it was *incomplete*. This argument is not simply one of hindsight. On the contrary, in the years and decades after the Revolution, thousands of Americans said the same thing.

A Revolution in Three Acts

To understand how Americans of the early republic viewed their revolution, we need to briefly review the history of the Revolution itself, for it was this history that shaped Americans' perceptions of the Revolution's legacy. To them—and to us still—it was a revolution in three acts.

Act I, usually dated from 1763 to 1775–76, was an era of revolutionary escalation. Every American middle schooler has been forced to memorize the series of almost interminable British parliamentary acts, from the 1764 Sugar Act to the 1773 Coercive Acts—"Intolerable Acts" to the Patriots—each of which generated a colonial response. Each colonial response in turn led to a British counterresponse. At first, the British government sought amelioration, but eventually British leaders decided to bring the colonists to heel. The early acts were spawned by Great Britain's stunning victory over France and its Native allies in the French and Indian War (the Seven Years' War in Europe), which gave the British nearly all French holdings in North America. This incredible military triumph was made possible by two crucial developments: First, the British government's willingness to assume massive debts to gain ultimate victory; second, after several years of military disasters in North America, British military leaders' recognition that colonial support was crucial for victory. By 1763, these developments caused two differing responses in Britain and the colonies: in Britain, a belief that colonists should help pay off the debt; in North America, colonists' belief that they had been partners in the victory and should now be treated as equal partners in the empire—or, at the very least, left to manage their own internal affairs.

It is all too easy to romanticize these years; what may be taught to American schoolchildren as a story of good versus evil was much more complicated. After all, two of the British acts so hated by the colonials were, by the standards of the time, quite enlightened. The Proclamation Act of 1763, passed in the wake of a massive Native rebellion against British expansion known as Pontiac's War, was an attempt by Parliament to keep British colonists from crossing the Appalachians and encroaching on Native land. The 1774 Quebec Act gave Catholics in Quebec more rights and autonomy. Both of these assurances—Native independence and Catholic autonomy—outraged most colonists, who desperately desired Native land and, as devout Protestants, were fiercely anti-Catholic.

At the same time, these years *do* deserve to be romanticized. These were the years when British colonists of both genders, and of all classes and races, took to the streets to protest British policies and banded together to boycott British goods. These were the years when colonial activists, many of whom had quite modest backgrounds (particularly in comparison to European nobles), started theorizing about natural rights, self-determination, representative government, and freedom of conscience—to name just a few of the revolutionary ideas they pondered. Although these years were hardly utopian, they were nonetheless years of hope and possibility, punctuated by a growing belief among thousands and thousands of Americans that first *their* world and eventually *the* world could be different—more just, more egalitarian, and more free. To realize their lofty goals, American revolutionaries embraced coalitions that spanned both sexes, multiple races, all classes, and different political ideologies, and they believed that everyone could be American and everywhere could be America.

The sense that anything was possible was best reflected in the two documents, both written in 1776, that marked the end of Act I: Tom Paine's *Common Sense* and the Declaration of Independence, authored primarily by Thomas Jefferson. Together, *Common Sense* and the Declaration embodied the Revolution's most noble ideals and most inspiring possibilities, which were representative of not just Paine and Jefferson, but the broader American public. It was not just Jefferson who believed in the natural rights of "life, liberty, and the pursuit of happiness," but tens of thousands of Americans. It was not just Paine who believed America could become a haven from tyranny—in his words, an "asylum for mankind"—but tens of thousands of Americans. Indeed, these same thousands of Americans had been saying similar things for years, haltingly at first, but, by 1776, ever more forcefully and coherently. No wonder both the Declaration and *Common Sense* have had long afterlives. Revolutionaries in Latin America resurrected *Common Sense* to explain their own rebellions decades later, while the U.S. Declaration of Independence became a model for many other declarations of independence throughout the world.[2] In the United States itself, rare is the presidential campaign speech that does not at least invoke the Declaration or its ideals in some fashion.

Yet these heady days of the Revolution would not last. 1776 was the culmination of Act I, but it also marked the beginning of Act II: the Revolutionary War. As with Act I, Americans have also overly romanticized Act II. The everyday valor of the Minutemen, the stirring leadership of George Washington, the stoic perseverance of Continental soldiers at Valley Forge, remarkable battlefield victories at Trenton, Saratoga, and Yorktown, to name just a few—all resonate in American lore. By focusing on the heroism alone, however, we mask the war's truly horrendous nature. In terms of casualties per capita, it remains, after the Civil War, the second worst conflict in all U.S. history. It was not just a war for independence, but a brutal civil war that pitted neighbor against neighbor, particularly in the South—and both sides perpetrated horrendous atrocities. Wherever soldiers went, misery followed, in the form of not just death on the battlefield, but rape, murder, disease, starvation, and horrendous conditions for prisoners of war. The war shattered much of the hope, optimism, and revolutionary fervor of the prewar years—but, crucially, it did not erase the memory entirely.

How, then, to rebuild this shattered world and bring back the best years of the Revolution? That was the question for Act III, which lasted from the final victory at Yorktown in 1781 to the election of George Washington to the presidency in 1789, which was made possible by the writing and ratification of the Constitution in the summer of 1787. For some, such as former Continental soldier Daniel Shays, the answer was *more* revolution—more protests and more armed resistance—hence, Shays's Rebellion, which challenged state authority in western Massachusetts. For others, the answer lay in the state governments, which could best respond to the diverse needs of their constituents while avoiding the centralization of power. State autonomy was further aided by the weak national government prescribed in the Articles of Confederation. It was centralized power in Great Britain, after all, that had spurred the Revolution in the first place. For the men who would eventually be dubbed the Framers of the Constitution, however, state power was the entirely wrong answer. Instead, these wealthy, well-educated men looked to form a new, more powerful central government—at first, entirely in secret. The result, after months of exhaustive, cantankerous deliberations in Philadelphia, was the U.S. Constitution.

It is no knock on the Constitution to state that nearly every American had at least some problem with it. There was certainly no eighteenth-century version of the "pocket Constitution" that became a fad among modern Tea Partiers in the late 2000s and early 2010s. This contemporary skepticism is hardly surprising. The document was a product of months of intense, often bitter, compromises—and this was among men who all believed a new government was necessary, to say nothing of the thousands of Americans who believed it was not. Some Americans believed the Constitution gave far too much power to the federal government, while others believed it did not give enough. Some Americans believed it was too proslavery, others it was too antislavery. Many attacked it for not containing a bill of rights, or for giving the federal government the power to tax or for its allowance for a standing army (at least for a certain length of time), or for a vast range of other reasons. During the state-by-state ratification process, most adult men weighed in, and nearly half rejected the document entirely. If women, enslaved people, and Native people had been given a vote (none of which was ever considered), many of them would have rejected it too. In the end, the required nine states voted yes on ratification, making the Constitution the supreme law of the land. It remained to be seen how, exactly, this government would really work in practice.

Post-revolutionary Americans may have still lived in an era of mutability, but not *everything* was up in the air. These certainties started with U.S. independence itself. Independence had been the primary raison d'être of American revolutionaries, and Americans still deem the Fourth of July, rightfully, "Independence Day." It had been won militarily—and definitively—at Yorktown in 1781, which was then codified diplomatically with the signing of the Treaty of Paris two years later. Another certainty was republican government, in which the American people (defined differently for different people) had some say in choosing their leaders. By the end of the war, the Loyalist population had either fled the United States or quietly accepted the new status quo: There would be no return to monarchy. All other Americans, including the country's leaders, supported some form of a republic, most crucially George Washington. He—and he alone—had the prestige and popularity to establish a dictatorship. Yet, like all his peers, his worldview would support no such vision.

One key measure that buttressed republican government in the early years of independence was the states' abolition of primogeniture and entail. Primogeniture was the European tradition in which property was transferred to the oldest son alone, while entail ensured that large estates remained intact over generations. As we shall see in chapter 6, Americans believed that these measures were necessary to help guarantee economic equality, which they believed was necessary for a republic to function successfully. At an even more basic level, however, these measures ensured that the United States would not develop its own aristocracy, which was further cemented by the Constitution's prohibition of noble titles. Ultimately, these measures did not guarantee economic equality, but they did guarantee that the United States—at least for the time being—would not be dominated by a few massively wealthy landed magnates who could undermine and then destroy representative government to suit their own interests.

The third certainty was religious liberty. The Constitution prohibited religious oaths, and it never established an official national religion akin to

Anglicanism in England or Catholicism in France. To be sure, in 1787 many states *did* maintain their own state religions, and more than a few maintained them for quite some time. Congregationalism remained the official religion of Massachusetts until 1833, the last state to uphold an official state religion. Yet even in states like Massachusetts that gave tax revenue to their established churches, religious liberty, broadly defined, was never in doubt. Even the most religiously inclined Americans recognized that the particular circumstances of the United States mandated against religious persecution, for there were simply too many Protestant denominations, not to mention about 25,000 Catholics and about 2,000 Jews. Anything but religious liberty would set the country against itself. No wonder, then, that some of the first official declarations of the Revolution were ones that mandated "freedom of conscience," as religious freedom was deemed at the time.

This is not a book that debates the specific merits (of which there are many) or flaws (of which there are also many) of the Constitution and its certainties. Instead, it focuses on what the ratification and implementation of the Constitution signaled to Americans at the time. To replace revolutionary idealism, the Framers created a systemic governing document that they believed would produce safety, structure, and order for the country, all while still preserving some form of representative government. In other words, they believed the United States and its people needed to get back to normal—or, perhaps, become normal for the very first time.

Yet many other Americans, of both genders and all races, from all regions, from the wealthiest to the poorest, did not want to get back to normal. The end of Act III did not mean people forgot Act I. The simple fact that the Constitution seemed to work did not mean that the ideological values of the Revolution—liberty, equality, harmony, self-determination—had been fully realized. To many Americans, the American Revolution may have ended, but the real work of revolution remained. Possibilities remained open, different futures beckoned. The Constitution, after all, was short and decidedly (and at times deliberately) ambiguous. Just what the United States would become was still unwritten.

There was unfinished business to attend to.

"By the Standards of Their Time"

In the Gettysburg Address, Abraham Lincoln deemed the Revolutionary generation "our fathers." Perhaps, looking back as Lincoln did in 1863, the Revolutionary generation was a parent generation (or, at least, grandfather generation) to his own Civil War generation. 250 years after the country's birth, however, the concept of "Founding Fathers" no longer holds water, because it implies too much of a similarity between now and a quarter millennium ago. Today, the Revolutionary generation should be considered much more like distant cousins at a large family reunion. They may share similar facial features and mannerisms with us, perhaps even shared interests, but they still grew up thousands of miles away and lived very different lives, without ever having met us. The Revolutionary generation and the few generations after were like us in some ways—*but they were not us.*

One constant refrain among Americans who lionize the Founding Fathers, particularly coming from conservative voices, is that we should not judge them by the standards of our time, but by theirs. In this line of reasoning, we should not condemn slaveholders because slavery was widely practiced at the time of the Revolution, nor should we condemn men's subjugation of women because that was simply the norm.

Yet the American Revolution was revolutionary precisely *because* these seemingly timeless practices of injustice were questioned, for the first time, on a widespread scale. Many Americans, including most of the Founding Fathers, expressed antislavery sentiments, and a few took deliberate antislavery actions. Many Americans—men as well as women—voiced various notions of gender equality, or at the very least supported more rights for women than they possessed at the time. In this vein, this book very much *does* judge Americans by the standards of their time. Indeed, Revolutionary-era Americans were often the ones doing the judging.

And yet, Revolutionary Americans conceived of social justice issues in very different ways than Americans consider them today. Could real economic equality be achieved without the redistribution of property? In the aftermath of the Revolution, Americans believed it could. Would gender equality involve women's full and equal political participation in the U.S.

government? In the aftermath of the Revolution, many women and men believed wholeheartedly in "the rights of women"—but most did not believe that women should vote, let alone hold office. And how would racial equality be achieved, between black and white people and between Native and white people, if black people and Native people needed to live apart from white people? At least some Americans, usually white people, believed this was the only way—although, as we shall see, more radical figures provided a different vision.

All these contradictions, blind spots, and impossibilities point toward a final, central argument of this book: The thousands of Americans who were unhappy with the results of the American Revolution had real grievances, ones that we should take seriously. They then made serious attempts to improve the United States for the better, at least as they imagined "better" to be. We should celebrate their attitudes and convictions, particularly in our modern world of cynicism and distrust. The men and women in this book believed in ideas and futures they thought were noble, and they fought for them; their stories deserve to be told. However, we do not necessarily have to celebrate the goals themselves. Certainly, some goals do deserve more celebration than others—but even the seemingly most principled of them possessed characteristics that would be unfamiliar to us today.

What This Book Is—and What it Isn't

Each of the following chapters considers a particular promise of the Revolution: the right to have rights; the right to revolution; gender equality; racial equality; political harmony and nonpartisanship; economic equality; universal revolution; Indigenous rights; the right to found a new nation; and, once again, racial equality. Each chapter recounts the featured promise through a story that best illuminates its history in the decades after the Revolution, in roughly chronological order from the First Federal Congress in 1789 (chapter 1) through Reconstruction in the 1860s and early 1870s (chapter 9).

I have partly chosen these episodes for their geographic, chronological, and demographic diversity. From New Jersey and New York in the 1790s through Kentucky in the 1820s, to Texas and Utah in the 1850s and Philadelphia in the 1870s, the stories in this book range widely. So, too, do its characters, from Judith Sargent Murray, a writer and women's rights advocate living in the 1790s, to Lansford Hastings, an overland trail guide and would-be founder of a western republic, to Octavius Catto, a black activist from Philadelphia in the 1860s. I have also chosen them, quite frankly, because I think they are good stories, some of which are more widely known than others.

This book is not a synthesis of the first century of U.S. history (frankly, there are just too many good ones already). Nor is it a history of the memory of the American Revolution,[3] and by no means does it make the provocative claim that the American Revolution was actually a century-long affair. There is a good case to make that the Revolution did indeed end with the ratification of the Constitution in 1789, or at the very latest with the election of Thomas Jefferson to the presidency in 1800. Rather, this book argues that, even if the Revolution ended, its legacy was not set in stone—and Americans of all backgrounds knew this. To use an extended metaphor: if the American Revolution birthed the United States, it remained only an infant in the 1780s, a toddler in the 1790s, and a child in the 1830s. Just as an infant or a child cannot change its core biological makeup, the United States could no longer change some of its fundamental characteristics, but its final form—its adulthood—remained a very open question. Indeed, to continue with this metaphor, the United States in its early decades was like a child who is asked, "What do you want to be when you grow up?" As with a child, answers to this question for the future United States ranged from the very achievable to the more difficult to the preposterous.

In this way, this book is a history of the *possible*. Like all human beings, Americans during the early republic made decisions about their lives and their actions based upon their predictions about the future, and many times their predictions were based upon the results and promises of the American Revolution. They imagined a different world than the world that the United States ultimately made, and we must understand how and why they imagined it, and how they hoped to realize that world, to understand the historical events they experienced and often propelled.

As part of understanding what is possible, this book sometimes strays outside the geographic boundaries of the United States (which, for nearly all this book, did not match the country's current borders). There are two reasons for this. First, to understand what was possible we need to consider the history of other revolutions, where events sometimes mirrored those in the United States—and other times dramatically differed, which is precisely the point. When considering the history of other revolutions, it becomes even more clear: Events *could* have turned out differently. There was no set path to U.S. history, and how that path could have been different is revealed in the paths of other countries. Second, these comparisons are not after-the-fact anachronistic comparisons, because *Americans at the time made the same comparisons*. For the first century of U.S. history, Americans lived in a world of revolutions: France, Haiti, Latin America, and the European revolutions of 1848, to name only the most famous. They read about all of them, for newspapers were both cheap and widespread, and when they did, they constantly considered how exactly these world events reflected on their own revolution and on the history of their young republic more generally. Radicals considered foreign revolutions as aspirational, asking, *Why did that* not *happen here? And how could we make it* eventually *happen?* Conservatives often considered the opposite: *How do we* prevent *that from happening here?* This book asks those same questions.

More broadly, to understand how Americans during the early republic considered the future, we need to restore a sense of openness, possibility, and—in the words of one historian— "boundlessness," because that is how Americans of the time thought about the next day, the next year, and the next decade.[4] When it came to the future of the United States and the future of everyday Americans, *everything* may not have been possible, but *most things* were. As Tom Paine wrote in *Common Sense* just before independence, "History sufficiently informs us that the bravest achievements were always accomplished in the non-age of a nation."[5] Just because the American Revolution had ended, the United States was *still* young—and Americans could *still* make the "bravest achievements."

The work of the Revolution was still unfinished.

A Note on Terminology and Sources

This book was written between 2019 and 2024, a time in which the conventions for describing various groups of people and ethnic identities have changed—and continue to change at the time of this writing. I have no doubt that these conventions will *continue* to change, and my words will, at some point, appear old-fashioned, perhaps even derogatory (although I very much hope not the latter). I accept this as one small hazard of writing the history of people and ideas that still matter today.

When referring to Americans of African descent, I have chosen to use the lowercase "black" rather than capitalized "Black." At the time of this writing, this terminology remains in flux. I have chosen the former because, quite simply, it is how black Americans in this book increasingly referred to themselves in the first half of the nineteenth century. They did this on purpose, abandoning the identity of "African," more common at the time of the Revolution itself, to emphasize their innate Americanness. They deemed themselves "black Americans" and "colored Americans"—and *American* was the most important identifier.[6] For the most part, I use "Indigenous" or "Native" instead of "Indian" to describe the people descended from those who first inhabited the continent, although I continue to use "Indian" when the passage is referring to how white Americans understood Native peoples. In every case possible, I use the more specific names of Native nations (e.g., Cherokees, Choctaws) for that is how Native peoples identified themselves first and foremost. I use "nations" instead of "tribes" because that is what they were: sovereign, sophisticated nations that were deeply rooted in North American history, not primitive tribes removed from the passage of time.[7]

Regarding sources: I began a PhD program in early U.S. history in 2011, and I started reading works of history for more than a decade before that. This book represents my own ideas about the early United States that I have formulated after reading so much on the subject. I have made the utmost effort to cite every direct quotation and every specific piece of information found in other works, but I have no doubt that I have made some mistakes and omissions. Moreover, I have made no attempt to cite *every* book and article on a subject, a choice I have made for reasons of word count and my own sanity. Nevertheless, my deepest and sincerest thanks are owed to the hundreds and hundreds of scholars who continue to produce fine history. It is more relevant than ever.

1

Revolutionary Finale: The Bill of Rights, 1789–91

It was June of 1788 in Richmond, Virginia's newly minted capital, where Virginians had arrived in droves to see one of the greatest orators in the young United States. He was none other than Patrick Henry, who, in the same city thirteen years before, had given one of the most famous speeches in American political history. In 1775, as Great Britain escalated its attacks on American liberties, Henry sought to raise the Virginia militia, believing that conflict with Britain was inevitable. Moderates in the Virginia colonial government opposed him for his radicalism, arguing it was too soon to resort to arms. At that point, Henry rose to challenge them. "What would they have?" he reportedly asked of the fence-sitters. "Is life so dear, or peace so sweet, as to be purchased at the price of chains and slavery? Forbit it, Almighty God! I know not what course others may take; but as for me, give me liberty or give me death!"[1] Thanks to the speech, Henry's motion carried the day. The Virginia House of Burgesses authorized the Patriot militia—and war would soon follow.

By 1788, Henry's leadership during the Revolution had made him a legend in his home state, particularly but not exclusively for his famous speech. His fellow Virginians knew that, if Henry felt passionately about something, his oratory would not disappoint. And, in 1788, he *did* feel passionately about something. As he did thirteen years ago, he rose to address his fellow delegates in the Virginia Assembly, using words that echoed some of his language from 1775. "The stile of the government (*We, the people*) was introduced perhaps to recommend it to the people at large; to those citizens who are to be levelled and degraded to the lowest degree; who are likened to a *herd*; and who, by the operation of this blessed system, are to be transformed from respectable, independent citizens, to abject, dependent subjects or slaves."[2]

This time, however, it was not the British government that would put Americans in chains. Instead, Patrick Henry was referring to the U.S. Constitution.

Betraying the "Spirit of '76"

This is not how most Americans think about their Constitution today. On the contrary, the document is revered as the culminating moment of the American Revolution, when the Framers tied a bow on the Revolution's achievements while simultaneously sparing the young nation from the calamities and atrocities experienced by other post-revolutionary societies—France, Russia, China, to name just a few. Yet this was not how many white American men viewed the Constitution at the time. To them, the Constitution portended a powerful centralized—they used the word "consolidated"—national government that would quickly slide into despotism. If the Constitution became the law of the land, they believed, it would be a betrayal of all they had fought for since 1775. Of course, this is to say nothing of women, the nearly half-million black Americans, and the thousands and thousands of Native people who also had a stake in the politics of the United States—but, with the exception of a small number of free black men who were able to vote for their representatives to the state ratification conventions, these groups were not asked to give approval. As we shall see in later chapters, they too would weigh in on the post-Revolutionary settlement, in various ways.

By 1787, nearly all Americans believed the governing document of the first national government, the Articles of Confederation, was deeply flawed. Under the Articles, the unicameral Congress, in which every state had a single vote, lacked the ability to tax, could not regulate interstate commerce, and was not allowed to raise an army—which, in the aftermath of a revolt of western Massachusetts farmers led by Daniel Shays in 1786, looked to be increasingly necessary. A broke and feeble national government of course needed fixing.

But, to the horror of many Americans, the Framers of the Constitution went way too far. Instead of amending the Articles as they had promised, the Framers threw them out entirely, crafting a government with sweeping powers over seemingly all aspects of American life—and behind closed doors, no less! Although the Federalists, as those who supported the Constitution deemed themselves, could argue that the powers of the central government were "enumerated," meaning the government could only do what it explicitly said in the Constitution and nothing more, Antifederalists could counter with words in the Constitution itself: Article I, Section 8 gave Congress the power to "make all Laws which shall be necessary and proper for carrying into Execution" the powers the Constitution gave it. The Antifederalists argued that, when combined with the Preamble that tasked the new government with "Promoting the General Welfare," the Necessary and Proper Clause gave Congress the power to do just about anything. As one fearful Antifederalist put it, Congress would possess "great and uncontrolable powers."[3]

Antifederalists had many, many more objections to the Constitution (the compiled papers of the Antifederalists runs to seven volumes), but at the heart of most Antifederalist concerns were lessons drawn from Americans' all-too-recent history. Before the Revolution, Americans believed they possessed a broad range of liberties enshrined in the unwritten British constitution, as well as in written documents like the Petition of Right (1628) and the English Bill of Rights (1689). Yet, beginning in the mid-1760s, the British Parliament started to chip away and eventually eliminate those rights, taxing Americans without their consent, eliminating trial by jury, sending professional armies to monitor the unruly colonists, and eroding local representative government by trying to take away power from the colonial assemblies. For most Patriots, the bulwark of liberty became their state governments, many of which codified their own bill of rights. States then defended these rights by raising militias and, much more inconsistently, sending men to serve in the Continental Army.

Now, however, by drastically curbing state power, the Constitution was destroying all the gains that had been made since the Revolution. In the words of one Antifederalist, the Constitution was a "total dereliction of those sentiments which animated us in 1775."[4] Another remembered how "a few years ago we fought for our liberty," but now, he argued, Americans were throwing it all away.[5] In the New York ratifying convention, Thomas Tredwell bluntly stated, "With this Constitution, we have departed widely from the principles and political faith of '76, when the spirit of liberty ran high."[6]

Opposition to the Constitution was not confined to members of the upper class. On the contrary, Antifederalism was a big tent that also found adherents among thousands of Americans who hailed from the "middling" and "lower sort"—from farmers in North Carolina to mechanics in Philadelphia. Unlike the Framers, these people believed in small-d democracy—the idea that power should originate with ordinary people. And, amid a dreadful postwar economic slump, they celebrated the fact that many state governments responded to the will of their constituents by offering tax relief for the poor at the expense of the rich. These leveling measures were just, for, as one Antifederalist put it, the wealthy were "useless and idle drones" who lived "on the common stock."[7] The fact that non-elites could not only be heard but also influence others was a product of the American Revolution's egalitarianism, one its most radical legacies. The Revolution gave space for middling and, in a few cases, even members of the lower sort to openly engage in politics. Throughout the 1780s, they were making themselves heard.[8]

In hindsight, some of the Antifederalists' arguments appear deeply naive, even silly. How could a national government *not* have the ability to tax, or to raise an army? What sort of fantasy world were the likes of Antifederalists like Patrick Henry and Samuel Adams living in? When some Antifederalists praised how well the United States was doing, were they serious? Patrick Henry, for example, declared, "I know of no danger awaiting us. Public and private security are to be found here in the highest degree. . . . Our political and natural hemisphere are now equally tranquil."[9] Meanwhile, the United States was only two years removed from Shays's Rebellion, and there was open talk that the young confederation would soon dissolve into warring regional factions.

Behind the seemingly deliberate naivete of people like Henry, however, was a deeper phenomenon that stemmed from the American Revolution itself. Much of the Antifederalists' mindset still stemmed from Americans' optimism in those early, heady days of the conflict, before the brutal war and postwar depression. During those days, all seemed possible.[10] Many revolutionaries believed that they really were creating a new type of society. Tom Paine famously voiced this optimism in *Common Sense*, writing, "We have it in our power to begin the world over again. A situation, similar to the present, hath not happened since the days of Noah until now. The birthday of a new world is at hand."[11] Even the cantankerous pessimist John Adams got swept up in the moment, writing only a month before independence, "We are in the midst of a revolution, the most complete, unexpected, and remarkable of any in the history of nations" (although Adams then complained about how much "drudgery" he was forced to do to ensure the Revolution's success).[12] By 1787, Federalists like Madison and in particular the Anglophilic Alexander Hamilton had long cast aside these sentiments as fanciful utopianism, but Antifederalists did not want to abandon the revolutionary moment so quickly. Were Americans really going to revert to the old ways of doing things, they asked, simply because the United States had suffered a rough patch?

At times, there was a certain mystical quality to Antifederalist rhetoric. Patrick Henry maintained that even if Europe once again threatened the United States, no standing army would be needed. "I would recur to the American spirit to defend us;—that spirit which has enabled us to surmount the greatest difficulties."[13] Antifederalists' optimism may have been naive, but it was sincere. At their best, Antifederalists posed real questions about how to ensure the broadest representation possible in a republic, and how that representation would ensure the greatest prosperity for the greatest number of people. In essence, they offered a democratic critique of the Constitution, arguing that the Constitution took power from the people and gave it to "aristocratic junto's of the *well born few*" (italics in original).[14]

Melancton Smith, a New York merchant and prominent Antifederalist, contended that the Constitution gave the American people only a "shadow of representation." The people directly elected only members of the House of Representatives (until 1913, the Senate was chosen by state legislatures), and even that body was deeply flawed. With each representative elected from thirty thousand inhabitants and serving for two years, the House of Representatives, like the Senate, would only serve the wishes of the wealthy,

Smith argued. What the people needed were a greater number of representatives elected annually, which would bring the "middling class of people" into the government. To Smith, only this class could actually represent all Americans. Unlike the wealthy, the middling class was forced to live "frugally" and felt "public burdens"—and therefore they would be hesitant to do anything that would harm people just like themselves.[15]

Federalists responded to Antifederalists like Smith with an ingenious bait-and-switch, first voiced by James Wilson at the Pennsylvania ratification convention. Alongside James Madison, Wilson was one of the intellectual giants of the Constitutional Convention, and at Pennsylvania's ratification convention he rose to defend his work. Antifederalists argued that the Constitution dangerously split sovereignty between the federal government and the states. They were basing this argument on a long-held political theory that stated that ultimate power needed to lie in only one body, or civil war would soon follow. Wilson denied this accusation. On the contrary, he argued, "all sovereignty rests with the people." The people could then dole out sovereignty to various other bodies—the state legislatures, the three branches of the federal government—as they saw fit (and retract it if necessary).[16] Wilson's argument implied that the Constitution would beget a democratic and populist government, far more democratic than that which the Articles of Confederation produced. Because the Articles were, in Wilson's words, "a CONFEDERATION of SOVEREIGN STATES," then the "PEOPLE . . . are not as such represented."[17] By contrast, in the Constitution, "the supreme power resides in the people."[18]

Wilson had a point about the state-centered nature of the Articles of Confederation, but presenting the Constitution as a populist, democratic document was thoroughly disingenuous. Nothing democratic or populist had occurred during the Constitutional Convention. Instead, it was fifty-five men behind closed doors trying to bring order to a disordered country that was obsessed with liberty. Many of the Constitution's electoral mechanisms—senators chosen by state legislatures, the president chosen by the Electoral College, Supreme Court justices nominated by the president and confirmed by the Senate—were specifically designed to *limit* the influence of the people. From a debating standpoint, however, Wilson's argument was inspired. After all, the Constitution even began, "We the People"—as Wilson himself noted.

But there was one problem that neither Wilson nor any other Federalist had a good answer for: The Constitution lacked a bill of rights. Some Federalists argued that a bill of rights was not needed, because most (but not all) states had their own bill of rights already. Others argued that a bill of rights was not necessary, because the people possessed all rights that were not explicitly given to the government in the Constitution. Other Federalists claimed a bill of rights would in fact be dangerous to liberty, for it was simply impossible to list *every* right the people possessed, and the federal government could exploit gaps where rights were not listed. All these relatively feeble arguments stemmed from a simple and understandable, but politically weak, explanation: The Constitution lacked a bill of rights because, when George Mason, author of the Virginia Declaration of Rights, brought it up near the end of the Constitutional Convention, the delegates had been at it for months and were simply exhausted. Probably many of the Framers recognized their glaring error, but debating a bill of rights would likely reopen old fissures and perhaps even open new ones. At best, debating a bill of rights would add several more weeks to the convention. At worst, the debate could chip away at the precarious unity that had been achieved over the final draft of the Constitution. The Framers would have to do their best at selling the Constitution without a bill of rights.

And they needed to sell it. Even though the Constitution restrained democracy in many ways, the Framers recognized that it nevertheless required democratic and populist legitimacy, for two reasons. First, practically speaking, they had no army by their side to impose the Constitution on the American people. Second, even though most of the Framers were conservatives and elitists, they were still creatures of the American Revolution and therefore ideologically committed to representative government, even if they wanted to circumscribe this representation in various ways. Some historians have labeled the implementation of the Constitution on the American people a coup (or at least coup-*ish*), but the process by which the document would become the supreme law of the United States was hardly coup-like.[19] For the Constitution to become law, nine states needed to ratify it. Ratification would be determined by ratifying conventions within each state, where delegates elected by the people of that state would vote up or down on the Constitution.

To be sure, there are valid reasons to question the democratic legitimacy of this process. Women and enslaved people did not get to vote, even though the Constitution would of course govern them as well. (Native people also did not get to vote, but for a sounder reason: They lived in separate nations independent from the United States, as the Constitution acknowledged. See chapter 7.) Yet, at the least, many states lowered the property threshold for voting, ensuring that more men could participate in this all-important, once-in-a-lifetime experiment in self-government. And, in most Northern states and even in a few Southern ones, some of these men were black.[20] When viewed in hindsight, the ratification process was not necessarily modern democracy in action—but, by the standards of 1788, it came close. Americans had not participated so widely in the public sphere since the early days of the Revolution itself.

We know the ending to this story, of course. On June 21, 1788, New Hampshire became the ninth state to ratify the Constitution, making it the supreme law of the land. Virginia and New York would follow later that year, North Carolina the year after that, with overwhelmingly Antifederalist Rhode Island holding out until May of 1790. The Federalists won.

But not completely.

"The People" Become the People

To understand how the Antifederalists gained a partial victory, we need to return to the middle of the ratification process, when ratification was not yet assured. By the end of 1787, four states had ratified the Constitution, beginning with Delaware (current license plate: the First State), followed by Pennsylvania, New Jersey, and Georgia. Delaware, New Jersey, and Georgia had all ratified unanimously. Not only did all three small states welcome the structure of the Senate that would somewhat preserve the outsized power they already held under the Articles, but Delaware and New Jersey looked forward to a time when their residents would not have to pay duties for goods coming through Philadelphia and New York City. Georgia's ratification records are sparse, but its residents likely looked forward to a time when a stronger national government would be able to better defend its borders against Native incursions from Spanish Florida. Perhaps, too, they appreciated the Constitution's built-in protections for slavery, as their neighboring South Carolinians certainly did a few months later.[21]

But if Federalists liked the seamless ratification process in these three small states, Pennsylvania's path to ratification was far more ambiguous. Yes, there too the Federalists had won, but strong-arm tactics by the Federalist-dominated Pennsylvania Assembly, followed by belligerent debates in the ratification convention itself, had left a legacy of bitterness in the state between Federalists and Antifederalists. Such was the toxicity that an Antifederalist riot even broke out in the central Pennsylvania town of Carlisle in early 1788, during which demonstrators burned James Wilson and Pennsylvania governor Thomas McKean, also a Federalist, in effigy.

Considering the Federalists' superior political resources, perhaps they could have continued to bully their way toward ratification, but what good would ratification be if half of Americans believed the process was illegitimate? The Federalists hoped to create a national government that could effectively manage crises like Shays's Rebellion, but what if the Constitution instead sparked a *series* of these rebellions? The only alternative would be rule by force, and, although the Framers wanted to limit the influence of the people on the U.S. government, no Framer wanted to eliminate republican government entirely.

After Pennsylvania, the ratification process moved to Massachusetts, the home of Shays's Rebellion. Federalists in Massachusetts knew they had to win legitimately, not only for the sake of their state, but for the sake of the Constitution's national prospects. They were boosted by their neighbors in Connecticut, which ratified the Constitution by a vote of 128 to 40 in early January. In Connecticut, state leaders were overwhelmingly Federalist, and from the scant records that survived from the ratification debates, they seemed to have swamped their opponents with both their arguments and their illustrious pedigree.[22]

Massachusetts Federalists would not have it so easy. The state, like all New England, had a long history of representative government. Since its founding 150 years before, Massachusetts's government was based upon the institution of the town meeting. In the case of ratification, each town would convene, debate, and eventually choose a delegate to send to the ratification convention in Boston. Sometimes these local debates lasted several days, for New Englanders, like all Americans, knew the stakes. And, as in Pennsylvania, Massachusetts was closely divided between Federalists and Antifederalists—but, unlike Pennsylvania, by early 1788 Massachusetts Antifederalists were fully organized for the forthcoming struggle.

The stakes were bigger in Massachusetts than in any other state, owing to both the *where* and the *when* of the Massachusetts convention. Boston had been the city where the American Revolution had first stirred, and the epicenter of revolutionary conflict between 1763 and 1776. Whichever way Massachusetts voted on the Constitution would send a powerful signal to the rest of the country. After Massachusetts would come conventions in other closely divided states: New Hampshire, South Carolina, North Carolina, New York, and most importantly Virginia, the largest state in the Union. Federalist leaders had placed much of their hopes for ratification on momentum: As more states ratified, other states would follow. But a vote against ratification in Massachusetts could also work the other way: If Massachusetts voted nay, then momentum could swing against ratification throughout the country. If Virginia then followed Massachusetts's lead, the Federalists' nightmare scenario would be well on its way to taking place, and the Constitution's prospects would be doomed.

Even before debate commenced, it was clear to both participants and observers at the Massachusetts ratifying convention that the final vote would be close. Both sides had tried to judge the results of the town meeting votes, but the results were ambiguous. Many towns sent their delegates to Boston voicing general support for the Constitution but also deep reservations about some of its characteristics—its proslavery tilt, its sweeping powers of taxation, its unelected judiciary, and its lack of a bill of rights, to name just a few. So, for nearly a month, the two sides battled each other rhetorically, with supporters and opponents trying to sway the broad middle.[23]

With ratification on a knife-edge, moderate Federalists eventually arrived at a compromise that they hoped would sway the doubters. Article VII of the Constitution stipulated that state ratifying conventions could only give an up or down vote, which was another of the Federalists' strategies. They realized that, if states were allowed to ask for changes prior to ratification, every state would seek its own conditions, and many of these conditions would be impossible to square with each other. But what if, a few Federalists at the Massachusetts convention asked, the convention requested changes not as a condition to be met *before* ratification, but as a humble request for the first Congress to take up *after* the Constitution took effect?

To persuade the fence-sitters, Federalists carried in the state's political big guns. John Hancock, he of big signature fame, was the current state governor and one of its most illustrious revolutionary leaders, but at the time of the convention he was ill and did not attend for the first several weeks. He had long held reservations about the Constitution, but the idea of suggesting amendments after ratification moved him to yes. To sway other delegates, Hancock arrived on a stretcher, then apologized for his "impropriety" for not arriving sooner. "Painful disposition of the body," he said, had prevented him from attending earlier, but now, due to "great dissimilarity of sentiments in the Convention," Hancock wished to "hazard a proposition for their consideration."[24] He then offered nine amendments to the Constitution that he would urge the first Congress to pass, following ratification.

Surprisingly, Hancock was joined by Samuel Adams, who had once been Hancock's ally in the early days of the Revolution, but since independence had opposed many of Hancock's policies and had become his main political rival. Adams, too, had reservations about the Constitution, but he also was mollified by the strategy of requesting amendments. The proposed amendments would "conciliate the minds of the convention," he argued, and they would also bear fruit nationally, for Massachusetts's "weight" would lead other states to adopt similar strategies. Tellingly, he also noted that requesting amendments would appease the "people without doors," a common eighteenth-century phrase that simply meant everyone who was not at the convention—in other words, the people in general. Adams was certainly one to know. Of all leaders of the Revolution, Adams had proven the most adept in his ability to respond to and subsequently mobilize the "people without doors" during the escalating imperial crisis in the late 1760s and early 1770s in Boston. In many ways, Massachusetts's revolutionary bona fides—its "weight," as Hancock put it—were due more to Adams than to anyone else.[25]

When the final vote was taken on February 6, the Federalists carried the day by a vote of 187 to 168. Massachusetts ratified the Constitution, but the state also asked for nine "amendments & alterations" that would "remove the fears & quiet the apprehensions of many of the good people of this Commonwealth."[26] These final amendments were the product of a committee of two delegates from every county in the state, one Federalist and the other Antifederalist. If only ten men had voted differently, ratification would have failed in Massachusetts—and, as Massachusetts would go, so too would go the country. Without question, there were at least ten people who voted yay thanks to Adams's and Hancock's presence, and it was the request for amendments that moved the ten to yes in the first place.

Just as importantly, even those who voted no were conciliated by the convention's general tenor. Unlike Antifederalists in Pennsylvania, Antifederalists in Massachusetts felt that they had been allowed to voice their opinions, and that they had been justly heard. Ultimately, they had lost, but the fight had been a fair one. As one delegate from rural Maine (then part of Massachusetts) put it, "I fought Licke a Good Soldier and have been Congared [Conquered] Like a man but Sir if it is adopted by the whole and becomes the foundation of the Law I am Sure I will Support it."[27] The letter's creative spelling also tells us that, at least in Massachusetts, regular people really did have a chance to weigh in.

And it proved true: As Massachusetts went, so too went the rest of the country. In the face of stout opposition, Massachusetts Federalists had eventually arrived at a formula that could swing the few delegates in the center: Ratify, but request amendments at the same time. Attitude mattered too: Unlike Pennsylvania Federalists, the decorum and respect exhibited by the Federalists of Massachusetts soothed Antifederalist defeat.[28] Of the seven states that still needed to hold conventions—by order of ratification, Maryland, South Carolina, New Hampshire, Virginia, New York, North Carolina, and, fighting it every step of the way, Rhode Island—all but Maryland followed Massachusetts's lead. This trend embodied what really was a national, popular consensus: A majority of Americans wanted a new government, and they liked many things about the Constitution, but were not totally sold—yet. The trend was also part and parcel of both America's recent revolutionary history and its long future: Illustrious authority figures request the American people to do something (in this case, to simply vote yes or no on the Constitution), and Americans respond by doing something entirely different.

James Madison, Closed Windows, and Open Doors

When James Madison learned of the Massachusetts convention's decision to vote yes but with suggested amendments, he was relieved—but he was not pleased. Writing to George Washington, Madison called the proposed amendments "a blemish," albeit, he added, "in the least offensive form."[29]

When it came to ratification, Madison had perhaps more at stake than any other American, for the very existence of the Constitution was due more to him than anyone else in the young republic. To be sure, many of the Constitution's compromises departed from his initial vision. To him, for example, the final structure of the Senate would mean small states would still be able to make mischief, and he believed the federal government needed the power to overrule state laws, which also failed to make it into the final version. Yet, more than anyone else at the Constitutional Convention, Madison set the terms of the debate by arriving with an established outline for the new government (eventually dubbed "the Virginia Plan"). It was Madison, too, who persuaded the indispensable George Washington to support the Constitutional Convention, and it was Madison who first argued that delegates needed to toss out the Articles of Confederation entirely rather than simply amend them. For good reason, posterity has dubbed him "the Father of the Constitution."

Born into the Virginia gentry class in 1751, Madison was raised on a tobacco planation in the state's Piedmont region. He was the oldest of twelve children (although only five of his siblings survived to adulthood), and his family enslaved more than one hundred people. He attended the College of New Jersey (now Princeton) in his late teens, where he focused his studies on law and religion, although he had no intention to make his career in either. By the time of his graduation, Madison had become particularly interested in religious and civil liberty, and he disdained the fact that Anglicanism was still Virginia's established denomination. True to his ideology, when the revolutionary crisis escalated he immediately threw his lot in with the Patriot side. Only in his mid-twenties, Madison was nevertheless elected a colonel in his local militia, helped write Virginia's state constitution and its Declaration of Rights, and eventually served in the House of Delegates. Frail and sickly for much of his life, Madison never actually fought in the Revolution, but as a political leader of the most populous and wealthy state in the country, his stock was on the rise.

Although he was passionate about civil and religious liberties, Madison was hardly a democrat, and he took a dim view of the United States' political trajectory after the Treaty of Paris, when many of the country's state governments started to bend to the democratic will on fiscal policy. Since the end of the Revolutionary War, many states had acceded to the wishes of their less well-off citizens and implemented "soft money" policies that allowed debtors to repay their loans with inflated paper bills. To Madison, this was no way to run an economy. Not only did soft-money policies hamper interstate commerce, international trade, and the general fiscal health of the nation; they also hampered Madison's personal ability to get a loan.[30] Madison's worldview was thoroughly in line with his background: He was an elitist who distrusted the ability of ordinary people to participate in day-to-day political affairs. In many ways, the Constitutional Convention was tailor-made for Madison to shine. He was widely read, a deep thinker, a diligent preparer, an assiduous notetaker, and a compromiser and pragmatist, though he was not a fiery speaker nor a commanding presence in debates. Perhaps his arguments could win the day, but he could not dominate a room by his sheer presence—let alone a more boisterous tavern or assembly.

And, at the Constitutional Convention, he did not need to. The doors and windows were closed, the proceedings kept secret from the American people for the entire summer and early fall of 1787. In such a setting, Madison more than held his own among his mostly older and more illustrious peers, elite men such as Benjamin Franklin, George Washington, and John Dickinson who had dominated American politics for decades. To be sure, he lost many battles at the Convention, with the final document only vaguely resembling his original Virginia Plan. When all was said and done, Madison voiced many reservations about the Constitution, but only in private. He believed the United States needed a new government, and the Constitution was the only opportunity to achieve it—therefore, in public, he would wax poetic about its virtues while staying largely quiet about its vices.

Madison's ability to see the proverbial forest through the trees when it came to the Constitution was part and parcel with his larger political outlook: Reaching the final goal was always more important than how to get there. For example, in 1780, during one of the nadirs of the Revolutionary War, Madison was confronted with Virginians' diminishing enthusiasm for militia service in the face of a British invasion, which spurred countless enslaved people to run to British lines. When one fellow Patriot suggested offering every white volunteer the ownership of one enslaved person, Madison responded to this "Negro bounty" with another idea. "Would it not be as well to liberate and make soldiers at once of the blacks themselves as to make them instruments for enlisting white Soldiers?" he asked in a letter. "It wd. Certainly be more consonant to the principles of liberty which ought never to be lost sight of." But his aim was more practical than ideological, writing, "Experience having shown that a freeman immediately loses all attachment & sympathy with his former slaves."[31] This measure, he believed, would turn the tables on the British invasion, transforming enslaved British allies into free Patriot soldiers. Madison was typical of many Virginia Patriots, in that he voiced abhorrence of slavery while owning slaves himself, profiting off their labor and doing almost nothing about it politically. Nevertheless, for Madison, winning the Revolution took precedence over maintaining the economic and racial status quo—just as producing a written constitution was more important than the parameters contained within it seven years later.

Once the doors and windows were opened on the Constitutional Convention, however, Madison was required to rapidly adjust in ways that did not play to his strengths. The Constitution was no longer secret, and it was time for the "people without doors" to weigh in. No longer could the genteel, soft-spoken Madison win with his acumen alone. He would need to confront the American people, and they were a very different animal than the fifty-five men secluded in the Pennsylvania State House.

Madison did this in two ways. More well known today is Madison's co-authorship, alongside Alexander Hamilton and John Jay, of what is now deemed *The Federalist Papers*. Writing anonymously as Publius, these three authors aimed to sway Antifederalist New Yorkers to ratify the Constitution by employing high-minded arguments about the document's many virtues. Yet, while Americans may see *The Federalist Papers* as sacrosanct today, their effect in the moment, even for New Yorkers, was muted. While some of the essays resonated, others, such as Madison's *Federalist No. 10*, arguably the most cited of the essays today (more on that below), were largely ignored.

At the time, it was Madison's public role in Virginia, not his anonymous authorship of *The Federalist Papers*, that was far more politically important. He was elected as a delegate to the state's ratification convention in June 1788, where he faced off against Patrick Henry himself. While other delegates weighed in over the three-week convention, it was Henry versus Madison that stole the show. Remarkably, not only did Madison hold his own, but in the end his performance outshined Henry's. To one observer, Henry was "never conquered," but it was Madison "among all the delegates, [who] carried the votes of the two parties. He was always clear, precise, and consistent in his reasoning, and always methodical and pure in his Language."[32] After three weeks of debate, ratification won the day by a vote of 89 to 79, reflecting the reality of a closely divided state. It turned out that Madison, despite his soft-spoken demeanor, was quite good at public politics.

But not *that* good, because, despite arguing again and again that the Constitution did not require a bill of rights or any other amendments, Madison could not prevent the convention from following Massachusetts's lead: Virginia ratified the Constitution, but also recommended the addition of a bill of rights and twenty other amendments, which were mostly designed to limit the power of the federal government. One amendment, for example, provided that Congress could only directly tax states that failed to pay their assigned quota. As in Massachusetts, ratification would not have passed without the recommendation for amendments. Madison knew this all too well, later writing that, without promising amendments, "in Virga. It would have been *certainly* rejected."[33] Once again, the Antifederalists had been defeated, but not without extracting concessions.

Madison himself was largely disdainful of amendments. He particularly loathed ones that would change the mechanisms of the Constitution by weakening the federal government. In his opinion, it had already been weakened enough in the Constitutional Convention. He was not particularly enthused by a bill of rights either. In his view, it was the carefully designed structure of the Constitution, with its many checks and balances, that would protect the people from a potentially tyrannic government. Enumerated rights would only prove to be "parchment barriers" if a powerful central government became bent on destroying these rights.[34]

Madison, however, had to reckon with the will of the American people. By the end of July 1788, when New York became the eleventh state to ratify the Constitution, it also became the fifth state to ratify alongside a request for amendments, and in most of these states the vote had been close. North Carolina and Rhode Island, fearing the Constitution's concentration of power, still refused to ratify. All these votes reflected a key truth: A majority of Americans were willing to give the Constitution a shot but they needed some reassurances.

For Madison, it was not just the American people writ large who needed reassurances, but the people in Madison's own Fifth Congressional District of Virginia. With Madison the key figure at both the Constitutional Convention and Virginia's ratifying convention, logic would dictate that the Virginia legislature would choose him as one of the state's two senators in the First Federal Congress. Yet, thanks to their face-off at the ratification convention, Madison had made a supremely powerful enemy in Patrick Henry, who himself was elected to the state legislature. Henry not only ensured that Madison was not chosen as a senator, but then tried to ensure he would not get elected to the House either. With Henry at the helm, the Virginia legislature passed a law that mandated representatives needed to live in their districts, and then drew Madison's district in such a way that gave it an Antifederalist majority. Henry then handpicked James Monroe, a young, popular, moderate Antifederalist, to run against Madison. To top it off, not only was Madison required to run against a well-liked opponent in a gerrymandered district (to use the term we would apply today), but the Virginia legislature sent him back to New York to serve in the final Confederation Congress. For months, he would be away from home, unable to answer Monroe's criticisms in person. Patrick Henry may have been defeated at the state ratifying convention, but it looked like he would still exact vengeance on the one person most committed to engineering that defeat.

It was under these difficult political circumstances, with Madison facing electoral political defeat, that he—to put it bluntly—changed his mind about adding a bill of rights to the Constitution. He was never secretive about his motivations being, for better or worse, largely political. He wanted to win his congressional election, and to do so he would need to sway at least some of his district's Antifederalist majority. He also wanted the U.S. Constitution to win, and he believed that a bill of rights would mollify just enough Antifederalists in North Carolina and Rhode Island to bring their states into the fold. Just as importantly, with so many states ratifying the Constitution based upon the addition of amendments, Madison believed that Federalists needed to keep their promises to retain popular support. This support was needed not only to ensure the precarious legitimacy of the Constitution, but to stave off a developing demand from some of the more strident Antifederalists: a second constitutional convention that would fix the errors of the Constitution. Madison and every other Federalist knew a second convention would likely crush any hopes for a new U.S. government. It had been hard enough to craft the Constitution with a group of people who all felt the need for one. With people like Patrick Henry and other, in Madison's words, "insidious characters from different parts of America," now at the table? It would be impossible.[35] The common denominator in all of Madison's stated reasons: The "people without doors"—in Madison's congressional district, in Virginia, in North Carolina and Rhode Island, and across the United States—demanded amendments, and he would accede to their demands.

For Madison, however, adding amendments was not just about naked politics. By the winter of 1788–89, his ideological stance had also changed. Ever since the Framers had unveiled the Constitution, Jefferson had been writing Madison from Paris, where he served as the U.S. minister to France, lamenting the defects of the new U.S. government. His most vehement criticism, voiced again and again, was its lack of a "Declaration of Rights." In a remarkable letter from March 1789, Jefferson answered Madison's objections to a bill of rights point by point. In response to Madison and other Federalists' argument that a bill of rights would be dangerous because it would be impossible to list *every* right, and therefore future governments would be able to trample these unlisted rights, Jefferson responded, "Half a loaf is better than no bread. If we cannot secure all our rights, let us secure what we can." To Madison's belief that a bill of rights would prove a "parchment barrier" in the face of a tyrannic government, Jefferson responded that, at the least, it certainly would not *hurt* in protecting rights. He argued, "A brace the more will often keep up the building which would have fallen with that brace than less."[36] From the lofty visionary Jefferson, these were solidly practical arguments, ones calculated to assuage the ever-practical Madison.

Madison's about-face went even deeper. He continued to believe that the best guarantee of the rights of the American people was embedded in the structure of government outlined in the Constitution. A bill of rights would only do so much to guarantee these rights if the structure collapsed. Yet, as the historian Jonathan Gienapp has argued, Madison also eventually arrived at his own ideological reason for adding a bill of rights: Listed rights would serve, in Gienapp's words, as "public markers." Over time, everyone would know them, everyone would cite them, and everyone would cherish them, thereby including personal rights not just in the document itself but, more importantly, embedding them as bedrock principles of the republic in the consciousness of the American people.[37] Over time, Americans would guard these hard-earned rights with increasing zeal, thereby increasing their effectiveness. Yes, Madison wanted to win his election and see the Constitution succeed, but, as he succinctly summarized in his notes, in the months since the Constitutional Convention, he had come to believe that a bill of rights would "improve the Constitution."[38]

In retrospect, it is not hyperbole to state that the fate of the Bill of Rights hinged on the few thousand people in Madison's district who would decide his political fate, for, as we shall see, few Federalists in Congress believed any amendments were needed. Once again, his support for a bill of rights put him over the top—doubly so, in fact. The votes all came down to a few hundred Virginia Baptists. This religious minority remembered Madison's continuous support for their own religious liberty in the past, and they trusted him to enshrine that right in the U.S. Constitution in the future. Meanwhile, Madison skillfully countered charges of his own hypocritical about-face through public letters and speeches at local taverns (a practice decidedly out of step with the formality of the era). Ultimately, a majority—57 percent—gave Madison their vote.

The Constitutional Convention and Madison's election to the First Congress were only two years apart, but they seem to be of entirely different worlds divided by more than two hundred years—or even more. The closed doors and illustrious names of the Constitutional Convention hearken back to the court politics of medieval Europe, while Madison's congressional election and all its political messiness—which included gerrymandering, petty revenge, shifting political narratives, and something resembling a modern public relations campaign—seems very much like current American politics that countless Americans claim to abhor.

This otherworldly nature and sheer unfathomability of the Constitutional Convention has led many Americans to romanticize it. It was a gathering of "plain, honest men" planning a "miracle at Philadelphia" that ultimately saved the United States—to quote the titles of two books on the Constitutional Convention.[39] Yet what Americans value most in the Constitution is not the various densely worded articles spelling out a complicated system of government, but the Bill of Rights. And these rights—*their* rights—were made possible not by a secretive gathering of great men, but by popular democracy, the same popular democracy that is often so derided today. It was the American people, not the Founding Fathers, whose collective skepticism of the Constitution's more controversial aspects paved the way for the eventual Bill of Rights. This popular pushback began in Pennsylvania, gained traction in Massachusetts, spread to a majority of other states, and culminated with Madison's promise to introduce a series of amendments in the First Congress. The Framers had tried to curb democracy and circumscribe the power of regular people in the Constitution, and to a significant extent they succeeded. Nevertheless, the ratification process, in particular states' demands for amendments, showed that the will of the people (at least, eligible male voters) still mattered in the United States. The American Revolution may have ended, but its democratic ideals lived on, despite—and even in opposition to—the purposefully antidemocratic features of the Constitution.

Forgetting Original Meanings

Read historically, the specific text of the Bill of Rights reveals a lost revolutionary world, one more radical and far more communal than is often understood, a world that reflected the fact that these rights were first demanded, then written and passed, in the immediate aftermath of the American Revolution. Of the ten amendments, half concern community action and participation, often in ways few appreciate today. Take, for example, the all-important five freedoms in the First Amendment: religion, speech, press, assembly, and petition. Freedom of religion was not simply the protection of one's personal beliefs, but a protection for groups of like-minded Americans to convene together, even if their beliefs ran counter to the dominant Protestant denomination of the respective state. Freedom of speech was not simply a protection of personal speech, but, alongside freedom of the press, it enshrined the right to speak to the broader public. Freedom of assembly was communal by definition, but it was far more radical than simply the right to picket or protest. Instead, it went as far as to enshrine the right to revolution itself—or, at least, the second-to-last step before revolution. After all, it was a public assembly that devolved into the Boston Massacre, which helped pave the way for U.S. independence. Finally, the right to petition was not simply an eighteenth-century version of "Call your local congressman." On the contrary: At the time public petitions were hallowed, and representatives were supposed to present every petition formally in the legislature. All in all, from an eighteenth-century perspective, the First Amendment protected the boisterous communal radicalism of American public life as it existed at the tail end of the American Revolution.

Other amendments followed suit. Until the 2008 Supreme Court case *District of Columbia v. Heller* and contrary to the arguments of modern gun rights advocates, the Second Amendment was never codified as a protection of an individual's right to own a firearm, but rather the right for that individual to serve in a "well-regulated" local militia—meaning a relatively egalitarian body of citizens organized to protect themselves and their local community. The importance of the amendment lay not in individual self-defense, but community self-defense (indeed, the expectation was that adult men *should* own firearms and *must* serve in the militia).[40] Amendments Five through Seven all concerned themselves with the right to trial by jury and juries more generally. Like militias, juries were also entities through which a relatively egalitarian group of American citizens organized themselves, in this case to make legal judgments. Today jury duty is seen by many Americans as a thankless task to avoid, but at the time juries were seen as the ultimate protection against a tyranny, the final populist backstop against political leaders and judges trying to wrest power for themselves. Indeed, the right to a jury in a criminal trial was the *only* right secured in *every* state constitution prior to 1787, and the legal historian Akhil Reed Amar has even argued that juries "were at the heart of the Bill of Rights."[41]

Assemblies, petitions, militias, and juries: Here were populist answers to the U.S. Constitution's antidemocratic and elitist tendencies. In the intervening 250 years since the amendments' passage, we must squint hard to see the revolutionary potential of the rights they guarantee. At the time, however, all these protections stemmed from the ideology and lived experience of the American Revolution. They had not been simply bequeathed on Americans by a benevolent, paternalist government, but had been demanded and enacted in the decades before Madison brought his proposal to the House floor in the spring of 1789.

In the lead-up to the First Congress, Madison spent weeks reading and synthesizing the rights proposed by the various state ratification conventions, which he then proposed to the First Congress. Yet many Antifederalists did not believe Madison's various proposals went far enough. They viewed a bill of rights as a starting point for amendments, and they hoped for many more constitutional changes alongside these protections. And, at the time and even more in retrospect, there was a clear dividing line between the *civil* rights guaranteed to every free person and the *political* rights promised to—in most cases—white men. Women and free black people could be protected by militias, but they could not join them (in the case of black men, the 1792 Militia Act would soon spell this out explicitly). Women and free black people could be tried by a jury, but they did not have the right to serve on them. Enslaved people, of course, were not even given civil rights. As we shall see in later chapters, these groups would not simply accept the status quo.

In addition to the rights that would protect the people from an all-powerful federal government, Madison turned to the relationship between the people and the states. One of his amendments read, "No *state* shall violate the equal rights of conscience, or the freedom of the press, or the trial by jury in criminal cases" (emphasis added).[42] Here was a shorter version of what would eventually be ratified as the Fourteenth Amendment after the Civil War, which protected Americans from not just the federal government abusing its powers, but *state* governments abusing *their* powers. As the Fourteenth Amendment stated: "Nor shall any state deprive any person of life, liberty, or property, without due process of law; nor deny to any person within its jurisdiction the equal protection of the laws." Madison's proposal was less expansive, but it rested on a similar principle: States, too, could act tyrannically.

Madison also suggested that the Constitution deserved a preamble—or, really, a *pre*-preamble, because it already had *the* preamble that began with "We the People." The text of this pre-preamble—what Madison referred to as a "declaration"—was very familiar: "All power is originally vested in, and consequently derived from the people. That government is instituted, and ought to be exercised for the benefit of the people; which consists in the enjoyment of life and liberty, with the right of acquiring and using property, and generally of pursuing and obtaining happiness and safety." The passage then became even more radical: "That the people have an indubitable, unalienable, and indefeasible right to reform or change their government, whenever it be found adverse or inadequate to the purposes of its institution."[43] It was not quite the language of the Declaration of Independence, but it was close. In essence, what Madison proposed was the incorporation of the right of revolution in the text of the Constitution.

The principles of the Declaration would not be a onetime deal, meant for the circumstances of 1776. They would be the principles by which the United States would continue to be governed.

For all the demand then and the reverence now for the Bill of Rights, Madison's fellow congressmen initially greeted his proposals with remarkable apathy. Most Federalists did not see the need for amendments, and the Antifederalist minority did not trust Madison and the Federalist-dominated Congress to pass them. Yet Madison commanded enough clout—Washington, after all, had supported amendments in his inaugural address as president—and enough of his colleagues begrudgingly admitted that a bill of rights could pay political dividends that his proposals were eventually referred to a Federalist-dominated committee—which, of course, included Madison himself. Over the summer months, this committee discussed the amendments privately, while business as usual continued in the House. By August, the committee gave its recommendations to the House as a whole, which then voted and referred seventeen amendments to the Senate, which in turn whittled the seventeen down to twelve.

Representatives from both the House and Senate then sat down in a committee to hammer out a few final issues over phrasing. On September 24, 1789, by a vote of 37 to 14, the House agreed to the Senate's amendments. In another moment of irony, many of the most virulent Antifederalists cast their votes *against* the amendments, many of which they had long demanded. Disgusted that Madison failed to take into account the structural changes they desired, and even more disgusted that the Senate further whittled down what they already considered milquetoast, they registered their protest for posterity.

With the amendments now through both houses of Congress, it was time for the state legislatures to give their assent. Three-quarters of their votes were needed.

Of Whales and Tubs

In August, during the most heated (literally and figuratively) debates in the House, Aedanus Burke, an Antifederalist from South Carolina, rose to offer one of the memorably phrased criticisms of Madison's amendments. He noted that Madison's proposals ignored most of the Antifederalist critiques and did little to actually reform the workings of the Constitution, as Antifederalists desired. Madison's amendments, he argued, "are not those solid and substantial amendments which the people expect; they are little better than whip-syllabub, frothy and full of wind, formed only to please the palate, or they are like a tub thrown out to a whale, to secure the freight of the ship and its peaceable voyage."[44]

No other critic described Madison's amendments as "whip-syllabub"—a British dessert that mixed cream and alcohol, with the alcohol curdling the cream—but many others attacked them as "throwing a tub to a whale." Today, it is a bizarrely obscure phrase, but it seems nearly every American at the time knew it, judging by the sheer number of references in letters and speeches attacking Madison's proposed amendments (the phrase even garners its own index line in the documentary history of the Bill of Rights).[45] The allusion referred to the Anglo-Irish satirist Jonathan Swift's immensely complex 1704 novel *A Tale of the Tub*, in which sailors throw a tub into the ocean in order to distract a whale from destroying the ship—in other words, what became the Bill of Rights was simply a diversion. Federalists leveled this attack at Madison just as much as Antifederalists. While Antifederalists like Aedanus Burke believed Madison's amendments did not do nearly enough, Federalists believed they simply distracted from the more important tasks at hand.

Were they right? If the Bill of Rights was a tub thrown to a whale, then it was certainly quite the tub, for it was one of the most politically successful distractions in all U.S. history. As Madison wrote Jefferson before the First Congress even met, his goal with amendments was to "extinguish opposition to [the Constitution], or at least break the force of it, by detaching the deluded opponents from their designing leaders"—designing leaders like Patrick Henry and Elbridge Gerry, who hoped to sabotage the Constitution before it even went into effect.[46] The Bill of Rights did just that, proving to the vast middle of the country, those wary of the Constitution but not overtly hostile to it, that Congress could be trusted to fulfill its promises. Soon after Congress sent the amendments to the states for ratification, a prominent Virginian wrote Madison,

"A very considerable change has taken place among the Anti's as to yourself, they consider you to be the patron of amendments." All the writer noticed now when it came to Virginians' attitude toward the Constitution was "acquiescence."[47]

Even North Carolina and Rhode Island, the states most hostile to the Constitution, soon "acquiesced." North Carolina ratified the Constitution in November. Rhode Island took longer. Although the state's governor, John Collins, wrote George Washington that the "amendments . . . have already afforded some relief and satisfaction of the minds of the People of this State," it still held out for nearly another year, ratifying the Constitution in May 1790.[48] The states that had already ratified the Constitution also approved. Three-quarters of them needed to ratify the amendments for them to be officially added to the Constitution, which was accomplished by December 1791—not lightning speed to be sure but, for the era, still rather quick. Virginia's state government, dominated by Antifederalists and led by Patrick Henry, took longer to ratify, waiting until after the Bill of Rights became law, but Madison believed this was politically beneficial to the Federalist cause. The pointless opposition of Virginia Antifederalists only further proved to Virginians that it was the Federalists who actually cared about the rights of the people. As Madison wrote Washington, this maneuver would only "have the effect of turning [Virginians'] distrust towards their own Legislature."[49] When everything was said and done, Madison's at first unpopular attempt to pass a Bill of Rights had fulfilled all his political hopes.

But, of course, the Bill of Rights was not simply a political distraction. Americans already took these rights for granted in 1789, and they continued to do so during the entire history of the early republic. Rather than seeing the Bill of Rights as a single definitive list, they saw it as one American document in a long history of English law that clarified the rights of the people, beginning with the Magna Carta in 1215, and continuing with the Petition of Right in 1628 and the English Bill of Rights in 1689.[50] Indeed, this long history of existing rights is found in the Ninth Amendment: "The enumeration in the Constitution, of certain rights, shall not be construed to deny or disparage others retained by the people." As Madison and other Federalists had argued when they at first declined to include a bill of rights, Americans *already* possessed rights—and they knew it.

In the end, the Bill of Rights showed that the American people still mattered, that however much the Constitution circumscribed democracy, it did not destroy it all together. It was part of what the historian Woody Holton deemed the "underdogs' Constitution," the various amendments that have empowered and protected individual Americans beginning with the Bill of Rights in 1789, followed by the Reconstruction Amendments and the Progressive Era Amendments more than a century later. It was also part of what we could term the Revolutionary era's "underdogs' constitution" (lower-case "c"), a collection of written texts and broadly held unwritten ideals from the Founding era that defined the promises and possibilities of the Revolution—not just the Declaration and the Bill of Rights, but various state bills of rights, statutes like the Virginia Statute for Religious Freedom, state constitutions (particularly those like Pennsylvania's that empowered local democracy), and radical writings like Tom Paine's *Common Sense*. All together, these documents and ideals made the persuasive case that the American Revolution meant more to Americans than a simple shift in the composition of the ruling elite. To them, the Revolution *was* a revolution—and they would continue claiming as such in the decades to come.

2

The Right to Rebel: The Whiskey Rebellion, 1791–94

It was 1794, and, for Herman Husband, it was time for rebellion—*again.*

As Husband surveyed local and national politics from his modest farm in Bedford County, located in the Allegheny Mountains of western Pennsylvania, he did not like what he saw. George Washington and his administration, at the urging of Secretary of the Treasury Alexander Hamilton, had passed an excise tax on distilled spirits. To the modern reader, this seems innocuous enough. After all, the federal government charges an excise tax of $13.50 per gallon on liquor, and every state also collects its own sales tax directly from the consumer at the time of purchase. Yet, in the 1790s, Americans who lived along the trans-Appalachian frontier viewed this seemingly minor tax as an economic and political injustice—economic because it taxed whiskey, the one item that westerners were able to move to distant markets because it was nonperishable; political because it came at the hands of a distant federal government that westerners felt did not represent their interests. Indeed, to Husband and many other westerners, the whiskey tax was a fundamental betrayal of the American Revolution. So, in August of 1794, the seventy-year-old Husband set off for the small town of Parkinson's Ferry, seventeen miles south of Pittsburgh, where he would convene with other western Pennsylvanians to draft resolutions against the hated whiskey tax and, in their eyes, the increasingly tyrannical federal government.

It was no surprise that Husband's neighbors chose him as a delegate. He had done this before, a quarter century earlier. At that point, Husband was a British subject who lived in colonial North Carolina. The American Revolution still lay in the future. Nevertheless, the list of grievances of western North Carolinians in the late 1760s was remarkably like the list of grievances western Pennsylvanians voiced in the early 1790s. In both cases—and throughout much of early American history, in most colonies and states—the western frontier was the edge of white settlement, always more dangerous and riskier than living in the East. There, westerners confronted numerous and well-armed Native people, whom they hoped to subjugate or drive farther west. To get there, they had to trek across the Appalachian Mountains, and, once there, they had to clear the land themselves and move their goods to market over many miles. They took these risks because, in the East, they were poor and landless, and in the West they could acquire land—maybe.

Maybe. The problem for western migrants was that, even though they did the actual physical labor of finding, clearing, and farming this land—in their words, carried out the work of "improvement"—wealthy easterners maintained political and economic control. In the courts and taverns of eastern towns and cities, wealthy and connected speculators bought and sold western lands that they had never actually seen, among them George Washington himself, who speculated in western lands nearly his entire life. These speculators were connected to the politically powerful, or were powerful politicians themselves, a situation that lent itself to corruption. Westerners who had done the work of improving the land found themselves at the legal mercy of these eastern speculators and politicians. To westerners, eastern courts discounted "improvement titles, and gave preference to the paper titles."[1] And, when westerners sought to curb speculation and corruption, they ran into the problem of their political powerlessness. Colonial and later state governments were situated in the East, and they were thoroughly controlled by easterners, who time and again refused to grant westerners equal representation.

Just as galling to western migrants, it was these out-of-touch easterners who desired to halt the western migration of white Americans, which would presumably preserve peace with Natives and provide order to the chaotic, violent frontier. To western whites, pro-Indian government policies stunk of hypocrisy, for eastern elites (or at least their ancestors) had also wrested land from Native people but, now that they had successfully acquired it, they refused to enact measures that would further the process of land confiscation and redistribution. When it came to Native relations, frontier whites felt they were on their own.

It got worse. Even as they refused to aid frontier whites, easterners implemented regressive tax policies that taxed everyone, rich and poor, an equal amount. And if westerners wanted to vote out a corrupt official, they did so at their own peril. Voting in the early United States was a thoroughly public act, so powerful officials knew full well who were their friends and who were their enemies. For a poor westerner to vote against the most powerful local official was a risk indeed, particularly if he was arrested for farming land he did not own and then dragged to court—which, again, was situated in the East, and dominated, once again, by wealthy and connected easterners.

It all added up to, in Herman Husband's words, westerners who "groaned . . . under the weight of these crushing Mischiefs."[2] Enough was enough. The time for revolution was at hand.

Again.

Worlds Upside Down

By their very definition, revolutions overturn the existing world order. That's the point. Revolutions are never safe, half-hearted, or drab, but radical, sweeping, and—crucially—open-ended. Once a revolution begins, who knows where, when, and how it will end. This uncertainty is precisely the reason why conservatives consider them so dangerous, and why moderates often oppose revolutionary activity even if they sympathize with many of its immediate goals.

Take John Dickinson, the wealthiest tobacco planter in Delaware. He spent a great deal of time in Philadelphia, and, although not Quaker himself, Dickinson was connected to Pennsylvania's powerful Quaker politicians through both his family and his wife's family, and he retained a Quaker-influenced worldview. The religious doctrine of the Society of Friends, as Quakers were known officially, was remarkably egalitarian for the time, and Quakerism made many of Dickinson's views quite radical. He was both a proto-feminist who argued for female spiritual equality and took political advice from women, and an abolitionist who emancipated all of his slaves in 1777.[3] He first made a name for himself in the American

Revolution by penning thirteen different *Letters from a Pennsylvania Farmer* in 1767, which made the case that Great Britain had the right to regulate commerce with its colonies but not raise revenue from them. *Letters from a Pennsylvania Farmer* was the most influential revolutionary writing of the era until Tom Paine published *Common Sense* in 1776.

Yet for all his radicalism, Dickinson refused to vote for full independence in 1776, a sin for which posterity has never forgiven him. Dickinson has been cast as the archvillain in two popular depictions of the American Revolution, the musical *1776* and the HBO miniseries *John Adams*. In both, he is John Adams's primary antagonist, arguing against independence until the very end. He comes across as learned but ultimately foolish and tragic.

But Dickinson was not foolish. Valuing the Quaker ideals of harmony and order, Dickinson searched for a way that Britain's North American colonies could remain politically connected to the mother country through a new, more equal political alignment. He feared deeply that full independence would bring American disunion—and with it, disorder and disaster. Independence, he argued, would invariably lead to a "multitude of Commonwealths, crimes, and Calamities—centuries of mutual Jealousies, Hatreds, Wars, and Devastations, until at last the exhausted Provinces shall sink into Slavery under the yoke of some fortunate conqueror."[4] Dickinson then devoted much of the rest of his political life to finding ways that would prevent such a catastrophe: He was one of architects of the first national government of the United States and its governing document, the Articles of Confederation, although his original version proposed a more robust central government. He then attended first the Annapolis Convention in 1786, and then the Constitutional Convention in 1787, both of which sought to fix the issues with the Articles that seemed to be leading the United States down a path toward catastrophe—the same sort of catastrophe Dickinson had predicted would occur in 1776.

"Jealousies, Hatreds, Wars, and Devastations": One did not need Dickinson's sophisticated, complex, Quaker-inspired political philosophy to make just such a prediction about the American Revolution—or any revolution, for that matter. A revolution can invariably lead to a world shattered, unable to be repaired as it was before. This shattering could be stirring and profound. It could also be murderous and disastrous—if the revolution went off the rails.

And, in the 1790s, Americans did not have to look very far to see a revolution that had gone off the rails. In 1789, when the people of Paris stormed the Bastille and their delegates swore the Tennis Court Oath, Americans were overjoyed that the United States' great ally during their own revolution was now joining them as another nation of liberty. The Marquis de Lafayette wrote the Declaration of the Rights of Man and of the Citizen with Thomas Jefferson literally at his side. All seemed to be going according to plan, at least in the minds of most Americans.

But before long Lafayette and Jefferson found their hopes dashed. Thanks to the militancy and newfound power of the common people of Paris, the political genius of rising radicals like Danton and Robespierre, the political stupidity of King Louis XVI, and the vagaries of international relations, soon Lafayette was fleeing for his life, ending up in an Austrian jail cell; King Louis and his wife Marie Antoinette were guillotined in front of raucous crowds; and the Committee of Public Safety ruled France through what posterity has dubbed the "Reign of Terror." What had once been a safe, liberal revolution had become a violent, dangerous, extremist conflict that rocked the foundations of European society from the coast of Ireland to the steppes of Russia.

It was not just in Europe where the French Revolution picked up speed, but across the Atlantic Ocean, in the French sugar colony of Saint Domingue. There, a small conglomerate of white planters reaped immense profits from half a million enslaved black laborers toiling under brutal conditions. Back in France, the Comte de Mirabeau, one of the giants of the first years of the French Revolution, wrote that these white planters were "sleeping at the foot of Vesuvius."[5] This was assuredly the case before the French Revolution, but the conflict's rhetoric of liberty, equality, and fraternity added ideological heft to slave resistance that had always existed on the ground. By 1791, slaves in the northern part of the colony were in open revolt; by 1794 the French revolutionary government abolished all slavery in its colonies; by 1803, black and mixed-race people on the island declared the independence of the Republic of Haiti, the first independent black republic in the world.

In Europe, meanwhile, General Napoleon Bonaparte slowly but surely made himself the indispensable man to the Directory, the last French revolutionary government. He then made himself First Consul in 1799, which made him de facto dictator of France. His authority was supported by a popular plebiscite that allowed Napoleon to maintain the appearance of a democratic government. Five years later, he no longer needed to maintain this veneer, crowning himself emperor of the French. None of his political maneuvers brought peace to Europe; on the contrary, his brilliant generalship threatened all the other great powers of the continent, leading to more than a decade of uninterrupted warfare across the continent, from Spain to Russia.

The guillotine. The Reign of Terror. Haiti. Racial violence. Napoleon. Ceaseless warfare. Millions dead. Such were the repercussions of the supposedly laudatory, safe French Revolution of 1789.

The Endless Specter of Western Rebellion

In 1794, Americans did not know how the French Revolution would end, but they knew that whatever it had become under Robespierre and the Reign of Terror, it was no longer mimicking the American Revolution. They also knew their European history. They knew that internal political struggles that started out small could expand dramatically and continue interminably, such as when a power struggle between the English king and the English Parliament in the late 1630s led to a series of civil wars throughout the British Isles that did not get fully resolved for more than half a century. They knew, too, that republics like the United States were fragile entities that could quickly collapse into tyrannies. This was the fate of most historic republics, with the collapse of the Roman Republic as the example par excellence. Such fragility meant that even a small conflict could lead to the failure of the American republican experiment.

And they knew that, if a new conflict did come to the United States, it would almost certainly emerge in the Trans-Appalachian West. Early migrants to the West would find their prospects dwindling as speculators, surveyors, and government officials followed in their wake. All these Americans were ideologically armed with the legacy of the Revolution and its principle of armed rebellion. Were they not still, as the Declaration of Independence famously proclaimed, suffering a "long train of abuses and usurpations" perpetrated by the government, which meant they had every right to "alter or abolish" it?

Thomas Jefferson agreed—at least rhetorically. To him, the American Revolution was not necessarily a onetime event. Writing to an acquaintance in 1787 in the aftermath of Shays's Rebellion, Jefferson claimed that the Shaysites acted on "ignorance, not wickedness." He then made the bold statement, "God forbid we should ever be 20 years without such a rebellion." In fact, if Americans did not rebel again, then this demonstrated "lethargy," which was the "forerunner of death to public liberty." Asked Jefferson, "What country can preserve its liberties if their rulers are not warned from time to time that their people preserve the spirit of resistance? Let them take arms." The Whiskey Rebels were about to do just that. As Jefferson famously concluded in this letter, "The tree of liberty must be refreshed from time to time with the blood of patriots and tyrants." Less famously (and much less eloquently), he went on, "It is its natural manure."[6]

Long before 1794, inhabitants of the West had been getting—in Herman Husband's words—"crushed," and western resistance against eastern political and social structures had become quite common. Indeed, by the time of the Whiskey Rebellion, frontier rebellions had become something of a tradition in British North America. It began with Bacon's Rebellion, which erupted in 1676 in Virginia when frontier landless whites allied with enslaved blacks to demand free land. While the rebellion fizzled, hardening racial lines in the process, western insurrections continued. In the 1760s, the "Paxton Boys" from western Pennsylvania marched on Philadelphia, while "Regulators"—Herman Husband among them—rose in North Carolina. In the 1770s, the "Green Mountain Boys" banded together to counter New York's claim to the region that eventually became Vermont. In the 1780s, Americans living in what became eastern Tennessee sought to secede from North Carolina and create the "State of Franklin." Most famously, in 1786 in western Massachusetts, Daniel Shays and several thousand "Shaysites" rose against the Massachusetts government. As one historian has argued, the frontiersmen who undertook the Whiskey Rebellion in 1794 were simply "Pennsylvania Regulators," part of a long frontier custom.[7]

These rebellions had varying degrees of success. The one, unambiguous rebel victory occurred in Vermont, where Ethan Allen and the Green Mountain Boys essentially carved an independent state out of territory claimed by both New York and New Hampshire. By contrast, the North Carolina Regulators failed abysmally when official colonial forces crushed their rebellion at the Battle of Alamance in 1771. Although the two thousand–plus rebels outnumbered North Carolina governor William Tryon's forces two-to-one, the Regulators had no command structure, had not trained together as a single unit, and quickly ran low on ammunition. In the end they were routed, and the North Carolina Regulation movement evaporated.

Which brings us back to Herman Husband.[8] In the mid-1760s, Husband was a merchant and landowner in the North Carolina Piedmont, and a man who, more than most American colonists at the time, had been successfully able to scale the political, economic, and social ladder of the colonies to achieve modest prosperity. This prosperity made him a logical leader of the North Carolina Regulators, who protested what they saw as unjust taxation and endemic corruption among eastern North Carolinians who ran the colonial government. In 1769, he was even elected to the North Carolina Assembly, one of several Regulators elected that year.

Unfortunately for Husband and his allies, their presence in the Assembly only exacerbated east–west tensions. Husband himself was a pacifist, and therefore he sought a moderate way forward, but most Regulators were far more radical. Frustrated with the Assembly's intransigence, during the next two years they rebelled against the government, until their calamitous defeat at Alamance. Husband, owing to both his pacificism and his belief that the rebels would invariably lose, fled the Regulator army just before the battle commenced. His flight did not spare him the wrath of the governor, who declared Husband an outlaw, confiscated his lands, and offered a £100 reward for his capture. Husband and his family fled north to Pennsylvania.

Nicknaming himself "Tuscape Death," Husband settled in Bedford County, where his entire life seemed to repeat itself. Once again he slowly acquired land, once again he became a moderately prosperous landowner, and once again he became a respected local leader. In the mid-1770s, Husband supported the American Revolution, and was particularly thrilled with Pennsylvania's radically democratic state constitution, which held annual elections to a unicameral legislative body. Most free men, white and black, were eligible to vote. Such was his growing influence and fame that he was elected to the Pennsylvania Assembly after the Revolution.

However, like so many of his backcountry neighbors, Husband became disillusioned by the late 1780s, when Pennsylvanians ratified a more conservative constitution, and, even more problematically, when Americans ratified a new conservative governing document that covered the entire Union: *the* Constitution. In both cases, the more populated East thwarted the goals of the more sparsely inhabited West. As we have seen, the Bill of Rights did help mollify many skeptical of the new Constitution, but it did not persuade everyone. Indeed, to many Americans, particularly westerners, the conservative order of both the U.S. Constitution and the new Pennsylvania Constitution seemed to run roughshod over the radical promises of the American Revolution. In western Pennsylvania, as unhappiness gave way to protest, and protest gave way to resistance, Husband found himself elected as a delegate to the meeting at Parkinson's Ferry, where a new set of Regulators would once again challenge the corruption and elitism of eastern governance.

As he did in North Carolina thirty years before, Husband stood out from the group, for he was an odd duck. Raised an Anglican, Husband became a Presbyterian during the Great Awakening, which he then abandoned for Quakerism. Several years later, however, his local Quaker Meeting excommunicated him over some social dispute. By the time Husband led the North Carolina Regulators, he was, essentially, a church of one. He continued to adhere to the pacificism of the Quakers and the evangelicalism of the Great Awakening–era Presbyterians, but he also embraced millennialism. By the time he settled in Pennsylvania, Husband was sure that the Old Testament prophet Ezekiel's visions matched the geography of the mountains of North America, leading him to believe that the United States was the "New Jerusalem." He even drew a map to prove it, placing at its center the yet-to-be-founded city of New Jerusalem—with a future population of

100 million, he predicted. When a German botanist visited Husband in Bedford County, he thought Husband's isolation had driven him to insanity. "So wholly was [Husband] absorbed in the glory of this future kingdom," the botanist remembered, "that it was quite impossible for him to admit a reasonable thought."[9] Husband's pacificism also made him an outlier, particularly on the often-brutal Pennsylvania frontier, a site of intermittent warfare between whites and Natives since 1755. It is a remarkable historical quirk that the person with the strongest link between two violent frontier insurrections espoused nonviolence.

Despite his oddities, Husband's life nevertheless illustrates the connective tissue between the Regulators in North Carolina and those in Pennsylvania—and, by extension, their connections to the other frontier rebellions of late colonial and early U.S. history. In all of them, rebels espoused economic and social equality, denounced corruption and speculation, and demanded political rights for white western settlers.[10] When the American Revolution erupted, these rebels seamlessly adopted its tenets, arguing that the revolution was not just a political revolution against Great Britain but a social revolution against inequality and injustice.

The antidemocratic, elitist measures contained in the U.S. Constitution, as well as in new state constitutions like Pennsylvania's, confounded these egalitarian hopes. The elite of the new nation may not have been the same as the old colonial elite (although some were) but, to western yeomen farmers like Husband, they were the elite nonetheless, still subject to corruption, still lusting for power, still translating their political power into financial wealth, and still using their financial wealth to accrue more and more political power. The constitutional order felt like a betrayal of the promises of the Revolution, simply replacing the distant despotic British with the closer despotic federal government. Once again, westerners felt they were bearing the brunt of unjust taxation, speculation, and deflationary "hard money" policies, in particular state laws that mandated tax and loan payments in specie, which was all but absent on the distant frontier.

While tensions between East and West had been present long before the early 1790s, it is clear the Whiskey Rebellion would not have happened as and when it did without the influence of one man: the tireless, brilliant, controversial Alexander Hamilton. President Washington had appointed Hamilton the secretary of the treasury, and, according to most historians and many contemporaries, there was no better man for the job. Even Hamilton's critics—then and now—knew he had a genius for political economy, and the policies that the federal government implemented, based upon his 1790 Report on Public Credit, are largely credited with rescuing a U.S. economy that was in shambles thanks to the chaotic violence of the Revolutionary War and the postwar disorder of the Articles of Confederation.

Hamilton's main goal was for the federal government to assume the many state and countless individual debts accrued during the Revolution, which would make the United States creditworthy in the eyes of European powers like Great Britain and France, as well as in the eyes of the wealthy and connected American merchants and manufacturers whose support the fledgling republic could not afford to lose. A crucial part in paying this debt was to find new sources of revenue, one of which was the excise tax on alcohol. According to Hamilton, revenue from the Whiskey Excise would pay a quarter of the nation's debts.[11] There were also other potential benefits. If, as many western distillers complained, the tax helped consolidate the whiskey business among large, eastern distillers at the expense of small, western ones, then this would only help modernize the U.S. economy.[12] And, because the tax would be collected by federal officers, it would expand the reach and power of the federal government in the process, thereby further securing the constitutional settlement.

These were highly controversial measures. For all his brilliance and his many virtues, Hamilton was an outlier among his peers. He was to the Founding Fathers what Herman Husband was to the Whiskey Rebels: an odd duck who was not broadly representative of the larger group. An orphan and self-made immigrant born on the Caribbean Island of Nevis and raised on nearby Saint Croix, Hamilton distinguished himself as a commander of an artillery company in the first year of the Revolutionary War. Washington then promoted him to lieutenant colonel and made Hamilton one of his aides-de-camp. With Washington now thoroughly in his corner, Hamilton's status rapidly ascended. In 1780, he married Elizabeth Schuyler, scion of a wealthy and powerful New York family. For all intents and purposes, Hamilton had made it.

Hamilton felt little concern about concentrated political power. On the contrary, unlike practically all his contemporaries, he felt the position of president was problematic not because it was a position with too much power, but not enough. In 1787, in one of his more tone-deaf political acts, he gave a five-hour speech at the Constitutional Convention, urging his fellow delegates to support the idea that the United States should be governed by an elected monarch who would serve until the end of his life. It was a speech that, thankfully for Hamilton's subsequent political life and later posterity, his colleagues chose to completely ignore. There was no need for the convention to even address his idea, for, as one member remembered, while Hamilton had been "praised by every body," he was "supported by none."[13] (Needless to say, this scene did not make it into Lin-Manuel Miranda's musical *Hamilton*.)

Considering how much Hamilton loved centralized power, displays of martial prowess, internal taxes, and getting his way—and considering how the unrest in western Pennsylvania played into his hands in all of these ways—historians have wondered the obvious: Did Hamilton *seek* rebellion?[14] By passing a tax on distilled spirits specifically, was he attempting to goad western settlers into action, which he would then use to demonstrate federal power, further strengthening Washington's administration and the federal government more generally in the process? After all, he could have chosen something else to tax. Why not imported goods? Or, better yet, why not land? There was plenty of that. Yet both options were problematic. As Hamilton noted, a tax on imported goods would hurt merchants who, more than any other group at the time, bought government bonds and therefore allowed Hamilton's finance schemes to succeed. A land tax was too extreme, and Hamilton believed it should be saved for a moment when the nation was in crisis, when it needed to call on its most valuable resource.[15] A tax on whiskey also had the added value of being what we would now call a "sin tax." It targeted a commodity that American doctors viewed as unhealthy and American ministers preached was immoral, thus widening its base of support. That whiskey was the only commodity western farmers could get to market? This was not Hamilton's problem.

While there were certainly good financial and political reasons for Hamilton to support a tax on distilled liquor above other taxes, the best argument against the "Hamilton was seeking rebellion" argument is this: Like the popular pushback that eventually gave way to the Bill of Rights, the Whiskey Rebellion also bubbled up from below, emerging from the actions of countless individual Americans living in western Pennsylvania who sought the fulfillment of Revolutionary promises—as did Americans in the western parts of Virginia, Maryland, and the Carolinas, as we shall see. Hamilton may have been brilliant, but even his brilliance could not have predicted the course western protest would chart—or if it would chart one at all. However, while there is no clear evidence he hoped for rebellion, Hamilton would seek to capitalize on its course once it happened. Indeed, there is good reason that historians still wonder if Hamilton was playing a deeper game: If he sought the perfect insurrection that the federal government could put down with minimal effort, proving its potency without risking its legitimacy, then chance served it to him on a silver platter. As one early account of the rebellion stated, the Whiskey Rebellion was a "fortunate occurrence" that allowed the federal government to flex its newfound muscle.[16] In effect, western Pennsylvanians played right into Hamilton's hands.

Rebellion Begins

The eruption of the Whiskey Rebellion was almost solely the result of the actions of John Neville. Neville was a Virginian and an Episcopalian of English descent, and he had served in the Continental Army with George Washington, eventually attaining the rank of general. All of these traits differentiated him from his western Pennsylvanian neighbors, most of whom were of Scots-Irish or German ancestry, practiced Presbyterianism or Lutheranism, and were not professional soldiers.

Even more important, Neville's neighbors were poor—and Neville, decidedly, was not. After the Revolutionary War, Neville and his family moved west into lands he had once speculated in, where he founded the plantation of Bower Hill. Not only was the house itself likely the largest and best furnished mansion west of the Allegheny Mountains, but the grounds held a large whiskey distillery, one of the very few in the region. The distillery was worked by several enslaved people, which angered frontier whites—not because they viewed slavery as immoral (although some did), but because they believed slave labor inherently harmed their profits as free laborers. Neville also made money from various business connections throughout western Pennsylvania as well as back east. In the early 1790s he added one more line to his résumé: He became the region's federal collector of the Whiskey Excise. Simply by doing his duty and collecting the excise tax, he would invariably be putting small distillers out of business, thereby augmenting his own sales. To top it all off, he was proud, stubborn, and arrogant. No writer of fiction could have created a better frontier villain.

When Congress passed the Whiskey Excise in 1791, opposition arose throughout the western United States. Westerners in Virginia and Kentucky (then still part of Virginia), in North Carolina and South Carolina all vigorously opposed the excise tax, and most refused to pay it. And, because federal tax collectors were often isolated among such a hostile population, most of them refused to even try to collect the tax. If they did, juries refused to convict, most of which were filled with fellow tax evaders who would not condemn one of their own. This opposition meant that, in the first two years following the passage of the Whiskey Excise, virtually no taxes were collected in most western counties.

Neville, however, had no intention to quietly submit to his neighbors' lawlessness. On July 15, 1794, he willingly helped a federal marshal serve dozens of subpoenas against tax evaders, all of which mandated that offenders not only pay a tax that most could not afford, but also defend themselves in court in Philadelphia, a journey most did not have the time nor money to make. As the day went on, some twenty or thirty armed men began shadowing Neville and the marshal as they continued to deliver the subpoenas, until everyone arrived at the farm of William Miller. When served with his summons, Miller, "mad with passion" and remembering later that he felt his "blood boil," refused to accept the summons and started berating Neville and the federal marshal.[17] At this point the nearby posse intervened in support of Miller, forcing Neville and his companion to flee. As they rode off, one man fired at them. Thankfully for Neville and the marshal, the shot missed, although whether the miss was deliberate or accidental remained disputed among the participants—as were most of the events that followed.

In such a circumstance—standing alone against an armed, dangerous, and angry population—a normal man would have bolted. The federal marshal was a normal man. That night he fled to Pittsburgh. Although he would eventually be captured by the rebels, he soon escaped and secretly made his way out of the town on a barge. John Neville, by contrast, was not a normal man. Whether because of his wealth, his pride, his local political power, his connections back east, or some combination thereof, Neville rode his horse back to Bower Hill and chose to make a stand.

By the time a group of anti-tax men arrived at his plantation at midnight, Neville was ready. He had barricaded himself in his house with his family, and when the group tried to break in and seize Neville, he and those he enslaved fired at the intruders. The attackers fired back, and a twenty-five-minute standoff ensued. Inside the house, Neville's wife, Winifred, reloaded Neville's guns, as Neville used his war experience and his defensive position to shoot five attackers, one of whom was William Miller's nephew Oliver. Of the five, four would survive, but Oliver Miller did not. Outside the house, the attackers were able to riddle Bower Hill with bullets but nothing more. By morning they realized they were at a decisive military disadvantage and withdrew.

The next day, both sides brought reinforcements. Neville requested aid from his brother-in-law, Major Abraham Kirkpatrick, commanding at nearby Fort Fayette. Kirkpatrick and ten other soldiers rushed to Bower Hill. They hid Neville and the enslaved in a nearby ravine, and then barricaded themselves in the house with Neville's wife and children before any opposing force arrived—which turned out to be a quite significant one. That afternoon, somewhere between five hundred and seven hundred militiamen descended on Bower Hill. They were led by James McFarlane, a respected local leader who, like Neville, had made a name for himself fighting in the Revolution. First both sides negotiated with each other, with McFarlane allowing all women and children to leave Neville's house. Then the shooting began.

It continued for an hour, until someone in the house waived a white flag from the second floor—at least, according to the accounts of the attackers.

McFarlane called for a ceasefire and stepped into the open. A shot rang out from inside the house. McFarlane fell, mortally wounded. His seeming death-by-treachery further enraged the already incensed crowd, and they set fire to the house. Eventually, the soldiers inside surrendered and were taken into custody. The "Battle of Bower Hill," as it became known, was over. By its end, at least two men were dead, although casualties were probably higher, as it is likely a few more also died of their wounds, including one of the soldiers defending Neville's house.

The West Aflame

In the aftermath of the Battle of Bower Hill, people throughout the surrounding counties of western Pennsylvania mobilized and organized to an extent not seen since the American Revolution itself. James McFarlane's death turned small-scale resistance into widespread rebellion, or at least the appearance of such. It enflamed much of the population of the region, bringing together westerners by the thousands in a show of opposition against the whiskey tax, and, by extension, against the federal government and the Constitution.

A few weeks after the battle, thousands of mostly propertyless men gathered nine miles south of Pittsburgh at Braddock's Field, so named because it was the location where, four decades before, British officer William Braddock fell mortally wounded when his force was defeated by the French in the early days of the Seven Years' War.[18] The gathering marked the largest domestic rebellion in U.S. history until the Civil War.[19] Among those gathered were prominent men who hated the whiskey tax and sought its repeal, but thought violent resistance, let alone outright rebellion, was both unlawful and foolhardy. Three of these men in particular, William Findley, Hugh Henry Brackenridge, and Albert Gallatin, were already successful politicians and therefore quickly assumed leadership roles during the crisis—to their lament. Findley had been a leading opponent of the ratification of the Constitution in Pennsylvania in the late 1780s, and currently served in the U.S. House of Representatives for western Pennsylvania.

Brackenridge was a former representative in the Pennsylvania legislature. Gallatin was originally from Switzerland, having emigrated in 1780. He was elected to the Pennsylvania legislature in 1790. Eventually, he would be elected to the U.S. Senate in 1794, where he would quickly emerge as an outspoken opponent of Hamilton's economic program. Soon, however, Federalists discovered that Gallatin had not yet been a citizen for nine years, the minimum amount needed to serve in the Senate, and they used it as a pretext to expel him. These three men sought to steer the rebellion into less tempestuous waters, but they needed to do so stealthily, lest they suffer the same fate as John Neville.

For the moment, these moderates were sidelined by a score of radicals, most notably David Bradford. As a deputy attorney general of Washington County, one of the centers of anti-excise action, Bradford was a man on the make—but only to a point. In recent years, he had struggled to rise any further up the local political ranks, and now he seized the opportunity to do so.[20]

While moderates like Findley urged caution, Bradford called for immediate action, rallying the crowd to march on Pittsburgh. Although still a small town compared to eastern cities, it was the largest, most prosperous settlement in western Pennsylvania. Unsurprisingly, rural Pennsylvanians regarded Pittsburgh's (comparatively) wealthier, Federalist-leaning inhabitants as embodying all the same evils as the whiskey tax. Whether the plan was to destroy the town as they had Bower Hill, find the most offending inhabitants and tar and feather them, or simply demonstrate their power and moral authority in a peaceful march remains disputed. Whatever the case, residents of Pittsburgh took no chances, sending the wealthiest inhabitants out of town while liberally providing the crowd with—appropriately—free whiskey (the irony seems to have been lost on the restless crowd). Meanwhile, the guns of Fort Fayette hovered nearby, serving as a warning to the marchers. In the end, the rebels marched, drank, broke some windows, searched in vain for their enemies, and, eventually, dispersed. At the same time, Bradford and other rebel leaders robbed the postman to prevent information from spreading to Philadelphia. They then planned to reconvene in two weeks at Parkinson's Ferry, where two delegates from each of the surrounding counties in Pennsylvania and western Virginia would convene to further plan their resistance to the whiskey tax—and, by extension, to the United States. To them, the American Revolution had begun again.

The march on Pittsburgh turned out to be the high point of the conflict. The next phase began two weeks later, when 250 men convened at Parkinson's Ferry. Among them was once again David Bradford, who continued to urge decisive action, as well as Herman Husband, who was elected as a delegate from Bedford County. Husband had not been present at Bower Hill or Braddock's Field, but both his radical ideology and his radical (albeit pacifist) past in North Carolina made him an obvious delegate. At the convention, delegates flew a flag of six stripes, representing the five rebellious counties of western Pennsylvania as well as Virginia's Ohio County.[21] Whether this flag simply represented defiance toward the federal government or was an overt demonstration of support for outright secession from the United States is impossible to tell. Indeed, at this point, the inchoate nature of the rebellion meant that every rebel could have sought a different future and envisioned a different outcome. One neutral firsthand observer of the conflict made just this point, arguing that some rebels had an "ancient aversion" to the Pennsylvania government and wanted to form a new state in the Union, while others wanted to go much further, seeking a "seizure of the Western lands, a union with Kentucky, the navigation of the Mississippi, and a connection with Great Britain." A third group was simply caught up in "the blind impulse of the moment."[22] No one knew what the rebels would do. It was at this point of chaos, defiance, and uncertainty that three federal commissioners arrived from Philadelphia.

The Federal Response

Since learning of the attack on Bower Hill in mid-July, George Washington, Alexander Hamilton, and the rest of Washington's cabinet had not been idle. Hamilton had been urging action against the defiant, tax-evading westerners for several years, but had found little support among his peers in the cabinet. Here, finally, he believed the moment (*his* moment?) had arrived.

As a focus for suppressing resistance, western Pennsylvania offered several benefits. First, and most obviously, the "Battle of Bower Hill" and the march on Pittsburgh could be portrayed as—and, to Hamilton, *were*—attacks against the federal government itself. It was much easier to justify an expedition against these rebels than against isolated incidents of tarring and feathering of excise officers (as had happened in western Pennsylvania a few years prior), let alone other, even more limited and much less obvious methods of resistance, such as offenders not showing up for subpoenas or sympathetic juries refusing to convict offenders. As Hamilton noted in a letter to Washington, western Pennsylvania "distinguished its resistance, by a more excessive spirit" than other places of unrest.[23]

Second, western Pennsylvania was the ideal location to quell a rebellion. Of all areas of western grievance, it was by far the closest to Philadelphia, the U.S. capital at the time. Doing nothing in response would appear at the very least embarrassing, or, much worse, invite further attacks on federal authority across the entire frontier.

Third, Hamilton believed that, in some fashion, the insurrection in western Pennsylvania was connected to the Democratic-Republican Societies that were coalescing throughout the United States in opposition to the administration's Federalist policies.[24] While there certainly were connections—many of the rebels had joined these societies, Hugh Henry Brackenridge among them—it was not the deeper conspiracy that Hamilton believed it was. Nevertheless, Hamilton, and Washington too, believed these societies were extralegal and therefore illegitimate, and crushing the rebellion would send a message to this potentially disloyal group. As Hamilton later put it, in the face of any significant opposition, the federal government "ought to appear like a *Hercules*."[25]

Behind the administration's opposition to the Whiskey Rebels lay a crucial ideological shift that had occurred since the American Revolution, and even more so since the ratification of the Constitution. Rebels like David Bradford could point to a long tradition of what was then termed "crowd action," in which the common people (or the mob, depending on one's perspective) made their voices heard through organizing and marching, raising liberty poles, burning symbols and people in effigy, tarring and feathering targeted officials, and, in some cases, destroying property. This latter option was rare, however, and, if property was destroyed, it was a specific target rather than randomized looting and arson. Crowd action was not about random anger, but rather forcing officials to change a specific policy or forcing local merchants to drop the price of goods, all for the welfare of the common people. The crowd was upholding its idea of a "moral economy."[26] Both the crowd and government officials viewed these actions as a legitimate attempt to make the people's wishes heard, and quite often the government responded to the mob's requests, at least to a certain degree. Governing officials viewed these actions as legitimate because the "middling" and "lower sort" were permanently barred from government. By the mid to late eighteenth century, the height of the European Enlightenment, the common people were not expected to simply agree to everything, particularly when a policy hurt their livelihoods—but they were not expected or allowed to take part in governing, either.[27]

In 1787, everything changed. Now "We the People" wrote and ratified the U.S. Constitution. Employing this half-truth, Federalists could argue that formerly legitimate crowd action was now illegitimate, for "the People" *were* represented, and, officially, "the People" were sovereign. If western Pennsylvanians did not like the excise tax, then they should simply vote for new representatives who would change federal policy. Because the government *was* the people, the people no longer had the right to challenge the government through extralegal means. As federal authorities later stated to the rebels, "Formal resistance . . . violated the great principle, on which republican government was founded. . . . It was manifestly absurd to oppose the national authority."[28] And so, while the Whiskey Rebels saw their actions as part of a long tradition of legitimate, antigovernment action, exemplified by Herman Husband's participation, Hamilton and his Federalist allies saw the disorder as fundamentally illegitimate. To them, because they lived under a republican government, Americans no longer had a right to rebel. The Whiskey Rebellion needed to be suppressed. The time for revolution was over.

While Hamilton had been urging the use of force for several years, George Washington was less sure. An impulsive "act first, think later" army officer during the Seven Years' War and the first year of the Revolutionary

War, Washington had learned from his military failures by the end of 1776. For the rest of the war, he fought a "war of posts," refusing to risk his army in an all-or-nothing battle. By the 1790s he had left his hotheadedness behind him permanently, becoming the Washington of lore: reflective, calculating, and careful, but determined. He listened to Hamilton, but he also listened to his attorney general, Edmund Randolph, who advocated sending a peace commission that would hear out rebel grievances. True to form, Washington did both. He sent three commissioners, all of them prominent Pennsylvanians, to parley with the rebels. He then readied U.S. forces for war.

When the commissioners arrived at Parkinson's Ferry, the moderates at the meeting were ecstatic. For weeks, men like Hugh Henry Brackenridge and Albert Gallatin had been pulled along by the radical crowd, fearful that if they did not participate in the Braddock's Field meeting and convention at Parkinson's Ferry, they would be singled out like Neville, and their homes and property would be attacked. They hoped to steer the resistance away from violence, especially outright rebellion, but they could only do so with nudges and whispers, lest they get called out by the radicals as being Federalists. Now they hoped the commissioners had opened space for a peaceful discourse.

Their hopes were quickly dashed. The commissioners saw the raised liberty pole, felt the hostility of most of the delegates, and heard from men like David Bradford. According to the commissioners, Bradford, "in a violent speech, was for resistance, stating the practicability of it,—that arms could be procured from the militia whom they could easily defeat, and the property and every thing else ought to be risqued in so righteous a cause."[29] Witnessing the tumult, the commissioners reported to Washington that only military intervention would end the rebellion.

A few weeks later, leaders of the insurgency met again, this time at the town of Brownsville, thirty miles south of Pittsburgh. Hoping to stave off a military intervention that seemed increasingly likely, they voted 34 to 23 to submit to federal authorities. They did not know that it was too late: the army was already on its way. *As it should be*, thought the federal commissioners observing the vote. The narrow vote for capitulation only further solidified their belief in the need for armed force. Forty percent of the rebel leaders (twenty-three out of fifty-seven) still voted for resistance. And, while statements of submission to the federal authorities had started to pour in from all the western counties of Pennsylvania, there were not enough statements to account for a majority of the population—although, as moderates seeking a compromise pointed out, ensuring these submission letters from remote areas of the backcountry actually got to the commissioners was a challenge.[30] Moderates hoped the federal government would wait just one week more, by which point they believed an overwhelming number of western Pennsylvanians would demonstrate their thorough loyalty.[31] The federal commissioners did not care.

Repercussions

The Whiskey Rebellion ended not with a bang but a whimper. In early September 1794, a thirteen-thousand-man federal force marched west to crush all resistance. It was far less formidable than it looked on paper. Most of the army was composed of militia, much of which was composed of draftees forced into the ranks—and some federal officials even suspected that the westerners who had been drafted would refuse to fight against their fellow westerners.[32] Nevertheless, thirteen thousand men was still thirteen thousand men, far more than the insurgents in western Pennsylvania could muster. More importantly, it was ostensibly commanded by George Washington, who was accompanied by Alexander Hamilton and General "Light Horse" Harry Lee, Revolutionary War heroes all. In reality, Washington came to oversee the army for just a week, and then left it in the capable hands of General Lee, whom he believed could easily quell what remained of the uprising.

Washington's presence, although brief, was nevertheless crucial. Even westerners who hated the Constitution and loathed the federal government and its policies did not want to take up arms against Washington himself. To anti-tax westerners, the luster of Washington's Revolutionary War service and leadership may have dulled, but it had not disappeared. It had been one thing to attack John Neville, but it was quite another to attack the "Father of the Country." Even David Bradford, the bellicose rebel leader who just weeks before had argued that the insurgents could defeat anything thrown against them, expressed "great embarrassment" over his earlier actions.[33] He then fled west, away from the approaching army.

He was not alone. Roughly two thousand rebels also escaped into the backcountry, some on a temporary basis, waiting until the army retreated until they returned to their homes. Others left permanently. Bradford himself fled to Spanish Louisiana, where he resumed practicing law. His wife, Elizabeth, twice petitioned Washington for clemency to no avail, but eventually President John Adams pardoned him in 1799.[34]

With so many insurgents gone, the army did its best to round up those who remained. In the end, they captured twenty men and marched them to Philadelphia to stand trial for treason. Yet, in most of the trials, either there were no witnesses or there was a case of mistaken identity. Everyone knew that the ringleaders had escaped, and those arrested were clearly bit players in the larger drama. Ultimately, most were acquitted. Only two men were sentenced to death, but Washington pardoned both.

Herman Husband was one of the twenty arrested. The evidence for his guilt lay in his many eccentric but explicit writings, in which he advocated resistance to what he saw as a nefarious federal government. True to form, Husband remained a pacifist throughout the entire insurgency. As a rebel delegate at Parkinson's Ferry, he advocated only peaceful resistance. To no one's surprise, he was quickly acquitted. Yet Husband, who had once nicknamed himself "Tuscape Death" after fleeing from North Carolina, could no longer escape the inevitable. The journey to Philadelphia and the long confinement had taken their toll on the seventy-year-old. Husband started the journey back to Bedford County, but he could not get farther than the outskirts of the city, where he collapsed and died in June of 1795.

Husband's death marked the end of an era. As first a North Carolina Regulator and then a Whiskey Rebel, he epitomized the tradition of simmering frontier discontent and periodic frontier rebellion that stretched back for over a century. He also embodied the legacy of the American Revolution, with its powerful rhetoric that justified rebellion against tyranny.

Legacy

History textbooks almost always argue that the Whiskey Rebellion proved, above all, the efficacy of the new Constitution. During Shays's Rebellion, the weak Confederation government failed to respond to a national crisis. A few years later, the newly created and newly empowered federal government crushed the Whiskey Rebellion. The lesson: the U.S. Constitution worked.

There is much to this argument that rings true. Participants on both sides and countless observers expressed as much. As one of the former rebels noted in his petition to Washington asking for clemency, "The total suppression of the late insurrection and the terror and submission which have succeeded to the late opposition to the laws of the United States, appear to render public example of justice unnecessary at the time with the view of preventing a repetition of similar acts of rebellion."[35] In other words, the federal government had so utterly crushed the rebellion that there was no need to double down with further imprisonment for the offenders. Although the plea was self-serving, it did not make it any less true. Hugh Henry Brackenridge, one of the moderates who had disliked the whiskey tax but did not support rebellion, agreed, writing of the rebellion, "An early and effective lesson was given in our republican government."[36]

Yet this traditional portrayal is only a half-truth that tells half a story. As we have seen, in the short term, very few of those who took part in the insurrection were captured. Two thousand fled farther west, some until the federal army departed, and others, like David Bradford, on a more permanent basis. Even after Bradford received his pardon from President Adams in 1799, he only returned to western Pennsylvania to settle his affairs, and soon traveled back to Spanish Louisiana and, it seems, a moderately successful legal practice.[37] In this sense, the thinly spread population of the West was both a curse and a blessing for the Whiskey Rebels. It was a curse because it prevented prolonged organizing: Even if the 7,000 men who gathered at Braddock's Field were passionate about sustained opposition to the government, they still needed to return to their homes to farm and provide for their families. That fewer and fewer insurgents attended each subsequent meeting (7,000 to 250 to 50) may have reflected cooling passions, but it also demonstrated that it was difficult for westerners to travel dozens of miles over poor or nonexistent roads. At the same time, the dispersal of the western population also meant that the former rebels were invariably one or two steps ahead of army officials tasked with arresting them, and they had plenty of places to go to hide out—for a short time or, like Bradford, forever.[38]

Furthermore, after the Whiskey Rebellion, it was not as if the coffers of the federal government suddenly filled with proceeds from the Whiskey Excise. With all resisters cowed into submission, there was a substantial increase in revenue from western Pennsylvania in 1795, but this did not last.[39] Just like disaffected distillers in Kentucky, Virginia, Maryland, and the Carolinas, after 1795 western Pennsylvanians once again stopped paying their taxes. William Findley later claimed that up to one-third of the revenue from the whiskey tax was spent paying tax collectors, most of whom were unable to do their jobs thanks to western opposition. To him, the excise tax was a waste of resources. Indeed, practically no taxes from the western United States were *ever* collected until after the Civil War, more than sixty years later.[40] Washington, Hamilton, and the U.S. Army may have suppressed outright revolt, but they clearly did not suppress the more restrained defiance of thousands of westerners. Ostensibly, the Whiskey Rebellion demonstrated a triumph of federal power. Looking deeper, however, it is more accurate to claim that the outcome of the Whiskey Rebellion was—quietly—a de facto armistice between the federal government and discontented westerners.

Textbooks and historians portray the Whiskey Rebellion as a sort of coda to the American Revolution. It was, in Tom Slaughter's words, the Revolution's "frontier epilogue." And it *was* an epilogue—but it also encapsulated the ongoing tension between Americans' hopes for the post-revolutionary world and that world's lived reality. The Whiskey Rebels were not alone among Americans who believed that the promises of the Revolution had not been fulfilled—although what these promises were varied from American to American. Most Americans, however, did not rebel. Instead, they hoped that their state governments and the new federal government would be able to see these promises fulfilled, at least to a certain extent, down the road. In other words, they would continue to hold their elected officials to account. Capital-r Ratification of the Constitution was a onetime event, but small-r ratification of the constitutional order was a continual process.

Thomas Jefferson understood this all too well—at least when it came to white men. While he had written that patriot "blood" was necessary for refreshing the "tree of liberty," it seems unlikely that Jefferson actually longed for periodic revolutions in the United States, with all their violence and unpredictability (neither of which would support Jefferson personally, with his genteel lifestyle predicated on the stability of Southern slavery). Rather, Jefferson was more concerned about a government that grew unconcerned about, perhaps even hostile to, the desires of its constituents, one that grew increasingly aristocratic and monarchic—one that, to Jefferson's horror, increasingly resembled the Federalists in power. Without a government that could respond to the will of the people, perhaps periodic rebellions *would* be necessary. The question was: Was the Constitution democratic enough to actually respond to the people's desires?

Perhaps surprisingly, considering the conservatism embedded in the Constitution's framework, it was. We can see this dynamic clearly when tracing the history of some of the famous moderates who got caught up in the Whiskey Rebellion, men like William Findley, Albert Gallatin, and Hugh Henry Brackenridge. While David Bradford and Herman Husband looked backward to the long history of western rebellions and the American Revolution to justify their actions, these moderates looked forward to an age of stability by effectively meeting Washington and Hamilton halfway. First, they recognized that, with U.S. independence secure and the Constitution ratified, rebellion was now problematic because it could start a pattern. As one submission letter stated, "If every corner of the United States claim a right to oppose what they dislike, no one law will be obeyed. . . . And, if ever, the fatal lesson is taught the inhabitants of this extensive republic to shed one another's blood, we may for ever bid farewell to harmony, to mutual confidence, and to peace."[41] The only way to avoid cyclical rebellion was to never start the cycle.

But if the Constitution did in fact reflect that the people were now sovereign, and these people elected representatives to run the day-to-day business of government, then these same people had every right to follow the parameters of the Constitution to peacefully oppose the status quo, and—eventually—peacefully replace it by electing new representatives. This was the premise of the fledgling, soon-to-be flourishing Democratic-

Republican Societies that countered Federalist policies, which became, in effect, the first legitimate opposition in U.S. political history. Led by Thomas Jefferson and James Madison at the federal level, and countless other politicians at the state and local levels, Democratic-Republicans began to amass power, first in the states in the mid-1790s and, in 1800, over the federal government itself. It was this election, known as the "Revolution of 1800," where Jefferson was elected president, and one party peacefully transferred power to another for the first time in U.S. history.

The moderates who had sought to steer the Whiskey Rebellion down a less violent path ended up taking power. William Findley continued to serve in the U.S. House of Representatives until 1799, and then was elected to the Pennsylvania State Senate for the next two decades. Hugh Henry Brackenridge ran for the U.S. House of Representatives in 1795 and was defeated, but he was then appointed to the Pennsylvania Supreme Court by Pennsylvania's Democratic-Republican governor Thomas McKean, which he served on until his death in 1816. The person who defeated Brackenridge in 1795 was none other than Albert Gallatin, who once again became a leading opponent of Hamilton's fiscal policies in Congress. In 1801, Jefferson appointed Gallatin secretary of the treasury, Hamilton's former position. At the impetus of Gallatin, one of the Jefferson administration's first measures was to abolish the hated Whiskey Excise. Federalists fumed, claiming Jefferson walked "arm in arm" with former Whiskey Rebels, but they were now the minority party with a diminishing grasp on power.[42] So much for Hamilton's great victory over the rabble of western Pennsylvania—some of that rabble now controlled the federal government.

While the United States changed much over the next several decades, the general relationship between white Americans living along the western frontier and the federal government did not. Westerners, particularly poor westerners squatting on unclaimed land, continued to complain that the federal government did not do enough to expel Indians, and they continued to find themselves at the mercy of speculators and their political allies. When federal officials invariably arrived, they pushed squatters off their land, who then moved west yet again to begin the process anew. As years went on, however, westerners did see some gains: In 1795, Pinckney's Treaty between the United States and Spain gained them access to the

Mississippi River. Then, in 1803, the Louisiana Purchase made the entire middle third of the continent U.S. territory (at least officially—Native people actually controlled most of the land for many more decades). Most westerners remained illegal squatters, but with so much more land available, it was much easier to get away with it. The Whiskey Rebellion, therefore, became the last of western rebellions, a frontier "epilogue" to *the* American Revolution rather than the first in series of American revolution*s*. To be sure, U.S. history has continued to be marked by violent riots and upheavals, but none has matched the Whiskey Rebellion in the rebels' explicit arguments (to some extent correct ones) that they were heirs to the "Spirit of '76."

Of course, the Civil War's Confederates were very much rebels, and they initiated by far the most violent and threatening rebellion in all U.S. history. Yet the Southern rebels of 1861 did not define themselves as such. Instead, they were "secessionists." Even in 1861, for millions of white Southerners who now gave their allegiance to the Confederate States of America—all seemingly united around a common effort that they believed honorable and justified—it was a step too far to deem their actions "rebellion," let alone "revolution." "Rebellion" implied illegitimacy, and "revolution" implied radical, chaotic change. By contrast, the Confederates' secession was, in their eyes, a constitutionally legal, morally vindicated, restorative counterrevolution. Indeed, for more than half a century, from the Virginia and Kentucky Resolutions in the late 1790s to South Carolina Nullification in the early 1830s, Southern slaveholders had developed a legal framework that saw secession as a defensive, conservative act. To Southern fire-eaters, it was Lincoln and the Republicans who were the potential revolutionaries, so Southerners had every right to withdraw from the Union to avoid calamitous revolution. Lincoln and his allies, meanwhile, believed secession was essentially the same as rebellion—and, because it was rebellion, the federal government had every right to suppress it.[43] For both sides, the right of rebellion no longer existed.

3

The Rights of Women: New Jersey's Radical Experiment, 1789–1807

In mid-October, 1800, in the northern New Jersey county of Somerset, in the small town of Pluckamin, at the tavern of John Van Duyn, a woman named Sarah Eoff did something that, after 1807, no woman would do in New Jersey for more than a century.

She voted.

She was not alone. Immediately following Eoff at the polls was Margaret McDonald, and two voters later came Eleanor Hodge Boylan. They were numbers 106, 107, and 109 on the voting list, out of 118 total people who voted that day in Pluckamin.[1]

Voting after McDonald and before Boylan, number 108 on the voter list, was a man named Hugh Gaston. Gaston knew all three women quite well, and he accompanied them to the polls. There was good reason for this. During the first decades of the early republic—and, indeed, until the early twentieth century—voting days were rowdy affairs. As with this election in Pluckamin, votes were frequently cast at local taverns and inns, where men drank and socialized for one or even two days. For them, election day was a party. For these three women, however, entering the raucous, masculine world of the tavern was thoroughly outside the ordinary, for they were wealthy, unmarried, and—of course—women. The music would have stopped and all tavern-goers would have gone silent, staring at these unwanted interlopers—or so we can imagine.

These three women could vote because they were property owners, and, in New Jersey, any "inhabitant" who owned property in New Jersey could vote. In the years after the American Revolution, the ownership of property was one of the key prerequisites for voting in almost all states, but only in New Jersey did this lead to female voters. In all other states, even men who believed that women with property should have the right to vote feared what would happen to women if they went to the polls. The Virginian Richard Henry Lee, signer of the Declaration of Independence and one of Virginia's most dynamic Patriot leaders, claimed he would "at any time give my consent to establish [propertied women's] right to vote." But he maintained that the "tumultuous assemblies" found at the polls were inappropriate places for women.[2] Best to leave voting to men, for their sex made them comfortable amid such "tumult."

For men, voting day may have been a party, but the actual process of voting remained something of an ordeal—one that these women also had to have gone through when casting their ballots on that October day in 1800. For much of colonial American history, voting was conducted *viva voce*, meaning the voter proclaimed his choice publicly. This practice could be subject to voter intimidation and blackmail—indeed, to the elite, that was the point. Voters would not vote against the choice of their employers or patrons if it meant losing their job or patronage.

No wonder, then, that in the aftermath of the American Revolution, American voters sought change. By the 1790s, more and more states, including New Jersey's Somerset County where these women voted, conducted elections via a written ballot.[3] Yet a written ballot was not necessarily a secret ballot, as we have today. Often, just before voting, a local partisan in the tavern would hand the voter a slip of paper with a particular set of candidates. Onlookers would know who that person was and what candidates were on that slip of paper. Perhaps, of course, a voter would come in with their own slip of paper, but that was still suspicious for its secrecy. In either case, the voter next swore a public oath to the sheriff of elections that they were who they said they were, and then placed the slip in the ballot box—once again, for everyone to see. With so many partisan and passionate onlookers, including the sheriff and inspector of elections, voting remained a thoroughly public act.

We have no firsthand accounts from any of these women, so it is impossible to determine how each woman actually felt about entering the inn, swearing an oath, and putting her choice of candidates in the box. Perhaps they were nervous, even intimidated, for they were taking an unprecedented step out in the open, in public, for all tavern-goers to see. They were, in essence, running a gauntlet of eighteenth-century masculinity. Judging by the fact that they traveled to the tavern together, and were accompanied by a male family friend, perhaps they felt the need for both female solidarity and a male chaperone.

On the other hand, all three women were distinguished and resilient. They all came from prominent Somerset County families, were well known in the local village, were over forty years old, and had seen hardship and experienced the difficulties of eighteenth-century life. Margaret McDonald and Eleanor Boylan were widows who had recently buried their husbands, both of whom had been paragons of Pluckamin. (The village's adorable name originated from either an obscure Scottish village, the French word for "date-plum" [*plaqueminier*], or a local landlord who wanted everyone in the village to come drink in his manor, and thus was "Plucking-them-in.")[4] Boylan's husband served as an officer in the Patriot militia during the Revolutionary War, and Boylan herself gave birth to fifteen children and would go on to outlive her husband by fifty years, dying in 1845 at the age of ninety-seven. Local lore claimed she had once danced with George Washington in 1779, at a ball that celebrated the founding of the U.S.-French alliance, making her famous by the standards of the village. With such a background, perhaps Boylan felt few qualms about voting. Sarah Eoff, by contrast, had never been married and never would marry, but, given that her father and then her brother owned another local tavern, perhaps she felt comfortable in such a raucous setting.[5] Considering that no other women voted at Van Duyn's tavern that day, at the very least these three women were willing to stand out in the crowd.

If we cannot know how they felt, we do know how they voted. They all chose Democratic-Republican candidates, the party of Thomas Jefferson, rather than the Federalists, the party of the sitting president John Adams. They did so in a county and a village that remained staunchly Federalist, with Federalist candidates usually receiving twice as many votes as Republicans. Here, too, was a reason these women may have been wary. They were out of place not just because of their sex, but because of their politics.

Whatever the reason they voted on that date and for those people, the fact remains: they voted. In the United States in 1800, no other women could vote, except in New Jersey. In New Jersey, some could—and some did.

How did this happen?

Women and the Revolution

There would never have been an American Revolution without American women.

Revolutionary wives, mothers, and daughters surely influenced their revolutionary husbands, sons, and brothers as the resistance to Great Britain swelled in the late 1760s and early 1770s, but it is nearly impossible to uncover how their influence specifically changed the political dynamics within each home. Starting in 1773, however, we can finally see the full-scale mobilization of women *as women*. Because women at the time were responsible for purchasing goods for the home, their participation was crucial for the "nonimportation" and "nonconsumption" policies of the First Continental Congress to have any effect. They did not just participate, however; they *led*, forming Daughters of Liberty associations in towns and cities throughout the colonies. They also gathered in groups, often organized through their church congregations, where they wove "homespun" to replace the now boycotted British-made cloth.

In a war that killed a higher percentage of Americans than any other war in U.S. history save the Civil War, thousands of women lost husbands and sons to the revolutionary cause. Some became "camp followers," accompanying their husbands into the Continental Army and state militias, where they knitted clothes, mended wounds, and foraged for food. Other women remained at home, where they independently managed finances and provided for children amid wartime violence and scarcity, all without the oversight of their husbands and fathers. A few even disguised themselves and became Continental soldiers themselves, most famously Deborah Sampson, a Massachusetts woman who served undetected for seventeen months in the Continental Army and was even wounded during her enlistment period.

New Jersey women in particular had it more difficult than most, simply because New Jersey was a center of wartime violence. Somewhere between three hundred and six hundred violent incidents occurred in New Jersey throughout the course of the war, most famously Washington's victories at Trenton and Princeton, as well as Monmouth Courthouse, the final large battle of the war's northern theater.[6] New Jersey women witnessed British and Patriot armies crisscross their fields, eat their food, and ransack their shops. For some it was far worse, as soldiers from both sides chose to take advantage of the chaos and violence to sexually and physically assault women. As in so many other brutal conflicts, rape became a weapon of war. For example, a thirteen-year-old girl from Huntington County was raped by passing soldiers over four consecutive nights in 1777, while another woman from the same county fought off a rape attack against both her and her ten-year-old daughter.[7] By the end of the war, New Jerseyites had endured the most revolutionary violence of any other state, and it was New Jersey women in particular who bore the brunt of it.

With such a history, it was no coincidence that New Jersey gave birth to one of the most famous legends of the Revolutionary War. When Mary Ludwig Hays's husband enlisted in an artillery regiment in the Continental Army, Hays stayed by her husband's side, becoming a camp follower like hundreds of other women. She was present at Valley Forge, where she cared for the sick and dying during that brutal winter. At the Battle of Monmouth six months later, the weather was torrid, and Hays did her duty—again, as so many women did—bringing water to Continental soldiers clothed in wool uniforms. When her husband collapsed from heat exhaustion, Hays reportedly took his place at his cannon until the battle ended at the close of the day. According to one—probably apocryphal—account, she even lost the bottom half of her skirt to a cannonball that traveled between her legs, reportedly shrugging it off with a phrase that could have been quipped by a superheroine: "Well, that could have been worse."

And so was born the legend of "Molly Pitcher," as soldiers reportedly yelled out "Molly! Pitcher!" when they called Hays to bring them water. Yet Hays was hardly exceptional (unless one counts her ability to generate wisecracks in the heat of battle).[8] In reality, there were many Molly Pitchers scattered throughout New Jersey and the rest of the colonies who gave everything they could to the Patriot cause. Other women dedicated themselves to the Loyalist side. Many more worked to ensure that they and their families simply survived. Ultimately, no matter what side they were on, the war brought death, trauma, and despair to women, just as it did to men.

New Jersey women knew they had sacrificed much. In 1780, an unnamed woman who referred to herself only as a "Lady in New Jersey" sought to emulate a group of Philadelphia women who raised thousands of dollars for the revolutionary cause. Writing in *The New Jersey Gazette*, this woman bristled with outrage, saying that the British not only "lay waste the fields" and "destroy[ed] our dwellings," but "desolated the aged and unprotected, and even waged war upon our sex." The paper then listed dozens of names of women throughout the state who had already contributed to the wartime fund, imploring more to do so.[9]

After the war, New Jersey women continued to make the case for their importance to the Revolution. In 1789, George Washington was famously greeted by the "ladies" of Trenton, the site of his most legendary victory, on the way to his first presidential inauguration. Trenton women erected a triumphal arch over a creek at the city's entrance, upon which they wrote, "THE DEFENDER OF THE MOTHERS WILL ALSO PROTECT THEIR DAUGHTERS." When Washington arrived, these mothers and daughters, all dressed in white and garnered with wreaths, lined Washington's path, with mothers in the back and daughters in the front. Women had been integral to U.S. independence, and they would not be ignored. Washington got the message, leaving them a note that stated (in Washington's typically halting, comma-laden phrasing), "General Washington cannot leave this place, without expressing his acknowledgment to the matrons and young ladies, who received him in so novel and grateful manner at the triumphal arch in Trenton, for the exquisite sensation he experienced in that affecting moment."[10] It seems New Jersey's husbands, fathers, and sons also got the message, for, by allowing limited female suffrage, they turned the revolutionary rhetoric of liberty and equality into reality.

The New Jersey Exception

Female suffrage in New Jersey probably started by accident. In 1776, only months after the Declaration of Independence was signed in Philadelphia, New Jersey revolutionaries wrote a new state constitution. In these early years of the Revolutionary War, Patriots sought to liberalize the old conservative structures of colonial governance. Some created governments that were quite radical for their time. Most famously, Pennsylvanians wrote a constitution that provided for annual elections to a single legislative body, with virtually no property requirements for voting. Pennsylvania's constitution ensured that electors would have to faithfully represent their constituents, or else they would face the wrath of the people in only a year's time at the next election.

New Jersey Patriots, by contrast, were less radical, implementing a bicameral legislature with steep property requirements for would-be officials—£500 for the Assembly, and £1,000 for the more elite Council. Voters themselves, however, did not need to be nearly as wealthy. A voter needed to possess only £50 of property in any form, which was quite a modest sum. It was low enough, in fact, that election officials would struggle to prove that any man was *in*eligible. Most importantly for what came next, the New Jersey Constitution allowed all "inhabitants" to vote, so long as "they"—not "he"—had resided in the state a year and were at least twenty-one years old.[11]

"Inhabitants" and "they": these two words were the crux of the issue. If they were not intended to become revolutionary, they soon became so. An inhabitant was someone who lived in the state—male or female, black or white. It seems unlikely that the men who wrote the New Jersey Constitution intended for women to vote, but these words were ambiguous, there for any New Jersey woman with £50 of property to seize the opportunity.

This property requirement still meant that most women could not vote, for most women over twenty-one were married. By the tenets of U.S. law (and its British antecedent), the doctrine of coverture stated that, when a woman married, her legal personhood merged with that of her husband. In real-world terms, this meant that any property she possessed became her husband's, and therefore, through marriage, she became propertyless—and subsequently unable to pass the £50 requirement to vote. While it may have been difficult to prove a man possessed less than £50, it was usually not difficult to prove a woman was married. Even if all women were inhabitants, only the single and widowed could actually vote.

Despite these restrictions, the exception nevertheless remained: *some* women *could* vote. New Jersey was not alone in its ambiguous language—quite the contrary. Of the thirteen original states, eight had statutes that did not specify voters by sex, also using words like "inhabitant."[12] Yet it was only in New Jersey that some women—very few, at first—seized the opportunity to vote.

In 1787, the same year that fifty-five men in Philadelphia met to draw up the document that would become the U.S. Constitution, two women walked into a polling place in Burlington, New Jersey, and voted. Members of the Society of Friends, more commonly known as Quakers, comprised a significant portion of Burlington's population, and they believed in the radical doctrine of spiritual equality—among all races and both sexes. Two Quaker women, coming from Quaker families who practiced an early, albeit modest version of gender equality, decided that they were as much "inhabitants" as anyone else and went to vote for their representatives. (To be sure, we cannot be certain they were Quakers, but given Burlington's demographics and the religious group's views on gender, this is the likeliest scenario.)[13]

They were 2 out of 225 voters that day in Burlington, such a small percentage that no one seems to have noted the anomaly, let alone raise any objection. Women may have voted in previous years but, because most voter rolls have not survived, we have no way of knowing for sure. What happened in the next few years also remains a mystery. With no objection raised, and no larger backlash, these two women may have told friends and family members about their experience, causing additional women to vote. Perhaps word trickled out from men at the polls, remarking to their wives and daughters that *women had been at the polling place!* Many radical Quakers may have noted this surprising occurrence with approval, while more conservative onlookers may have deplored the practice. Some men, those who were involved in or at least understood politics, saw this as an opportunity for more voters, and thus more victories, for their party of choice—as we shall see. Whatever the case, and however it happened, word eventually got out to the rest of the state, and then beyond: In New Jersey, women voted.

The names and numbers of most of these female voters are probably lost forever. Most election records were simply tallies of votes rather than lists of names. How many of those tallies represented the votes of women remains impossible to determine. Nevertheless, some of those downward slashes of the quill, among the dozens and hundreds of votes in each township, represented a radical and revolutionary development. The anonymity of each tally is a powerful symbol of this revolution: A woman's vote was equal to a man's, so equal that we cannot distinguish which tallies stand for women and which for men. A vote was a vote.

In 1790, New Jersey politicians acknowledged that women could and did vote, as evidenced by the new references to voters as "he or she" in the records of the seven counties in southern New Jersey.[14] The transition from 1787, when a few women took advantage of the ambiguity of the word "inhabitants," to 1790, when unmarried, propertied women were legally enfranchised, remains mysterious. There is no evidence of any public outcry, whether by women or their male allies, to officially extend the franchise and eliminate the ambiguity of "inhabitants." If women did advocate for the vote, then they did so in private places, within the confines of their homes and in the company of family and close friends. If they did, their words are lost to the fog of history.

The Rights of Women, Affirmed

The halting progress toward women's political empowerment in New Jersey shifted into a much higher gear in the early 1790s, driven partially by developments across the Atlantic. In 1789, the people of Paris stormed the Bastille while their representatives at Versailles swore the Tennis Court Oath, twin events that commenced the French Revolution. In the tumultuous years that followed in France, through every twist and turn of the chaotic, epoch-defining drama, there were women—marching to Versailles in 1789, invading the Tuileries Palace in 1792, and carrying the body of Marat, the murdered radical journalist, in a public procession in 1793. In 1791, the Parisian Olympe de Gouges responded to the lack of attention to women in the 1789 Declaration of the Rights of Man and of the Citizen with her pamphlet, "Declaration of the Rights of Women and Female Citizen."

Across the English Channel, Mary Wollstonecraft further amplified female demands. This self-educated Englishwoman was caught up, like so many women and men, with the possibilities of the French Revolution. Yet she was disappointed when French revolutionaries implemented national male education but neglected the education of women.[15] In response, she published *A Vindication of the Rights of Woman.* It would prove to be the most influential argument for women's rights for the next century.

Employing fiery rhetoric, Wollstonecraft blasted the "tyranny of men" and advocated for women's full and equal incorporation into civil society. She did not explicitly advocate for women's political rights, only mentioning the prospect of women voting in a sidebar that stated she was "dropping a hint" that may "excite laughter."[16] Nevertheless, *A Vindication of the Rights of Woman* was a revolutionary document, and, across the Atlantic, countless Americans—women *and* men—were inspired by its incendiary rhetoric. In Philadelphia, writer and newspaper editor Mathew Carey printed 1,500 copies, an astounding number for the era.[17]

Wollstonecraft may have been the loudest and most influential proponent of female equality at the time, but she was not the first—as we should expect. After all, the French Revolution came more than a decade after the American Revolution. It was in the United States, not France, where the first stirrings of liberty could be found—for women as well as for men. New Englander Judith Sargent certainly felt these stirrings. Thanks to her family's wealth, Sargent had the privilege of a regular tutor as a child, making her far better educated than most women in British North America. Her education soon became a source of frustration, however, for while her brother went off to Harvard and a wide-open future of myriad possibilities, Sargent had only one future: marriage and children. She married a local merchant in 1769 at the age of eighteen, but she did not become pregnant, which was essentially her societal duty as a married woman. During these early years of marriage, she and her family converted from Congregationalism to Universalism, a liberal Christian denomination that denied the existence of hell and maintained that all humans would one day be saved. Universalism gained adherents at the same time that the American Revolution entered its most radical phase. The synchronicity followed a certain logic, because both the denomination and the Revolution embraced a belief in the power and goodness of rational thought and envisioned a future of universal redemption.

Unfulfilled and lonely, influenced by both Universalism and the revolutionary fervor engulfing New England, Sargent penned a 1779 essay that she simply called "The Sexes." The nondescriptive title disguised its revolutionary radicalism. Addressing her essay to men, Sargent was nothing if not direct: "Yes, ye lordly, ye haughty sex, our souls are by nature *equal* to yours." And yet, equality of soul did not lead to equality of condition. Instead, women were "degraded." The reason, Sargent argued, was because they were excluded from an education, setting men "so far above" them. Instead of real learning, women were only trained for work around the home, "allowed no other ideas" than the "mechanism of a pudding, or the sewing the seams of a garment." If only women were educated, Sargent asserted, they would demonstrate that they were equal to men in everything but physical strength. Bold and sarcastic, Sargent did not mince words about how she felt men were not superior but ignorant, writing, "Strange how blind *self love* renders you men; were you not wholly absorbed in a partial admiration of your own abilities, you would long since have acknowledged the force of what I am now going to urge."[18]

Sargent did not publish her essay—yet. The time was not right, neither for the ideas nor for Sargent personally. Things changed a few years later, however. The Revolutionary War devastated her husband's merchant business, and in 1786 he fled his debts for the West Indies, where he soon died. Sargent quickly remarried, this time to John Murray, one of the first Universalist ministers of the United States—and thus someone who was clearly sympathetic to her arguments. She also gave birth to two children, although one died in infancy. Her personal life more secure and less lonely, Judith Sargent Murray now had the confidence to release her ideas to the public. By 1790, an increasing number of American women were fully entering the public sphere, writing pamphlets and books, putting on plays, making speeches, and even marching in the streets.[19] And so Murray published her essay in *The Massachusetts Magazine*, retitling it "On the Equality of the Sexes."

As the New Jersey congressman Elias Boudinot stated, "The Rights of Women are no longer strange sounds to the American ear; they are now heard as familiar terms in every part of the United States."[20] Thomas Cooper, an English radical who immigrated to the United States in 1794, was even more forthright. He noted that Wollstonecraft's *Vindication of the Rights of Woman* had made him rethink his prior assumptions of who counted as "the people." Placing men above women, he explained, was no more justified than placing men above other men. Indeed, Cooper argued, men treated women like the rich treated the poor, in that both subjugated groups were taught only those things that would help the powerful—men and the rich, respectively. Cooper continued, "We first keep [women's] minds and then their persons in subjection," which ensured that they could not govern themselves, thus making them slaves. He thunderously concluded, "Let the defenders of male Despotism answer, if they can, THE RIGHTS OF WOMEN."[21]

In 1797, the New Jersey Legislature further modified the language on its suffrage laws. Now "he or she" could vote not just in the southern counties, but throughout the state. The vote ultimately passed 34 to 4 in the New Jersey Assembly. In contrast to the earlier ambiguity of "inhabitants," this measure could never be mistaken as an accident. The New Jersey Legislature had deliberately endorsed limited female suffrage.[22]

Three years later, the support for women's suffrage received an even bigger boost when a New Jersey assemblyman made a motion to explicitly spell out the suffrage law's inclusion of women. The text of his motion stated that election inspectors "shall not refuse the vote to any widow or unmarried women of full age." Yet the Assembly voted the motion down—not because of any backlash against female voters, but because it was redundant. It stated the obvious: women with property could vote—and everyone in New Jersey already knew this. As the Newark-based newspaper *Centinel of Freedom* explained, "Our Constitution gives this right to maids or widows, black or white."[23] No further legislation needed.

New Jersey was one of only three places *in the world* that allowed women the right to vote, alongside extremely limited female suffrage in Sweden and lower Canada.[24] The fruits of the American Revolution may have been borne belatedly for (some) New Jersey women, but they were borne nonetheless.

Radical Names and Revolutionary Lists

Who were these women voters? It is a difficult question to answer. Few poll lists survive, and even fewer that record the names of voters instead of tally marks. Personal accounts from women voters themselves are also of little help, simply because there are so few. The documents of powerful men—these survive in droves. There is a reason why books the size of cinder blocks are published regularly on the likes of George Washington, Alexander Hamilton, and Thomas Jefferson, all of whom kept careful records of their lives, which were then saved, revered, and treasured by their descendants and later historians. But for women? Even wealthy, propertied women? Not so much.

But we do have a few poll lists—with names—that can get us at least somewhere. To be exact: nine poll lists, from four townships, in elections that date between 1800 and 1807.[25]

These poll lists tell us several important things about what voting was actually like for women in New Jersey. First, the three women who voted together in the village of Pluckamin in 1800 were not an anomaly. In all the poll lists that survive, women frequently voted together. Sometimes they were members of the same household, other times they were family friends. To be sure, there were women who voted alone, and there was nothing inherently female about going to vote with other family members or friends. Men did the same thing.

Circumstantial evidence, however, points to a desire among at least some women to seek out other women to navigate the potentially intimidating, thoroughly masculine world of the local tavern on election day. Take a woman named Christianna Holton—or, to be more exact, *two* women named Christianna Holton. They were mother and daughter, and they voted together in Upper Penns Neck Township in 1800. The elder Christianna was a widow, whose husband James had died in 1796. In his will, James left Christianna a horse and bridle and £10, and divided the rest of his lands and £161 between his surviving seven children, one of whom was the younger Christianna. Yet, after 1800, only one Christianna Holton continued to vote. This Christianna was almost certainly the older one, as the younger Christianna married in 1803, and thus her property became her husband's and she lost the right to vote. Although she could no longer vote with her daughter, the elder Christianna continued to vote with other women: one woman in 1801, three women in 1803, and two women in 1806. Only one of these women—a woman named Mary Katts—voted with Christianna more than once.

After her daughter was no longer eligible to vote, did Christianna Holton actively seek out different women to travel to the polls? It seems likely. After all, by this time Christianna was in her mid-fifties and had been widowed more than a decade, and the list of fellow female voters whom she knew would have been fluid. Every year, single women like her daughter would get married, making them ineligible. Every year, aging widows would either die or become too unwell to travel to the polls. Every year, younger widows would remarry. For someone like Christianna Holton, there would be a need to find new voting companions on an annual basis. Unfortunately, we cannot be certain of Christianna's motivations, as we know only two additional pieces of information about her life: First, thanks to church records we know she was a member of the Oldman's Creek Moravian Church; second, thanks to a single newspaper advertisement printed in 1807, we know that her daughter Christianna, the onetime voter in 1800, had a six-year-old horse stolen from her by a man with a "long face and nose pock marked." Perhaps the younger Christianna got the horse back, for her husband did not print the advertisement again.[26]

And that's it. That's all we know of Christianna Holton. Such are the vagaries of early-nineteenth-century records.

Sarah King was likely a young, unmarried woman when she first voted in 1800, alongside two other young, unmarried women. She next voted in 1801, accompanied by Jacob King, who was either her brother or father. She voted again with Jacob in 1802, the third- and fourth-to-last voters that day. The following year she was the very last voter of the day, just behind another woman and, once again, Jacob King. By 1806, however, Sarah and Jacob King voted separately, with Jacob's vote following Sarah's by more than a hundred people. Perhaps Sarah voted accompanied by a male family friend, or perhaps she was simply comfortable going to the polls alone. After all, it was her fifth time voting.[27]

Whatever Sarah King's background or motivations, the very presence of her name, listed again and again in the poll lists, speaks volumes. Her willingness to vote at different times, with different people, perhaps even alone, suggests a doggedness to get to the polls, particularly in 1803 with her name the last on the list of all voters. Clearly, voting mattered to Sarah King—as it did to other women as well, many of whom also voted in multiple elections.

Even though only a handful of voter rolls have survived from the early nineteenth century, there is real revolutionary power in these lists. They may not be original copies of the Declaration of Independence or original printings of Tom Paine's *Common Sense*, but they nevertheless demonstrate the expansive possibilities of the American Revolution. In just one example, in the poll book from the 1801 election in Montgomery Township, held at the Rocky Hill Inn in October of that year, the list of voters begins unsurprisingly: On the first page (of four total, each divided into three columns), we see that sixty-seven men voted, but no women. On the second page, however, the names begin to change.[28] First comes Mary Hagerman, about halfway down the first column. Then, in the second column, three women voted together: Mariah Totton, Live Totton, and Liley Varnardale. A few more female names appear in the third column of the second page.

Yet it is on the third page that the revolution appears full force: first the name Hanah Shelton, then Elonor Leonard, and behind her Mary Robertson (whether "Hanah" and "Elonor" were correct spellings or failed attempts by an election official is unknown). A few names later comes a Sarah, and then another Mary. At this point, the female names relentlessly pop off the page, one after the other: Mary, Carly, Sarah, Susan, Betsy, Mary, Phoebe, another Phoebe, Sarah, Grace Lidia, Mary, and Kelly. A few dozen more names come later: Amy, Charity, Mary, Elizabeth, Caty, Nelly, Mary, and Elizabeth. On the fourth page, a Rebekah, Catherine,

Jane, and Sarah vote, one after the other, followed later by another Elizabeth. Finally, about twenty names from the end of the list, Margaret Dinner is the last female voter.

Women acting politically, and doing so in overt ways, was nothing new in the early 1800s. On the contrary, they were crucial Republican and Federalist constituents at partisan celebrations during the Fourth of July and other politically important events.[29] Yet women *voting—that* would have been a stunning and remarkable sight. Historians have long argued that women's suffrage in New Jersey was a profound revolutionary step in the early United States, yet they have also argued that such limited numbers of voters made scant difference in terms of who actually won elections. In the words of one such historian, "Female suffrage was important in New Jersey in every way except numerically."[30] Recently discovered poll lists reveal that this assumption is definitively false. Of the 343 people who voted at Rocky Hill that October day in 1801, roughly forty voters have unambiguously female names, representing more than 10 percent of the day's voters. Ten percent of voters is a significant share, whether in 1801 or 2000, when George W. Bush won the presidential election by winning Florida by a margin of 0.0009 percent of the votes cast in the state. Despite the limitations on suffrage that prevented most New Jersey women from voting, widowed and unmarried women still existed in substantial enough numbers that they could easily swing an election.

And, in New Jersey and much of the early republic, anything that could swing an election mattered a great deal, as the country split along increasingly bitter partisan lines. In New Jersey, partisanship fueled women's participation at the polls. While a handful of women voted before 1800, it was only after 1800 that women voted in significant numbers. They voted for both parties, which seems curious on the surface. From an ideological perspective, the Federalists should have been the natural partisan home for women, for Federalists envisioned a top-down, deferential style of politics, in which wealthy white men watched over their dependents—poor white men, African Americans, and women—and, in turn, these dependents voted for their protectors. In this way, there was space for women and black people within the Federalist fold, as long as they knew their place.

By contrast, most Jeffersonian Republicans believed, at least rhetorically, in the equality of all white men, thus elevating poor whites while diminishing the importance of black men and all women. Politically, however, Republicans needed to win elections, so they needed to find votes—and, in New Jersey, the vote of a qualified woman was just as good as the vote of a man.[31] A tally mark was a tally mark, no matter who cast the vote. And so, for a time at least, New Jersey Republicans would uphold limited female suffrage like their Federalist rivals.

Both New Jersey Federalists and New Jersey Republicans needed all the votes they could get. In the first years of the nineteenth century, the state was narrowly divided between the two parties, so each side needed to mobilize as many voters as possible to eke out electoral victory. Whatever a male politician may have thought of New Jersey's suffrage requirements, now was not the time to criticize women's political participation, but to encourage it. This gave women very real political power—and this power had consequences. Because women could swing a close election, no substantial outcry against women's suffrage emerged in any New Jersey newspaper, nor did any politician try to rally voters against the measure. There was too much to risk by alienating this small but crucial voting bloc.

Certainly, some New Jerseyites did voice varying levels of disapproval. Frequently this took the form of sarcasm. In late 1797, for example, in the aftermath of the new suffrage law, the Newark *Centinel of Freedom* reported that seventy-five women voted in a recent election in Essex County. It then editorialized that New Jersey "outstrips" Tom Paine and other democrats in the "science of government." In the paper's estimation, New Jerseyites "not only preach the *Rights of Women*, but boldly pass it into practice." It then made an outlandish claim: "Women are now to take part in the jurisprudence of our state, we may shortly expect to see them *take the helm*—of government."[32] Of course, the *Centinel* was being derisive at women's expense. Voting was one thing, but actually governing? That remained out of the question. Nevertheless, despite his misogyny, the editor never called for women to stop voting.

Nor did anyone else. Instead, when critiques of the suffrage law came, they revolved around not single women voting legally, but married women voting illegally.[33] When the New Jersey Assembly investigated these claims, however, it found few voting irregularities—and even these were understandable. For example, in one case the Assembly found that one married woman voted in an 1802 election in Hunterdon County, but this was not an issue because her "husband had left her for several years, and that she had retaken her former name and under that name she paid taxes."[34] Here again we see the continued importance of property and property owners in early U.S. politics. While this anonymous woman may have still been officially married, she controlled her own property, and she paid taxes in her own name, making her an "independent" voter. Her vote still upheld the spirit of law, even if she technically violated its letter.

As these investigations made clear, women had done nothing wrong. They kept voting.

New Jersey and the United States

Americans living outside New Jersey looked at the state's suffrage laws with a mix of curiosity, amusement, and indifference. They certainly saw the state as abnormal, but abnormal did not mean unacceptable or threatening. It was simply an oddity. *The Philadelphia Gazette* merely reported that forty "female electors" voted in the New Jersey town of Bordentown, while other papers mimed the criticisms of their fellow partisan newspapers in New Jersey by sounding the alarm that married women were voting.[35] Once again, the problem was not women in general, but a certain type of woman who was not eligible to vote. Sometimes these mentions hinged on party, as some partisans celebrated female suffrage in New Jersey because they believed women would vote for their party of choice. As one Federalist paper put it, "The Ladies of New Jersey are very handsome or very *federal*; and they have a privilege which none of their sisters in other states enjoy" (emphasis added).[36]

What American women outside New Jersey thought about the state's curious voting laws remains largely inscrutable, for several reasons. First, by the 1790s, a majority of Americans, both men and women, ascribed to the ideology of what one historian famously termed the "Republican Mother." This ideal held that, because all men in a republic participated to some degree in politics, they had a duty to be informed about the world around them. This meant that women also had a duty: They needed to be educated, so, once they were mothers, they could then educate their sons and thus create good (small "r") republicans.[37] Because women's political rights continued to be restricted, and also because of the general dearth of sources, finding statements by women about New Jersey politics is nearly impossible. After all, as we have seen, male politicians and newspaper publishers from New Jersey, whose duty was to be informed of politics *in their own state*, rarely referred to female suffrage. If women did discuss the New Jersey exception, it was almost certainly among each other in personal conversations, and these conversations have been lost to time.

Not all women, however, sought to become Republican Mothers. A minority of American women remained, in the phrasing of the time, "female politicians." These were women who did engage in politics, or hoped to, particularly after they had read Mary Wollstonecraft's powerful tract. While (outside New Jersey) these women could not vote, they could give speeches at partisan celebrations, publish public pamphlets, write private letters, hold salons, and prod men toward various policies in the proverbial smoke-filled backrooms of early American political life.[38]

A few of these political women did mention New Jersey's curious law, most famously Abigail Adams, wife of President John Adams, and undoubtedly a political woman to her core. As John Adams himself put it, Abigail was a "Disciple of Wollstonecraft."[39] In 1776, while her husband debated independence in Philadelphia, Abigail famously urged John to "Remember the Ladies" and argued that men were "Naturally Tyrannical."[40] Her reward for her boldness was to be mocked by John, who called her "saucy," and claimed men were already "subjects" of women "in Practice." If women gained real power to match this behind-the-scenes power, John continued, men would be subjected to "Despotism of the Petticoat."[41] We have no idea how Abigail received John's remonstrance. At the very least, we can take comfort in the fact that John was someone obsessed over how he would be remembered—and, in this instance, he decisively lost the battle for posterity. We remember Abigail's words, not John's.

In 1797, Abigail Adams wrote her sister about her sister's friend's husband, who had recently run for office. In the letter, she claimed that, if

Massachusetts's constitution were as "equally liberal with that of New Jersey and had admitted females to vote, I should certainly have exercised it on his behalf."[42] In reality, of course, Adams could not have voted even had she lived in New Jersey, for she was married. Yet her statement demonstrates how New Jersey's limited suffrage law could—in capable rhetorical hands—take on a life of its own, and act as a symbol of greater female equality and political power.

Stirrings of Discontent

With New Jersey women potentially holding the balance of partisan power in the state in their hands, few men attacked women's suffrage outright, for partisanship overrode any ideological concerns over women voting. William Griffith, however, did not care. Griffith was a lawyer from Burlington and a staunch Federalist. He would eventually be elected to the New Jersey Assembly in the late 1810s and mayor of Burlington in 1824, but at this moment in his career he practiced law and was not yet a career politician. New Jersey's constitution nevertheless rankled him, and he refused to remain silent. In 1799, Griffith published a fifty-one-page pamphlet under the nom de plume "Eumenes." The choice of name was interesting. The historical Eumenes was one of Alexander the Great's generals who fought to maintain the ruler's empire after his death, but Eumenes was then betrayed and killed by his fellow Macedonians—in essence, a figure who brought tragedy upon himself by trying to do the right but unpopular thing. Griffith, it seemed, also imagined he was doing the right but unpopular thing—in his case, attacking New Jersey's state constitution.

Griffith wrote that he had two purposes in publishing his pamphlet: First, he wanted to expose all the "errors and omissions" of the New Jersey Constitution, and second, he aimed to "prove the necessity of calling" another constitutional convention to amend these errors.[43]

The first major "error"? Women could vote. As Griffith wrote, "To my mind (without going into an historical, or philosophical deduction of particulars on the subject) it is evident, that women, generally, are neither, by nature, nor habit, nor by education, nor by their necessary condition in society, fitted to perform this duty with credit to themselves, or advantage to the public." At this point in the text he moved on to other subjects, leaving his biggest diatribe to a footnote: "It is perfectly disgusting, to witness the manner in which women are polled at our elections. Nothing can be a greater mockery of this invaluable and sacred right, than to suffer it to be exercised by persons, who do not even pretend to any judgment on the subject."[44]

When he published his pamphlet in 1799, Griffith and like-minded dissidents opposed to female suffrage remained in the minority—and so, for a time, a semblance of democracy flourished in New Jersey. Indeed, state residents frequently discussed the numerical importance of the female vote, usually filtered through the lens of partisanship. One Republican paper, for example, noted that Federalism was dying out in Middlesex County, and in response Federalists were trying to rally their "petticoat electors" to hold on to some semblance of power.[45] Similarly, a Federalist paper claimed that the Republicans of Amwell Township "dragged their women voters out by waggon-loads through the rain and the cold" to win the local election. Surprisingly, the paper used this development not to attack female suffrage or Republicans, but to attack Amwell Township's Federalists for their laziness. Instead of going to find their own female voters, they simply waited for their voters to appear—and few voters showed up.[46]

And yet, while these partisan papers did not attack female suffrage, neither were these statements ringing endorsements. Both Federalists and Republicans recognized that female voters were necessary to win elections. But were those votes desired? Commentators portrayed women as passive voters, obedient to the wishes of their husbands and sons who "dragged" them out by "the waggon-loads," not as active citizens with their own political viewpoints. This limited approach was not the misogyny of William Griffith, but neither was it the powerful rhetoric of Judith Sargent Murray or Mary Wollstonecraft. The tide was subtly turning against female suffrage.

So far as we can tell, every single female voter listed in the voter rolls was white. We cannot tell this from the voter lists themselves, for they did not record a voter's race. Instead, this evidence comes from our ability to match names in voter lists to New Jersey residents identified in other sources (tax lists, wills, newspapers, etc.). Of course, many of these names remain unidentifiable, so it is certainly possible that some of these female voters were black. There was nothing in the New Jersey voting requirements that would have barred black women from voting, as long as they were not enslaved and possessed property worth £50 as required of all New Jersey voters.

Yet these two prerequisites meant that, if a black woman did vote, it was an extremely rare occurrence. While roughly fifteen thousand African Americans lived in the state, only about three thousand were free—and most of those were living on the economic margins. At this point, we can identify only a handful of black *men* who voted. The numbers of black women voters would have been far lower, for both poverty and marriage would have made them ineligible.

But unlikely does not mean impossible. Historians will keep looking.

The Rights of Women, Denied

When William Griffith demanded New Jersey's constitution be rewritten in 1799, few of his fellow New Jerseyites seem to have been paying attention to his cantankerous misogyny. Contrary to Griffith's wishes, women only increased their political participation in the years following the publication of his pamphlet. But, as the less-than-full-throated endorsements of female suffrage in New Jersey newspapers demonstrated, attitudes toward New Jersey's curious exception began to shift. This shift was part and parcel of a larger trend throughout the United States during these years: counterrevolution.

Revolutions inspire radical change but, as the historian David Brion Davis once wrote, "revolutionary time" is "perishable."[47] Revolutions do not last forever, and the time when radical change can occur will inevitably fade. Eventually, most people desire stability, and, if not a return to the prerevolutionary days, at least a step back from radicalism. In the United States, counterrevolution did not mean a return to British rule, the death of the republic, the splintering of the Union (not yet), or anything comparably catastrophic. Instead, counterrevolution occurred at the local level, in fits and starts, as the United States backtracked from some of its most inspired developments of the first decades after independence.

In neighboring Pennsylvania, for example, counterrevolution meant a step back from the radicalism of a unicameral legislature elected each year. Pennsylvania's new constitution was far more conservative, balancing a lower house elected annually with an elite senate elected every four years, thus stabilizing and inoculating the upper house from popular whims—a development the Whiskey Rebels disliked. Counterrevolution also meant the massive federal response to these same rebels, as Alexander Hamilton and George Washington sought to close the book on the American Revolution for good.

Counterrevolution also mean a gradual silencing of women in politics, in states throughout the republic. While women could not vote in any other state besides New Jersey in the 1780s and 1790s, for a time women still gave speeches, petitioned legislatures, and rallied their respective political parties. By the early 1800s, however, the time of the "political woman" was beginning to wane. For most men and some women, the progress toward gender equality, even though small by today's standards, had gone too far.

The counterrevolution against women's rights first began across the Atlantic Ocean, which then reverberated back to the United States. The political opening seized by Mary Wollstonecraft and the women of the French Revolution had definitively closed. By the late 1790s, the French Revolution was dead, co-opted by Napoleon Bonaparte to fulfill his dream of forging a French empire. Domestically, the recently crowned emperor famously instituted a new series of laws known to posterity as the Napoleonic Code. Part of this law code mandated that women give their husbands unquestioned "obedience." A wife could not "plead in her own name," and she was "obliged to live with her husband, and to follow him every place where he may judge it convenient to reside."[48] Gone were the days when the women of Paris asserted their political power.

Conservatism was also ascendant across the English Channel. With Great Britain engaged in a global struggle against France, British leaders were wary that dissent could lead to domestic instability. Mary Wollstonecraft was a particular target of revulsion. She had died in 1797, and in the aftermath of her death her similarly radical husband William Godwin honored her by writing and publishing her biography. In it, Godwin revealed that Wollstonecraft had given birth to a child out of wedlock, had carried on multiple affairs, and had tried to take her own life multiple times. Amid the rise of British conservatism, Wollstonecraft's radical, proto-feminist ideas may not have been able to weather the counterrevolutionary decade simply on their own merits, but these revelations about Wollstonecraft's private life immediately sounded the death knell for her influence. Critics did not mince words. Wollstonecraft was an "unsex'd female," one claimed, and another deemed her a "whore whose vices and follies had brought about her providential end."[49] *A Vindication of the Rights of Woman* would not be published again for another fifty years. (However, Wollstonecraft and Godwin's daughter, Mary Wollstonecraft Godwin—soon to be Mary Shelley—would find fame within two decades, publishing *Frankenstein* in 1818.)

Wollstonecraft's American counterpart Judith Sargent Murray would have none of it, arguing in private letters that Wollstonecraft's only "real *crime was her able defence of the sex*."[50] Yet, in public, Murray remained silent on Wollstonecraft's end. She, too, was feeling what one historian called a "revolutionary backlash" against women at the turn of the nineteenth century.[51] Murray published a three-volume collection, *The Gleaner*, in 1798, which contained her poems, essays, letters, and plays, all of which built up to her essay in the third volume, "Observations on Female Abilities." In many ways, her miscellaneous writings before this essay were the evidence for this final essay's argument: women did have remarkable "abilities."

Yet *The Gleaner* came too late to be embraced by an American public increasingly wary of female independence. This ideological shift was due not only to Wollstonecraft's precipitous fall from grace, but to larger developments in the American intellectual world. By the early nineteenth century, a growing group of (mostly white and male) writers and thinkers began to make the argument that women and men had fundamentally and permanently different mental and physical traits and therefore had different roles to play in the world. The man's world was the public world, corrupt and chaotic. The woman's world was the domestic world, safe and secure. Behind this permanence lay science—or, more accurately, "science"—that stated men and women's differences stemmed from biology, which was forever unchanging. This biological essentialism, as it would eventually be called, would not fully cohere for another half century, but even in its infancy it laid the groundwork for women's exclusion from the public sphere.

Judith Sargent Murray did not want to be excluded, and she continued to write, but it was difficult to find the time. She was burdened by both her family's uncertain finances and her responsibilities as a mother. She also began to self-censor in ways she had not before, as her later writings were never as radical nor as interesting as "On the Equality of the Sexes" and *The Gleaner*. Her new work was safe for the increasingly conservative times. Unsurprisingly, the little fame Murray had once possessed quickly dissipated. She died in 1820, disillusioned with her life's trajectory. The epitaph her daughter inscribed on her gravestone was fitting. "Dear spirit," it read, "the monumental stone can never speak thy worth."

In 1807, the backlash finally reached New Jersey, when county voters were asked to vote in a referendum on whether the new county courthouse should be built in Newark, the site of the older courthouse, or moved to Elizabeth Town. The question pitted two Republican factions directly against one another.[52] The stakes were high for both sides. Victory in the referendum could pave the way not just for the erection of a certain building, but for the permanent ascendancy of one particular faction. As the referendum drew near, a Newark newspaper accused Elizabeth Town Republicans of plotting to steal the election with a "scheme laid deep as hell," but Newark Republicans would not show any restraint either.[53] The stage was set for corruption on a massive scale.

During the three days of voting, both sides stuffed the ballot box on an unprecedented level. A local nineteenth-century historian memorably recaptured the scene:

> Repeating [i.e., voting multiple times] was resorted to, by many who would in any other cause have scorned such action. Men usually honest seemed lost to all sense of honor, so completely were they carried away by the strife. Women vied with the men, and in some instance surpassed them, in illegal voting. Only a few years ago there were living in Newark two ladies, who, at the time of

> the election in their teens, voted six times each. Married women, too . . . cast their ballots. Governor Pennington is said to have escorted to the polls a strapping negress. Men and boys disguised themselves in women's attire, and crowded about the polls to assist in winning the day for Newark.[54]

Judging by the results, much of this account is true. Newark did indeed carry the day with 7,666 votes, to 6,181 for Elizabeth Town, yet these numbers totaled *279 percent* of the eligible voters in the county.[55] Fourteen thousand votes were counted in a county with a *total* population of 22,000.[56] Whether the mass of illegal votes came from repeat voters, ineligible women, enslaved people, or underage boys is impossible to determine. In all likelihood, all of these groups were involved in this chicanery on some level—although, considering who ultimately benefited, it is almost certain that powerful New Jersey politicians were behind all of it. The Elizabeth Town Republicans protested the result to the New Jersey Assembly. The Assembly readily agreed that the election results were impossible and egregious, and it declared the election null and void.

The intraparty strife between these two local Republican factions boded an irreparable break in the state party as a whole, which in turn would threaten the Republicans' recent dominance of New Jersey politics. If the Republican Party split, the Federalists could regain power with only a plurality of votes, especially because they were on their way toward a national resurgence. In 1807, the same year as the Essex courthouse referendum, President Jefferson declared an embargo on all transatlantic trade to curb British interference in U.S. politics, reasoning that Britain needed this trade more than the United States and would soon capitulate. He reasoned incorrectly. The embargo punished American merchants, and it was exceedingly unpopular throughout the country, particularly in coastal states like New Jersey. The law gave New Jersey Federalists their first hope for statewide victory in several years, which would be nearly assured if the Republican split continued. New Jersey Republicans desperately needed to unify.

They did so by compromise: In return for building the courthouse in Newark, the more radical Republicans of that town, who in the past had supported New Jersey's liberal suffrage requirements, now agreed to support a new bill in the New Jersey Legislature that defined a legal voter to be a taxpaying, "free, white, male citizen of the state."[57] Federalists also got on board. For all parties, it was time to eliminate the vagaries of New Jersey's suffrage requirements.

Supported by both Republican factions and the Federalists, the bill sailed through the legislature with overwhelming majorities. The new law stripped the right to vote not just from women but from black men, immigrants, and the non-taxpaying poor.

Women would not vote again in New Jersey for more than a century.

The Legacy of the Exception

As time went on and as most nineteenth-century Americans forgot the New Jersey exception, a handful of female radicals emerged to challenge the male-dominated status quo, and they eventually found inspiration in New Jersey's early history. Their origins were rooted in the radical abolitionist movement that arose in the 1830s in the North. Activists like William Lloyd Garrison demanded the immediate abolition of slavery throughout the United States, countering the long-dominant moderate abolitionists who always coupled emancipation of the slaves with their "return" to Africa. But it was hard to isolate such radicalism, and soon abolition fused with another sweeping demand: equal rights for women, among them the right to own private property, the right to maintain legal personhood after marriage, and, most radically, the right to vote.

To women's rights advocates like Elizabeth Cady Stanton and Lucretia Mott, all these demands were entirely consistent with the United States' founding principles as embodied in the American Revolution and its defining statement the Declaration of Independence. Indeed, the central statement on women's rights, the 1848 "Declaration of Sentiments," penned largely by Stanton and signed by one hundred women and men at the legendary Seneca Falls Convention, was directly modeled on the Declaration of Independence.

There was no subtlety about this: On the contrary, the first two paragraphs of the Declaration of Sentiments are nearly word-for-word copies of the Declaration of Independence, but instead of "All men are created equal,"

Stanton wrote, "All men *and women* are created equal." Then, as in the Declaration of Independence, Stanton provided a list of grievances, this time not against King George III but against American men. The list included denying women the right to vote, making them "civilly dead" if married, denying women education, and holding a double standard for "moral delinquencies," in which men paid no price for their own sexual dalliances, yet if women were guilty of the same transgressions, they were "exlude[d] from society."[58]

It was in this context that New Jersey's curious but long neglected history became relevant again. For the writers of *The Lily*, the first American magazine produced by and for women, first published in 1849, New Jersey's history proved that extending suffrage to women would not have any negative repercussions. As one such article began, "The Matter of Women's Voting, is, after all, *not* so terrible." This same article went on to describe a conversation between two elderly "Quakeresses," one of whom was from New Jersey. The New Jersey woman remembered how she had voted for John Adams in 1800, to which her friend asked, "'Did'nt thee feel strangely?'" The first woman responded, "'Why no . . . I went with my father and brothers, and we quietly returned together.'"[59] In another instance, *The Lily* mentioned how, when New Jersey stripped women of the vote in 1807, no women protested. To the writer, this "acquiescence . . . demonstrated nothing but the degradation of the injured party." It showed that women were like freed slaves who pleaded for re-enslavement, for both women and enslaved black people desired "animal wants supplied without being troubled with human rights and duties."[60] This portrayal played into a trope, common at the time, that argued the enslaved deserved their fate unless they actively tried to escape their bondage.[61] The message from *The Lily* was clear: Women, like slaves, needed to break free from their daily humiliation. They needed to demand their political rights.

As radical activists discussed and demanded women's political rights, they also discussed and demanded women's property rights. In particular, they blasted the legal doctrine of coverture, which mandated that, once married, a woman's property automatically became her husband's. Beginning in 1839, certain states began eliminating coverture, allowing married women to retain the property they had held before marriage. These changing laws were not necessarily a reflection of changing attitudes toward women, but of changing economics. In the aftermath of the devastating Panic of 1837 that threw tens of thousands of Americans into debt, allowing married women to retain their property would help protect indebted families from creditors.[62]

For advocates of women's rights, however, changing the law, not the justification for it, was what mattered. Not only was eliminating coverture just in itself, but if married women *did* own property and therefore *did* pay taxes, they were being taxed without representation. In this way, ending coverture opened the road not just to a woman's *economic* rights within a marriage, but to her *political* rights. As the reformer Lydia Jenkins argued, in the United States "'No Taxation without Representation' is a cherished motto," but "one half of the adult population of our country, is not represented in the Legislature, yet laws are made for their government."[63] Elizabeth Cady Stanton took the argument one step further, predicting that "the right to property will of necessity compel us in due time to the exercise of our right to the elective franchise, and then naturally follows the right to hold office."[64] To these women, property rights for married women would provide a pathway for voting rights, and, eventually, full equality.

No wonder, then, that New Jersey's curious history of women's suffrage was of interest to advocates of women's rights. Not only was this history mentioned in publications like *The Lily*, but Susan B. Anthony wrote a New Jersey historian asking for more information on the subject in 1881.[65] By contrast, more recent feminist activists have largely ignored New Jersey—and the entire Revolution for that matter, as have most historians of women's suffrage. In their view, the story of women's suffrage in America *begins* with Seneca Falls.[66] Women's suffrage in early New Jersey, so this story goes, was just a weird historical accident.

On the contrary, the New Jersey exception was simply the most visible sprout from the many seeds sown for women's rights during the American Revolution. Indeed, the Revolution represented the first great step forward for women's rights in the United States. That these rights were incomplete and imperfect—and then lost entirely—should not take away from the Revolution's very real attempt to realize "the rights of women," at least as those rights were considered in eighteenth-century terms. Women's rights, too, were present at the Founding.

4

Racial Equality, Part I: Gabriel's Revolutionary Plan, 1800

In the fall of 1800, only a quarter century after the United States declared independence, two Americans worried that the gains of the American Revolution were about to disappear for good.

One of them was none other than Thomas Jefferson, who had not yet become the third U.S. president but whose revolutionary legacy was already firmly established: primary author of the Declaration of Independence, governor of Virginia during the Revolutionary War, minister to France, author of the Virginia Statute for Religious Freedom, the first secretary of state under George Washington, and, in 1796, the vice president by virtue of finishing second in the Electoral College to President John Adams. He also, crucially and infamously, enslaved roughly six hundred people during his lifetime—the most of any president—and he was the father of several children by Sally Hemings, a woman who, legally, was Jefferson's property.

Jefferson may have been John Adams's vice president, but Adams was also Jefferson's opponent in the 1800 presidential election. To Jefferson and his Republican allies, a second term for the Federalist Adams was a point of no return that would forever destroy all that was good in the fledgling American republic. In a letter Jefferson meant for private eyes but, to Jefferson's chagrin, was quickly made public, he described Adams and his like-minded Federalists as "an Anglican, monarchical and aristocratical party," composed of "timid men who prefer the calm of despotism to the boisterous sea of liberty." He continued, "We only need to awake and snap the Lilliputian cords with which they have been entangling us during the first sleep which succeeded our leaders." ("Lilliputian" refers to the small people who tied up Gulliver in Swift's famous novel.)[1] In other words: Americans needed a second American Revolution to consummate the first.

The second American who was concerned about the United States' seemingly counterrevolutionary trajectory certainly agreed with Jefferson's sentiments, although whether he ever read them in any one of the countless newspapers that reprinted the famous letter will forever remain a mystery. Yet the very fact that this man *could* read them at all was surprising, for one simple reason: he was enslaved. His name was Gabriel, still deemed "Gabriel Prosser" in many books despite there being absolutely no evidence that Gabriel took his enslaver Thomas Prosser's surname for himself.[2] At the same time that Jefferson sought to wrest the United States from its counterrevolutionary trajectory by defeating the elitist, antidemocratic Federalists, Gabriel sought to wrest the United States from a very different counterrevolutionary trajectory, one embodied by the likes of Thomas Jefferson himself. Under a banner inscribed with the words "Death or Liberty," Gabriel planned to enlist hundreds of enslaved and free blacks and, perhaps, sympathetic whites in a rebellion to overthrow slavery.[3] Like Jefferson, Gabriel too hoped to consummate the American Revolution—but in a far more radical, inspiring, and violent way.

Of Life, Liberty, and Domestic Insurrections

On the eve of the American Revolution, nearly all the black people who lived in what became the United States were enslaved, forced to work under the ever-present threat of brutal violence, from northern New England to southern Georgia. Slavery varied widely from place to place, both across states and within them. Yet, for the most part, a single maxim held: The farther south one traveled, the more slaves there were in proportion to the total population. Enslaved people in New England counted for 4 percent of the area's total population, while in Maryland and Virginia slaves numbered 40 percent, and in South Carolina, the only North American colony founded explicitly to exploit slave labor, they comprised a majority (60 percent). With the exception of Pennsylvania, the Middle Colonies confirmed this trend. Thanks to its long history as a highly lucrative port under first Dutch then English rule, New York, particularly New York City, was the center of Northern slavery, with nearly 14 percent enslaved.

Pennsylvania, by contrast, bore the mark of its Quaker foundations, with only 2 percent enslaved.[4]

Most British colonists shared several key beliefs when it came to the institution of slavery. First, very few ever questioned its legality or necessity. While some colonists may have lamented the brutal treatment visited on individual slaves, slavery as an institution was considered both ancient and normal, accepted in such foundational texts as the Bible and the works of Aristotle. While there had never existed a time when human beings were not at least somewhat troubled by human bondage, rarely did moral qualms outweigh the benefits that slavery brought to the enslavers. In this way, British colonists held largely the same views as Spanish, Dutch, Portuguese, and French colonists in the Americas.

Yet colonists also perceived that, while slavery may have been a human practice since time immemorial, what was happening in the Americas during the eighteenth century had a reached a level that was both quantitively more important to the American economy and qualitatively more brutal than anything that had come before. These phenomena went hand in hand.[5] By the time of the American Revolution, slave societies—meaning, societies that did not just have slave labor but were based upon it—dominated European settlements in the Americas, stretching all the way from Maryland to Brazil.[6] In British North America specifically, half a million people were enslaved. Wherever they lived, whether British North America, the Caribbean, Brazil, or other parts of Latin America, enslaved people had almost no rights, endured horrific punishments for the slightest transgression, and frequently suffered early deaths. Slave owners knew all this, but it did not matter. Profits always took precedence.

The issue of slavery was bound together with the issue of race, although the two were not the same. While the earliest generation of European colonists undoubtedly harbored ethnocentric and xenophobic prejudices against the Africans they enslaved (the historian David Brion Davis aptly labeled this "protoracism"), it was the growth of slavery that officially birthed racism, and racism in turn birthed the idea of race.[7] By turning black people into a permanently subjugated underclass, white colonists maximized both economic profits and social stability.[8] Unlike a white indentured servant, a black slave would never need to be given freedom, land, or a political voice, and every baby birthed by a black woman would only enlarge the workforce of the next generation—even when, as was often the case, the baby's father was a white enslaver. In this way, not only racism but sexual violence reaped profits for the enslaver.

The American Revolution eroded the ideological basis undergirding this brutal hierarchical system. Attacks on slavery had begun even before the Revolution, as more and more people in the British Empire noticed that this inhumane practice was no longer a troubling appendage of Britain's growing wealth and power but, much more appallingly, the very *centerpiece* of its empire. Small, disjointed, inchoate antislavery sentiments began to evolve into *the* antislavery *movement*. The Revolution, however, gave this movement a coherence and relevance that it lacked prior to widespread discussions of liberty and natural rights.

The Declaration of Independence reveals this relevance and coherence all too well, not just for Americans today, but for Americans living in the Revolutionary era. The famous post-Preamble first line, "We hold these truths to be self-evident, that all men are created equal . . . ," most clearly articulated a case against slavery and for racial equality. The next lines carry on the radicalism: "That they are endowed by their Creator with certain unalienable Rights, that among these are Life, Liberty, and pursuit of Happiness." It sparked an obvious follow-up question: If human beings had the right to liberty, then how could they be enslaved? And did not these all-too-human yearnings—to be safe, free, and happy—apply to blacks as well as whites?

William Cushing, the chief justice of the Massachusetts Supreme Court, certainly thought so. In 1781, Cushing was asked to rule on the status of an enslaved person named Quock Walker, who had sued his master for his freedom after enduring a brutal beating. In his ruling, Cushing began by citing the Massachusetts Constitution, ratified in 1780, which began with words that mirrored the Declaration of Independence: "All men are born free and equal."[9] To Cushing, slavery was clearly incompatible with this statement, even though the writers of the Massachusetts Constitution never intended for their words to be used to sanction abolition. In Cushing's words, a "different idea has taken place with the people of America, more favorable with the rights of mankind, and to that natural, innate desire for Liberty." Without anything in Massachusetts law written that supported slavery, Cushing concluded that slavery was "inconsistent" with the state's constitution.[10]

No other state abolished slavery via judicial fiat. Instead, states abolished via legislative action. Although Vermont's constitution freed the few dozen Vermont slaves in 1777, it was not yet an official state (it was, briefly, an independent republic), which meant that the distinction of first state legislature to act against slavery belonged to Pennsylvania and its 1780 abolition law. This is hardly surprising, considering Philadelphia, with its long Quaker history, was ground zero for abolitionism. However, during the Revolutionary War, Quakerism became tainted by its pacifism, and therefore the writers of the law invoked not Quakerism but the Revolution itself to push for abolition. They also argued that, so long as the king had been in charge, "no effectual legal Relief [for slaves] could be obtained." Since independence, however, "a long Course of Experience" had "weaned" Pennsylvanians of "narrow Prejudices and Partialities."[11] Other New England states soon followed Pennsylvania's lead, followed by New York in 1799 and New Jersey in 1804.

For enslaved people, these laws were tragically conservative. Designed to balance an enslaved person's right to freedom with the enslaver's right to property, all these laws except Vermont's provided for *gradual* abolition. This meant that anyone who was enslaved before the law was passed remained a slave for life, infants included. Children born to an enslaved woman remained legally indentured to their mother's enslaver until their twenties. Even in 1861, the first year of the Civil War, eighteen slaves still lived in New Jersey.

And yet, despite these very real and tragic limitations, Northern abolition was, in the context of the wider world, still revolutionary. In 1760, in the very beginnings of the American Revolution, slavery was legal, accepted, and deemed necessary by enslavers throughout all North and South America. By 1800, as the historian Edward Countryman points out, slavery was illegal in New England, dying in the Middle States, banned in the Old Northwest, and "shaken" in the Upper South. In his words, "the American revolutionary era marked the beginning of slavery's end."[12] James

Otis, the influential early Bostonian revolutionary, first made the argument in 1763 that black people, too, deserved natural rights. He asked, "Does it follow that tis right to enslave a man because he is black?"[13] Rhetoric like this continued over the next decade, culminating in the most radical antislavery step during the entire Revolutionary era. In 1774, the First Continental Congress decided to ban the slave trade altogether as part of its decision to boycott all British imports, which, according to Countryman, was the most universal antislavery decision in U.S. history until the Thirteenth Amendment, which abolished slavery for good in 1865.

In the South, where slavery was both more economically and ideologically important, antislavery sentiments were not as strong—but neither were they absent entirely. While colonies in the Lower South (and, later, states) like South Carolina briefly flirted with vague antislavery rhetoric and then quickly abandoned it, the Upper South took real action. Virginian slaveholders responded to the Revolution's slavery dilemma by making several modest changes to slave laws in the colony that made them feel better—and, to give them a smidgeon of credit, did improve the lives of a small percentage of black Virginians. First, in 1777, the General Assembly prohibited all slave imports from outside the state, although, because Virginia already had an overabundance of slave labor, this law mattered little except as window dressing for antislavery sentiment. The next law, however, did matter. Beginning in 1782, slave owners could free whomever they chose without the need of government approval, and many chose to do so. Most famously, George Washington manumitted all his slaves in his will.[14] Whether planters like Washington were playing the part of the benevolent master or were actually benevolent mattered little when it came to on-the-ground results. Hundreds, and eventually thousands, of black Virginians became free.

Thanks to the rise of individual manumissions, by 1800 nearly 10 percent of black Virginians, twenty thousand people total, were free. Virginia's enslavers, however, had little conception of the long-term ramifications of what they had just done: They had slightly opened the door to a post-slavery revolutionary world, providing inklings of hope to the almost 350,000 slaves who resided in the state—and then went no further.

Black Founding Fathers—and Mothers

There is another side to the American Revolution's antislavery story, one that is much more radical and provocative—and, ultimately, one that is closer to the truth. The above narrative locates antislavery agency in white revolutionaries, focusing on how their rhetoric about freedom and equality caused them to suddenly realize that slavery was inconsistent with their revolutionary principles. To tell the antislavery trajectory of the Revolution in this way is like telling the story of *Obergefell v. Hodges*, the 2015 Supreme Court ruling that legalized same-sex marriage throughout the United States, through the changing attitudes of the five justices who decided the case. Yet conservative Justice Anthony Kennedy's key swing vote did not arrive in a vacuum. Instead, his decision came in response to decades of fearless and relentless agitation by tens of thousands of gay activists in the United States, who slowly, resolutely, in the face of virulent, often violent pushback, demanded their constitutional rights. *Obergefell* was not a triumph *for* queer people, but *by* queer people.

With regard to the rise of antislavery sentiment during the American Revolution, it was not the Founding Fathers who magnanimously bequeathed antislavery ideas on the fledgling nation, but the unrelenting, courageous actions of enslaved black people who pushed the Founding Fathers and thousands of other white Americans toward antislavery actions. Indeed, when white Patriots publicly voiced antislavery sentiments, as they did so to an increasing extent in the mid-1770s, they were usually basing their arguments on ones that had previously been voiced, in both print and in person, by black activists.[15]

The list of black Americans who emerged from obscurity in the Revolutionary era is long. There was the Boston Massacre's famed martyr Crispus Attucks. There was Quock Walker and Mum Bett, the two Massachusetts slaves who separately sued for their freedom. There was lifelong friends Richard Allen and Absalom Jones, both former slaves, both ministers and activists, who founded the Free African Society in Philadelphia 1787 to aid fugitive slaves and newly freed black Philadelphians. Thanks to the persistent racism of Philadelphia's Methodist community, each of the men had no choice but to found an independent black church in the city, the first two of their kind. There is little doubt that their actions, in particular their friendship with Philadelphia politician Benjamin Rush, helped make Pennsylvania the first state to pass a gradual abolition law and made Philadelphia ground zero for abolitionism in the United States during the early republic. Most fascinatingly, there was the improbable story of teenage poet Phillis Wheatley, whose innate talent catapulted her to international fame, which included a face-to-face meeting with George Washington in 1776. Then there were countless others whose stories cannot be detailed here: Ona Judge, Benjamin Banneker, Prince Hall, Paul Cuffe, James Forten, and Venture Smith, to list but a few.

There was also Gabriel. He was born in 1776, so he was only a small child when the United States gained its independence, but he nevertheless grew up in a world remade by the American Revolution. His birth year, moreover, seems tailor-made for a legendary tale: In 1776 (the year of the Declaration), in Virginia (home to the writer of that Declaration), there was born an enslaved man named Gabriel (in the Bible, the angel bringing word of a coming Messiah). The opening lines of a film or novel practically write themselves.

But, of course, Gabriel was not a prop for a film or novel, but a real person, with thoughts, feelings, and dreams that were all too human. Almost certainly, he did not believe his birth year was significant (how many thousands of Americans were born that same year?), nor thought Virginia itself was special for its connections to the Revolution. He and his followers *may* have felt his name was significant, but ultimately the records are unclear. What is certainly true is that, in the year 1800, more than a decade after the Constitution had supposedly tied a bow on the Revolution for good, Gabriel planned to use violence to permanently end slavery in Virginia. In essence, he would restart the American Revolution.

In 1800, Gabriel was twenty-four years old, but what seems young to us today would not have been by the standards of the time—not for most people at the dawn of the nineteenth century, and certainly not for an enslaved man who worked as a blacksmith for much of his life. We can know this simply by his appearance: Gabriel bore several visible scars on his head, and he was missing several front teeth. Whether these marks were the result of physical beatings, a life of hard labor, or some combination thereof is uncertain, but whatever their origin, his hardships were written permanently on his face and his body. One newspaper even noted that he was "24 or 25," but "appears to be about 30."[16]

Gabriel was enslaved to a man named Thomas Prosser, who lived six miles north of the small city of Richmond, established as Virginia's capital in 1780. Gabriel's life and his world, as well as the wider world of Virginia, all embodied the contradictory proslavery and antislavery currents that the Revolution had birthed simultaneously. His enslaver Prosser owned a tobacco plantation, but with tobacco production declining thanks to the crop's destruction of the soil, he began speculating in local real estate. He also began to hire out Gabriel to work jobs in Richmond or on other surrounding plantations, which meant that Gabriel had the ability to move relatively freely, crossing frequently between rural and urban worlds. When compared to most enslaved people in Virginia, Gabriel's situation made him both lucky (if anyone enslaved can be called lucky) and atypical, but he was not unique. Thomas Prosser was hardly the only planter who realized that he needed to diversify his business dealings, and Gabriel would have encountered many other slaves who had likewise been hired out or, in an increasingly common practice, had hired themselves out, and thus lived for days and weeks at a time beyond their master's purview. He also could read, which made him again different but not exceptional, part of the 5 percent of Virginia slaves who were literate in 1800.[17]

Indeed, that Gabriel could both read and travel with few restrictions was proof that the small antislavery measures Virginians had enacted in the aftermath of the Revolution had real-world results, even if they affected only a small portion of the enslaved population. Even more broadly, the fact that we can uncover the lives of all these black women and men, even imperfectly—not just Gabriel, but Phillis Wheatley, Quock Walker, Richard Allen, and so many others—is a testament to the revolutionary trajectory of the era. As any historian of slavery in colonial North America will lament, the individual lives and thoughts of nearly all enslaved people in this era remain impossible to uncover—further evidence of the dehumanizing effects of the insidious practice. Yet, during and after the Revolution, the lives of individual black Americans begin to emerge from more than a century of obscurity, as increasing numbers of black Americans found a sympathetic white audience that was willing to listen to, write down, and publish their accounts of their enslavement. To be sure, many readers may recognize all the names mentioned above, as their stories have been told and retold for more than two centuries, for good reason: black Patriots whom we can describe in detail still number no more than a few dozen. Yet their influence outweighed their numbers: They were the forerunners of the black abolitionists who would so profoundly influence the antebellum North, and, as the historian David Waldstreicher has argued, this first generation pioneered the slave narrative that would eventually drive Northern public opinion a century later.[18]

Perhaps Gabriel also had heard tales of the countless black men who had fought for the Patriot side a quarter century earlier. Roughly five thousand served in the Continental Army during the Revolutionary War, a vast majority of them from Northern states. Some, for example Salem Poor, a legendary hero of the Battle of Bunker Hill, signed on with the Patriot forces before independence was even declared. Soon after that battle, George Washington took command of the Continental forces, and in one of his first decrees, he prohibited the further recruitment of black troops, although he allowed those already serving to reenlist. While this ban officially held for the duration of the war, in practice Washington and other officers were forced to ignore it, as most Northern states continued to send him black recruits to fill their state quotas. Volunteers for the Continental Army were always in short supply, and Washington needed every man who would be willing to serve, regardless of race. Even more concerning was the prospect that, if these black recruits did not fight for the Patriots, then, in Washington's words, "they may seek employ in the [British] Army."[19]

For black soldiers, fighting for their own freedom trumped fighting for the freedom of the United States. They were not shy about their motivations. Of the 292 African Americans from Connecticut who served in the Continental Army, 18 gave themselves the surname "Freedom" or "Freeman," and five more gave themselves the surname "Liberty."[20] Black Americans made up roughly 1 percent of the Northern population, but over the next seven years of often brutal warfare, they comprised perhaps 15 to 20 percent of the Continental Army—I say "perhaps" because race was often not recorded in Continental Army muster rolls.

These remarkable numbers made sense. If Patriot men had the choice, they preferred to serve in the local militia. Only the most desperate and destitute agreed to dedicate years of their lives to service as enlisted soldiers in the Continental Army, which offered poor pay in exchange for daily hardships and a high chance of death (more likely from disease than battle). And, thanks to more than a century and a half of racialized chattel slavery in North America, African Americans *were* usually desperate and destitute. Few were free, even fewer owned land or possessed a stable source of income, and the nearly universal, pernicious racism of the infant United States meant that their prospects were not going to improve any time soon. Many enslaved blacks served in place of their masters (with their masters receiving their payment!), or state governments compensated slaveholders for freeing their slaves so they could join the army. Other enslaved black men were promised their freedom if they served until the end of the war. Life in the Continental Army offered very few incentives, but, for black Americans, these were still better than the alternatives. Numbers showed this. In Rhode Island, for example, one of the few all-black regiments in the Continental Army counted 25 percent of the state's slaves in its ranks.[21]

Black women could not join these ranks, but they could and did run away at much greater numbers than they had before the Revolution. Whereas women comprised a little more than one in every ten escaped slaves before the 1770s, during and after the Revolution they made up one in every three runaways.[22] Others, most famously Mum Bett in Massachusetts, sued for their freedom, or, like Phillis Wheatley, were manumitted by their enslavers, often thanks to a combination of gratitude for their years of service and the growing traction of the Revolution's natural rights ideology. (In the case of Wheatley herself, she had simply become too famous for her enslavers to keep her in bondage in the face of public opinion.)[23] Black women's quest for freedom was arguably the most revolutionary undertaking of the entire era, for they were simultaneously challenging both white supremacy and male patriarchy. Even more profoundly, black women quite literally embodied the dream of freedom and the nightmare of slavery for every person descended from them, since enslavement was determined by the legal status of the mother. Therefore, if a black woman could achieve freedom, no matter how precarious, she could ensure freedom for generations of her descendants.[24]

For those black women and men who ended up supporting the Patriot cause, the reasons did not have to do just with desperation. Blacks, before all other Americans, understood the *revolutionary* potential of the American Revolution. They saw that white colonists demanding rights from Britain opened doors for black colonists to demand rights of their own from these same white colonists. They quickly realized the hypocrisy of Patriots protesting their "enslavement" by Great Britain when these same Patriots held slaves of their own. As one black antislavery petition noted to the Massachusetts legislature, "We expect great things from men who have made such a noble stand against the designs of their *fellow-men* to enslave them."[25] The petitioners lamented slaves' "deplorable case," and then demanded that the Massachusetts legislature "give us that ample relief which, *as men*, we have a natural right to." *Men* with *natural rights*. In other words: potential revolutionaries.

At first antislavery petitions were halting, humble, and sentimental, playing to slaveholders' heartstrings by pointing out the wretched lives of the people they enslaved. As the Revolution continued, however, black rhetoric became more radical. Take the example of twenty-three-year-old Lemuel Haynes. Son of a black father and white mother—and thus born free—Haynes was as an indentured servant in Connecticut until his indenture ended in 1774. The following year, Haynes served in the Connecticut militia in the months before and after Lexington and Concord, ending his service after he contracted tuberculosis. After the war he became a Congregationalist minister in Vermont.

At some point in the latter half of 1776, Haynes wrote the essay "Liberty Further Extended." It began by quoting the Declaration, which served as the backdrop for the entire essay. Haynes's thesis was clear: Liberty for the colonies must be followed by liberty for the enslaved. In his words (which he emphasized with italics), "*A Negro may Justly Challenge, and has an undeniable right to his Liberty: Consequently, the practice of Slave-keeping, which so much abounds in this land is illicit.*"[26] Jefferson, of course, had meant no such thing, but the power of the written word is that it can always be torn away from its author's original meaning. In this way, the Declaration of Independence became used as an antislavery document within months of its publication. In the coming years, many more black and white abolitionists would follow Haynes's lead.[27] It all added up to, as one Virginia slaveholder wrote, a "prodigious change" in how black Americans argued over and fought against their enslavement. According to this slaveholder, blacks had always fought for their freedom, but before the Revolution they "fought . . . merely as a good; now they also claim it as a right."[28]

These sentiments were lost on most white Patriots thanks to the racist leanings of their own rhetoric. As the historian Robert Parkinson has recently uncovered in an exhaustive study, white Patriots required rhetoric that would knit together the vast diversity of British North America into what they called the "common cause."[29] One sinister but eminently logical way to do this was to use race. The circumstances of the Revolutionary War were tailor-made for such a strategy. Lord Dunmore *did* offer freedom to enslaved blacks who fought for the British, and fifteen thousand black men *did* serve in British forces. Even more important than these wartime actions was the 1772 court case that hovered above everything that had to do with the British Empire and slavery. That year, Lord Mansfield, the chief justice of the King's Bench, issued a momentous ruling in favor of an enslaved black man named James Somerset, who, with the aid of British abolitionists, had sued his master for his freedom when he was taken to London. Mansfield held that slavery was "odious" and contrary to natural law, therefore it required positive law—meaning, enacted written law—to maintain the practice. Because no such law existed in England, Mansfield declared, "the black must be discharged."[30]

The Somerset Case, as posterity has dubbed it, did not actually free any slaves other than James Somerset, but symbolically it positioned England as a land without slavery—as it soon would be, when it became clear that any slave brought to England could now sue to avoid being taken beyond its shores. The decision quickly reverberated across the Atlantic, where slaves numbered not in the hundreds or few thousands as they did in England, but nearly half a million. The decision did not affect slavery in the colonies, where positive law *did* exist that protected the practice. To argue that Southern Patriots declared independence *because* of Mansfield's decision is a bridge too far. Yet when the Somerset case became a backdrop to Lord Dunmore's Proclamation, it created the perception—and, to a certain extent, the reality—that a newly abolitionist Great Britain would free Southern slaves to destroy Southern Patriots and win the Revolutionary War.

And white Patriot printers leaned into this perception. Whenever blacks did anything to aid the British, printers howled with indignation. Whenever blacks did anything to aid the Patriots, however, printers stayed silent. A bystander witnessing Continental soldiers triumphing at Trenton on Christmas Eve or enduring the winter of Valley Forge would have seen firsthand how racially integrated Washington's army really was, but someone reading an account of the victory of Trenton or the hardships of Valley Forge would have never known—and there were far many more newspaper readers than eyewitnesses. This relentless pattern continued throughout the entirety of the war, creating an unresolvable contradiction for African Americans: While the American Revolution had made antislavery thought not only possible but widespread, it was quickly countered by the racist rhetoric of the Revolutionary War.

In this vein, slavery would disappear in the North over the next generation, but racism would only be amplified, becoming, in Parkinson's words, "a cornerstone of the American republican edifice."[31] In the 1780s, black people were acknowledged as full citizens in at least five states of the Union, but this was a high point.[32] Increasing numbers of Northern states began transforming their colonial poor and vagrancy laws, which were originally designed to keep poorer nonresidents out of various communities, into anti-black laws, which restricted black migration and curbed black civil rights.[33] It was even worse for black people in the South, where a few years of modest antislavery legislation would be quickly subsumed under measures that were designed to strengthen the entire slave system. In the West, these trends were further exacerbated. In 1787, the Confederation Congress prohibited slavery in the Northwest Territory via the Northwest Ordinance, which was to prove one of the most effective and longest-lasting antislavery measures taken in the early United States. Despite pushback by some white migrants from the South, Ohio, Illinois, Wisconsin, Indiana, and Michigan became free territories and then free states—but, even more so than states in the Northeast, they also were virulently anti-black, as they repeatedly tried (but repeatedly failed) to prohibit all black migration. The 1790 Southwest Ordinance, by contrast, opened states like Mississippi and Alabama to slavery. Once the cotton gin was invented and the cotton boom erupted, these states would be the most rabidly proslavery states in the entire Union.

Infamously, the Constitution itself strengthened the political power of slaveholders via the Three-Fifths Compromise, while it forbade any interference with the international slave trade until 1808. Although much has been made of the antislavery rhetoric of most of the Framers (essentially, all but those from South Carolina and Georgia), when all was said and done the Constitution protected slavery in the moment while making it more difficult to do anything about it in the future.[34]

Soon after ratification, the First Congress continued the onslaught against black Americans. In 1790, the federal government passed a naturalization act that limited American citizenship to "free White person[s]" who had resided in the United States for two years—meaning a white foreigner was seen as being more American after two years in the United States than a black person who was born in the country. Two years later, the Militia Act mandated that only white Americans could serve in the militia. A year after that, the first Fugitive Slave Act provided means by which enslavers could recapture their slaves who had fled into free states. Like the Constitution, this act never used the word "slave." Even as white Americans turned away from antislavery, directly acknowledging slavery in a free republic remained embarrassing.

It is here, in the intersection between thoughts, words, and actions, where we can most condemn the Revolutionary generation, particularly its white elite leaders, for their relationship to slavery. The oft-peddled trope used to defend them—they were just "men of their time"—does not hold water when considering that antislavery thought in fact permeated their time and was indeed voiced by slaveholders themselves. There is a reason why historians criticize Jefferson and Washington for enslaving others, but do not similarly condemn Pericles, Cicero, or Caesar, who also enslaved others in an ancient world where notions of antislavery scarcely existed. Because slavery was nevertheless still accepted, deemed economically necessary, and sometimes celebrated by thousands of people in the Americas, Europe, and

Africa, neither do we need to judge the Founders utter monsters, as we would if they lived in *our* time. The bottom line is that, even though they were inundated by antislavery thought that was further amplified by the Revolution, most of the Founding Fathers at best did nothing when it came to slavery. In some cases, they strengthened it and made it more horrific.

Meanwhile, in the face of these proslavery measures, the words and actions of the American Revolution's black Patriots—Crispus Attucks, Quock Walker, Richard Allen, Absalom Jones, Phillis Wheatley, Lemuel Haynes, and countless others—would soon disappear into the counterrevolutionary fog of the early republic. To be sure, antislavery activism did not simply cease, and there remained a small but dynamic interracial coalition of abolitionists.[35] Yet, overall, the renowned historian Winthrop Jordan's words still provide a powerful statement on the relationship between black Americans and the American Revolution: "When the Negro grasped desperately at freedom too, he confirmed America's great expectations as well as one of America's greatest fears."[36]

In Virginia, in the years after the Revolution, Gabriel would ensure that those expectations and fears were going to be fully realized.

The Contradictions of Virginia

Gabriel grew up in a world of contradictions, all of which were spawned by the moderate antislavery trajectory of his home state of Virginia. As he traveled between Richmond and his enslaver Prosser's plantation in Henrico County, he would have met not only other hired-out slaves, but countless free black people. Small-but-growing Richmond boasted 5,700 residents in 1800, of which slightly more than half were black, and about 400 of them were free. These numbers were a direct result of the liberalized manumission law passed in 1782, in the midst of the American Revolution, which led to a slow but steady growth in the number of free blacks in the state.[37] In some cases, enslavers took to heart revolutionary ideology and freed their slaves thinking it was their moral duty. Most famously, Robert Carter, scion of one of Virginia's oldest, most illustrious families, freed more than five hundred of his slaves. Defending his decision, Carter argued, "Slavery is contrary to the true principles of Religion and justice."[38] More often, enslavers manumitted "favored" slaves as a reward for their years of loyal service, or they allowed individual slaves to purchase their own freedom. By 1800, 10 percent of the state's black population was free.[39]

Once manumitted, free black people remained intimately connected to the much larger number of enslaved blacks. Because slaves were usually freed in Virginia as individuals and in small groups, this meant that free blacks had husbands and wives, parents and children who remained enslaved. Free blacks, and to a lesser extent enslaved blacks, traveled between and among Virginia plantations to visit their family members, often using the state's extensive waterways for quicker transit. The boats and barges that traveled these rivers were often captained by black boatmen, some free and some enslaved. Alongside skilled slaves who were hired out like Gabriel, these boatmen lived lives in which white supervision was intermittent. This situation was exacerbated in Richmond itself, which, while a comparatively small city compared to the likes of Philadelphia and New York, nevertheless offered black people greater anonymity in a more densely populated urban world.

For Virginia's black population, these gains were very real. An enslaved person born in the 1770s had a far greater chance at obtaining freedom or at the least having some small measure of autonomy than an enslaved person born in the 1750s. But for all its seeming liberality, particularly in comparison to slavery in South Carolina, Georgia, and the Caribbean, Virginia's slave system was still a *slave* system. Like all slave systems, it required surveillance and brutality to be enforced. Enslaved people were still whipped and beaten. Enslaved families were still ripped apart. Enslaved women were still raped.

These developments meant Virginia's slave regime rested on increasingly precarious foundations. Virginia slaveholders maintained the viciousness of slavery but gave slaves more freedom away from white eyes to talk to each other about that viciousness. Enslavers cared little that most plantation communities boasted a few enslaved people who could read and write, which would allow them to pass information more easily to other enslaved communities throughout the state. Enslavers did not see how the Revolution had opened antislavery possibilities that were never really fulfilled—

and they did not see that enslaved people noticed. Most prominent Virginia slaveholders like Thomas Jefferson and James Madison were blind to the problem. Their racism led them to believe that slavery and republicanism could harmoniously coexist, for they believed black people were incapable of contemplating revolutionary ideas like natural rights, liberty, equality, and the right to revolution itself.

But what if they could?

Not all slave owners were so blind. As one wrote, "The negroes are in every family; they are waiting on every table; they are present on numerous occasions when the conversation turns on political subjects, and cannot fail to catch ideas that will excite discontentment with their condition."[40] But in all likelihood, even this slave owner did not grasp what his words could potentially mean in practice: Revolutionary ideas would only add fuel to enslaved women and men's desire for freedom. By the year 1800, Virginia's slave system had become a powder keg. All that was needed was for someone to light the fuse.

National and international developments made the situation even more explosive. As the autumn of 1800 approached, the young republic was immersed in a bitter, dangerous political battle between Federalists and Republicans. That year the Federalist president John Adams faced off in a rematch for the presidency against his vice president, Republican Thomas Jefferson. The two men and their two respective parties disagreed about nearly everything, but above all they disagreed on how a young, weak United States should navigate a world at war. Should the United States be more partial to Britain or to France in the Napoleonic Wars? And, after that decision was made, what if the opposing side decided to wage war on the United States in retaliation? How much were American citizens allowed to criticize their government if they disagreed with its direction? How should the federal government respond to this criticism? As the election approached, there was consistent talk of civil war.

Yet even potential civil war in the United States could not compare in gravitas to the history-shattering event spawned by the French Revolution: a second revolution, this time in the French sugar colony of Saint Domingue. In August 1791, enslaved people in the northern part of the colony launched a full-scale slave rebellion that quickly became a cataclysmic revolution, which ultimately killed more than three hundred thousand people. After a complicated series of invasions, decrees, and battles, France abolished slavery in the colony. By the late 1790s, Saint Domingue was nominally still French, but it was effectively ruled as an autonomous republic under the famed revolutionary leader Toussaint Louverture.

The Haitian Revolution exemplified how revolutionary ideas could take on a life on their own regardless of their origin. The revolution in France, itself influenced by the American Revolution, had spread across the Atlantic to Saint Domingue, where both white planters and *gens de couleur* ("free people of color," the French term for the colony's large mixed-race population) demanded more autonomy. In 1790, Vincent Ogé, a wealthy *gens de couleur*, demanded the right to vote, citing the principles of the Declaration of the Rights of Man. When the governor refused, Ogé led a brief rebellion until he was captured, tortured, and killed. One year later, it was enslaved people's turn to make the same demands, and this time French authorities were not able to snuff out the uprising. For some Haitian rebels, it was not their first revolutionary war. Men like Henri Christophe and André Rigaud, both vital leaders of the Haitian Revolution, had served with French forces during the American Revolution, fighting in the Siege of Savannah in 1779.

To be sure, it was not as if Haitian revolutionaries required the American and French Revolutions to begin their own—one that was far more revolutionary than both of its predecessors. Enslaved people have always resisted their enslavement. Yet the American and French Revolutions provided a language through which enslaved people could imagine a future that went beyond personal liberty from bondage, where former slaves took their place as equal citizens alongside their former enslavers. In this vein, the principles of 1776 and 1789 did not give rise to slave resistance, but these principles gave that resistance more revolutionary power. Virginia would soon witness the same phenomenon.

Whereas the American and French Revolutions had bequeathed revolutionary language to the Haitian revolutionaries, Haitian revolutionaries gave something back to enslaved people in the United States. Thanks to the American Revolution, slaves in the United States already were adept in their revolutionary rhetoric about natural rights, liberty, and equality, but now Haiti gave them something else: proof of success. Slave rebellions *could* succeed. To slave owners like James Monroe, governor of Virginia in 1800, even news of Haiti was a "contagion" that could destroy the American South's slave society. Events in Haiti, Monroe wrote, "must produce an effect on all people of colour in this and the States south of us, more especially our slaves, and it is our duty to be on our guard to prevent any mischief resulting from it."[41]

Despite his words, however, Virginia authorities were very much not "on guard." On the contrary, they were wholly unprepared for what was about to happen.

Gabriel

Nearly all we know about Gabriel comes from the after-the-fact words of either prejudiced white Americans or black Americans testifying under threat of violence, both of which are not very reliable sources of information. We have no words directly from Gabriel himself. But from these limited sources we can still make several important claims. First, at six foot two or six foot three, displaying scars and missing teeth, Gabriel was a physically imposing presence. Second, Gabriel was enslaved, but, as a literate blacksmith, he was able to take full advantage of the more lenient, less surveilled slavery that had taken root in Virginia since the Revolution. Third, Gabriel had a prior history of violent resistance, having already confronted and attacked his enslaver in 1799—but, thanks to what seem to be sympathetic judges (or, at least, judges disdainful of Gabriel's enslaver, due perhaps to the enslaver's perceived inability to successfully manage his human property), he was jailed for only a few weeks.

At some point in the years after this incident, Gabriel began to think bigger. Instead of challenging just his enslaver, he decided to challenge the entire slave society. His plot was brilliant in its simplicity. Gabriel and his allies would congregate by night outside the center of Richmond in a district named Rocketts Landing, taking advantage of the liberalized world of post-Revolution Virginia, where enslaved people could travel and congregate beyond white supervision. There, they would set fire to the city, which would act as a decoy that would draw white Richmonders out of their homes to Rocketts Landing to fight the blaze. With the city now largely empty, one rebel group would convene at the armory to seize weapons. Another group would take Governor James Monroe hostage. Fully armed and thoroughly organized, Gabriel and his black allies would then confront the leaderless, disorganized, unarmed group of whites in the streets of Richmond. Ahead of the attack, the rebels had made sure to spread news of the plot well beyond the Richmond area, as they hoped more and more black allies would filter into the city to join the fight, turning hundreds of rebels into thousands—and thus make it a second American Revolution that would rival recent events in Haiti.

Perhaps, Gabriel envisioned, he would even find white allies on the streets of Richmond who would come to his aid. His belief was not quite as preposterous as it may seem in retrospect. The unsurveilled streets of Richmond were places where black and white laborers interacted on a daily basis, and they may have found common cause in their day-to-day conversations. After all, poor whites, too, had reason to dislike the haughty planters who dominated the state and federal governments—just like the Whiskey Rebels only a few years before. The composition of Washington's army in the Revolutionary War proved that white and black men could fight together. Whether class solidarity could have actually overridden racial solidarity seems unlikely, but one historian of the rebellion attests to definitive existence of at least a few white co-conspirators.[42]

Unfortunately for Gabriel's carefully laid plans, the night of the planned rebellion witnessed what Governor Monroe later called "one of the most extraordinary falls of rain ever known in our country."[43] The storm may have saved Monroe's life. Such was its intensity that the rain washed out many of the bridges to Richmond, causing Gabriel to postpone the rebellion for one night.

He likely had no other choice, but the postponement nevertheless proved fatal to the uprising. On the day the rebellion was actually launched, two enslaved people who knew of Gabriel's plans revealed them to their enslavers. At first they were not taken seriously, but then white Richmonders observed black people *leaving* Richmond on Saturday night, a day of the week on which they usually traveled *to* Richmond to visit family and socialize. Something was up.

When white authorities started to investigate the rebellion, they found concrete proof of the plot: the existence of "scythe swords," which had been fashioned by Gabriel and his allies to use in the first salvo of fighting, before they seized the armory. In response, Governor Monroe took measures to snuff out the rebellion in its infancy. He ordered all weapons to be secured by moving them from the armory to the city penitentiary. At the same time, he moved to defend the capitol by calling up the Richmond militia, which numbered a paltry thirty-three men and did not have enough gunpowder to be anywhere close to effective.[44] For a little while, this was the best Monroe could do, again testifying to the revolutionary potential of Gabriel's plot. If Gabriel *had* been able to seize the armory . . . It was a thought that white Richmonders hardly wanted to contemplate.

As the militia pretended to secure the capitol, authorities fanned out across the region to uncover all they could about the conspiracy. Within a week, they had arrested many of the chief plotters, and over the course of the next two months, the state would put on trial more than sixty suspected black rebels. All were hauled before a special court reserved for enslaved criminals, known as a court of "oyer and terminer" (Latin for "to hear and to determine"), which consisted of five judges and no jury. Thoroughly tainted by racism and an overwhelming power imbalance, the trials were hardly fair or impartial, but neither were they simply show trials. Guilty verdicts needed to be unanimous, and in a few cases a single dissenting judge allowed a likely guilty person to go free (one unsympathetic observer blamed this judge's pattern of sympathy on his Baptist faith, which led him to believe in "impractical notions of liberty").[45] If Virginian authorities employed torture to induce confessions, then it was likely done at the stage of the arrest and initial imprisonment (although the record is unsurprisingly silent), not during the trials themselves.

Gabriel himself escaped the initial dragnet. He used his intimate knowledge of Virginia's many waterways to his advantage, staying one step ahead of his pursuers. His escape led to one of the more remarkable moments of the entire rebellion. Several miles outside Richmond, the fleeing

Gabriel hailed a passing boat captained by a white man named Taylor. By this time, guilty conspirators were already being hung on the streets of Richmond, and a black man without any papers and clearly running from *something* should have raised suspicions, but Captain Taylor let Gabriel on board without asking any questions. He then allowed Gabriel to remain on the ship for eleven more days as it made its way to Norfolk. When the ship arrived in the coastal city, it was not Captain Taylor but an enslaved man named Billy who alerted authorities that the man on board was likely the rebel leader himself. As with the two enslaved men who betrayed Gabriel's plan, it is easy to deem Billy a traitor to the cause of freedom, but the $300 he hoped to gain from turning over Gabriel would have gone a long way to secure his own freedom. In this insidious way, enslaved people were used against each other to uphold the "peculiar institution."[46]

As the report to Governor Monroe noted, Captain Taylor was hardly a novice when it came to Virginia's slave system. He was a longtime Virginia resident and a former overseer, so, as the report stated, he "knew much better than he acted." The report maintained that Taylor's "conduct appears extradinary [*sic*] to me & I think deserves punishment, instead of a reward."[47] Certainly his conduct deserves historical scrutiny, for it seems likely a white man in Virginia in 1800 had knowingly harbored a runaway slave who was guilty of the largest slave conspiracy in U.S. history. Perhaps Taylor aided Gabriel out of class solidarity. Existing beyond the prying eyes of Virginia's planter elite, the multiracial world of Virginia boatmen was the closest thing the state had to a sort of class-based proletariat. By aiding Gabriel, perhaps Taylor was simply sticking it to the snooty, powerful planter class whom he disliked. Or perhaps he was motivated by religious solidarity, as he was a Methodist who had promised to free the one enslaved person he owned (a promise he had not yet fulfilled).[48] In either case, Captain Taylor's actions testify to the plausibility of Gabriel's belief that, at some point, at least *some* whites would aid his rebellion.

Remarkably, when Gabriel was captured in Norfolk, roughly a hundred miles from Richmond, there were enslaved men who lived in Norfolk who had been part of the rebellion's original planning. Circumstantial evidence suggests that the conspiracy reached more than a hundred miles, not just southeast toward Norfolk, but in every direction, thanks to the ubiquity of black boatmen who passed on plans of the rebellion throughout Virginia's unobserved waterways. It involved at least hundreds, perhaps even thousands, of black Virginians.[49] These numbers were as amorphous as those of the numbers of Patriots in the American Revolution itself: Like white Patriots of 1776, would-be black Patriots of 1800 variously committed to, or withdrew from, Gabriel's Rebellion based upon the likelihood of success. If Gabriel had been able to seize the armory and Governor Monroe, perhaps thousands would have joined Gabriel, just as thousands of whites joined Horatio Gates's forces in upstate New York in 1777 before Saratoga, after it became clear that the British invasion from Canada was in dire straits. Of course, such a tipping point never occurred. On the contrary, one of the enslaved men who betrayed the rebellion did so almost when it was too late for authorities to do anything, suggesting he remained on the fence until the last possible minute, at which point he sided against Gabriel and what he probably deemed a suicidal endeavor.

One of the ironies of Virginia's racist court system was that, in making it illegal for blacks to testify against whites, it proved impossible for Governor Monroe to uncover the real extent of the conspiracy. If there really were white sympathizers, there was still no way to uncover them, for nearly all knowledge of the conspiracy came from the testimony of the caught rebels. Some did indeed provide names of a handful of white men who had offered to aid the rebellion, all living well beyond Richmond, but none of this testimony could be acted upon. For Governor Monroe, this may have been extremely convenient. After all, if authorities did discover white sympathizers, then it would have ripped off Virginia's facade of white solidarity and further unsettled the precarious system of racial slavery and white supremacy. Better to execute the slave rebels and claim the rebellion had been thoroughly uncovered.

Gabriel himself was executed on October 10, 1800. According to newspaper reports, he asserted that he was indeed the leader of the rebellion when he was captured, but he nevertheless pled not guilty. He did not speak at the trial, for he knew his fate. Monroe was probably right when he wrote, "[Gabriel] seemed to have made up his mind to die, and to have resolved to say but little on the subject of the conspiracy." By saying nothing, the man who knew the most individuals involved in the conspiracy would not implicate anyone who had not yet been arrested. Legally, of course, he *was* guilty, but in the eyes his followers, he was no more guilty than George Washington when he took command of the Continental Army. Some white observers inadvertently acknowledged this when they gave him the title "black General Gabriel."[50] This moniker revealed a simple truth: With the American Revolution still a part of living memory, Gabriel's goal was, like the Revolution, equally legitimate.

Gabriel was one of twenty-seven conspirators who were executed by hanging. Knowing they faced death, most nevertheless stood with Gabriel to the end, declining at their trials to portray themselves as Gabriel's dupes. Instead, they chose to maintain their own agency in joining the conspiracy, accepting the ultimate punishment.

Thanks to the dearth of direct evidence, historians have long debated just what, exactly, were Gabriel's motivations for launching a slave rebellion and what, exactly, he hoped to achieve upon its success. Was Gabriel primarily motivated by his belief that his rebels could gain white allies, as some historians have argued? Did notions of class consciousness really underlay the explicit racial dynamics of the slave rebellion? Or, as other historians have countered, was it not class solidarity but evangelical Christianity and local slave culture that helped spawn the conspiracy?[51]

Whatever the answer, on both sides of the argument lies the same crucial fact: The social, political, and cultural developments that gave way to Gabriel's plot were born during the American Revolution. If Gabriel really did think the white artisans of Richmond would join with black rebels in class solidarity, then it was because of the egalitarian principles that had taken hold among the "lower sort" during the Revolution. Supporting this interpretation was the conspirators' euphemism for rebellion, which they frequently termed "the business." This curious phrasing had emerged in the Atlantic world to describe all sorts of revolutionary activity, suggesting that at some point black rebels may have been in contact with white radicals, likely sailors, at a waterfront tavern at some Virginia port.[52] There is also the testimony of several enslaved people, in particular Gabriel's brother Solomon, who claimed that Gabriel's stated goal was to "conquer the white people & possess ourselves of their property."[53] Presumably, Gabriel hoped that at least some of the poorer whites, those without any property, would join him and his black allies in the endeavor.

If, on the other hand, the rebellion's roots lay in evangelical Christianity, then it was the Revolution that swept away established state religions (Anglicanism in Virginia) and made possible the spread of Baptist and Methodist teachings among enslaved communities. During these years, white and black Virginians frequently attended church together, briefly becoming spiritual equals in the eyes of God even as their respective roles in the secular world were permanently defined by Virginia's racial caste system. One of Gabriel's brothers was a preacher, potential rebels were recruited at Baptist gatherings, and Gabriel's speeches were known as "sermons." It is even possible that the rebels believed black Americans were God's chosen people, ready to be redeemed just as God had redeemed the Israelites in Egypt during the Exodus.[54]

Whether Gabriel's primary motivations were rooted in class or religion or something else, the language of the American Revolution—and, by extension, the Haitian and French Revolutions—infused the rebellion with ideological meaning. Countless plotters stated that they were fighting for larger ideals just as much as they were fighting to make their own lives better. A man name James defiantly proclaimed that he would "fight for my freedom as long as I have breath."[55] Another remembered how, before the plot was launched, one conspirator embraced another and asserted, "We have as much to fight for our Liberty as any Man."[56] White observers noticed this rhetoric. Wrote one, black people "manifested a sense of their rights, and contempt for danger, and thirst for revenge."[57] Massachusetts colonial governor Thomas Gage could have written the same thing about the New England Patriots fighting at Concord's North Bridge a quarter century before.

To announce their rebellion, Gabriel and his allies planned to raise a flag with the words "Death or Liberty." Whether this was a play on the famous words of Patrick Henry or a rallying cry informing onlookers that they only had these two options, it revealed how Gabriel and his allies co-opted revolutionary rhetoric and made it their own. As one apprehended rebel later proclaimed, "I have nothing more to offer than what General Washington would have had to offer, had he been taken by the British and put to trial by them. I have adventured my life in endeavoring to obtain the liberty of my countrymen, and am a willing to sacrifice in their cause."[58] Clearly the rebels knew recent American history.

And the similarities between the rebellion and the American Revolution extended beyond the rebels' language. The very existence of the conspiracy stemmed from the world that the American Revolution had wrought in the republic's most populous state. Antislavery thought had permeated Virginia society, but very little antislavery action was ever taken—and, for the most part, any antislavery actions that enslavers *did* take simply gave slaves more time away from suspicious enslavers to plot something like a massive slave rebellion. If there were actual white allies, as the plotters later testified and Gabriel believed existed, then this alliance, too, was one that was based upon the principles of the Revolution. Gabriel and his allies would have met white artisans in the streets of Richmond and along the waterways of the Virginia Piedmont. From these artisans, likely Jeffersonian Republicans, they would have heard rhetoric about "monarchical" Federalist merchants whose very existence threatened all that had been won during the Revolution. Briefly, then, Gabriel's and Jefferson's viewpoints of the Revolution met. In Gabriel's eyes, it made sense that these same people, people who still treasured the Revolution's egalitarian principles, would aid his rebellion.[59]

Even if white allies never emerged, Gabriel also knew that the young American republic was experiencing its most significant domestic political crisis since the Revolution itself. Federalists accused Republicans of being radical Jacobins and atheists, while Republicans countered that Federalists were anti-republican monarchical aristocrats. As the election of 1800 approached, Gabriel may have even heard talk of domestic strife and civil war. Such discord was an opportune time to launch a rebellion. After all, the Haitian Revolution taught just such a lesson, as Haiti's rebels had used the domestic and international turmoil of the French Revolution to their own, ultimately victorious, advantage.[60] Thanks largely to a rainstorm, Gabriel never got the chance to test the similarly unsettled waters of Virginia's slave society.

Counterrevolution

Some white Virginians had always believed that loosening the reigns of slavery would increase rather than forestall the possibility of revolt, and Gabriel's Rebellion seemed to validate their stance. As one writer noted, "If we will keep a ferocious monster in our country [i.e., slavery], we must keep him in chains."[61] There was no middle ground. Governor Monroe had long embraced the tentative liberalizing of Virginia's slave regime, and at first thought it "strange" that the state's slaves would seek rebellion despite their "more favorable" treatment since the Revolution.[62] After Gabriel's plot, however, he came around, writing, "Unhappily while this class of people exists among us we can never count with certainty on its tranquil submission."[63] To enforce this submission, the state created a public guard that would permanently fortify the state capitol. As one abolitionist author wrote much later, during the second year of the Civil War, this "cordon of bayonets . . . was the lasting memorial of Gabriel's insurrection, the stern heritage of terror bequeathed by his defeat."[64]

And with that, the Virginia General Assembly rolled back every single post-Revolution law that had made enslaved people's lives just a little more bearable. In 1802, blacks were permanently barred from becoming boatmen, the job that provided for both freedom of travel and the most amount of time beyond white supervision. In 1804, nighttime gatherings of slaves were prohibited. In 1805, free black schools were eliminated, and any black person who traveled north to receive an education was not allowed to return. In 1806, all newly freed slaves were required to leave the state within a year, and their future exodus needed to be guaranteed by their former enslaver upon manumission. While this law did not prohibit private manumissions entirely, the effect was largely the same, and it quickly curbed the population growth of free black Virginians. In 1808, the "hiring out" process, by which owners could hire out their slaves to other employers who needed labor, was banned (although this law only made the practice go underground). With this final law, the process was complete. To Virginia lawmakers, it was a job well done: They had slammed the door shut on domestic insurrections.

At least, they *tried* to slam it shut. They and their proslavery brethren throughout the South were stymied by a population they wished did not exist: free African Americans. Because while the expansion of slavery in the South was one legacy of the American Revolution, the growing population of free black people, mostly but not exclusively in the North, was *also* a legacy of the American Revolution. And while most Northern states denied free blacks their political and civil rights (which would only get further repressed over time), thereby providing a version of freedom that was often partial and highly circumscribed, free blacks were still free *enough* to mobilize against slavery on a large scale, as they wrote pamphlets, published newspapers, gave speeches, petitioned assemblies, aided fugitive slaves, and eventually armed themselves, all to fight the maintenance and growth of slavery in the United States. In their struggle, they had a rhetorical ally: the American Revolution itself, for whatever Jefferson did in the early 1800s to suppress antislavery agitation, what he wrote a quarter century before in the Declaration of Independence could not be unwritten. Free blacks, too, had natural rights—and they would continue to assert them, even in the face of increasing white opposition.

By the early nineteenth century, nearly all white Americans had turned their backs on antislavery arguments. The counterrevolution that had eroded women's rights also eroded black rights and nearly extinguished all but the most tepid antislavery thoughts among whites. Soon, only two abolition societies remained, in Pennsylvania and New York. And whatever energy remained in the white abolition movement, most of it was focused on lingering milquetoast colonization efforts that had died in Virginia but were still alive in the Northern states. With very few white allies, black Americans were left largely on their own to fight against both slavery and the right to be fully equal Americans.

As they fought, the memory of Gabriel and his conspiracy remained alive, both in written form in the North and as a folk memory passed down over generations by enslaved people in the South. Songs were sung and stories were told about Gabriel in enslaved communities, to such an extent that formerly enslaved people still mentioned him in interviews with the Works Progress Administration *in the 1930s*.

Most whites, by contrast, wanted to forget Gabriel and what he stood for. It was easier to misremember, to believe that the American Revolution had never been an antislavery struggle, to trust that enslaved black people were content to live in a world without their natural rights, to wish the free black population did not exist. But at least one anonymous New England poet understood the future implications of Gabriel's actions:

Remember ere too late,
The tale of St. Domingo's [i.e., Haiti's] fate.
Tho Gabriel dies, a host remains
Oppress'd with slavery's galling chain.[65]

The fight against slavery was not over.

5

Political Harmony: The End and Beginning of the Two-Party System, 1816–24

In November 1816, now more than fifteen years removed from his role suppressing Gabriel's Rebellion, President-elect James Monroe was in the throes of the arduous process of selecting the men who would form his presidential cabinet when he received a piece of advice in the mail on just that topic. "In every [cabinet] selection," the letter read, "party and party feelings should be avoided. Now is the time to exterminate that *monster*, called party spirit. By selecting characters most conspicuous for their probity, virtue, capacity, and firmness, without any regard to party, you will go far to . . . eradicate those feelings which, on former occasions, threw so many obstacles in the way of government; and, perhaps, have the *pleasure* and *honor* of uniting a people heretofore political divided."[1]

Monroe wholeheartedly agreed—but he did not need the lecture. After all, he had just won the presidency in the most lopsided result since the Electoral College unanimously reelected George Washington in 1792. Monroe's election twenty-four years later was not unanimous, but it was close. A Republican and Virginian like his predecessors Madison and Jefferson, Monroe lost only three states to his Federalist opponent Rufus King, taking 183 electoral votes to King's 34. Who was this writer to pontificate on the importance of political unity? Monroe was the embodiment of it.

And it was not as if the letter writer was suggesting something novel. In 1816, a vast majority of Americans—of both political parties—abhorred what the Framers called "faction," but by 1816 most Americans were calling it something else: "partisanship." Like them, Monroe also loathed partisanship. With the Federalist Party seemingly on its last legs, he believed that it was now time to pursue what he called "amalgamation," by which he meant the final destruction of all political parties.

Whether he was perturbed or not by this presumptuous letter writer, Monroe could not ignore him, for he was, in fact, none other than General Andrew Jackson. In 1815, Americans had christened Jackson "the Hero" (always with a capital "H") for his victory over the British at the Battle of New Orleans, the final battle of the War of 1812.

For our purposes, Jackson's anti-partisan letter was not particularly important in the moment, but important for what Jackson would eventually become: one of the most vociferous partisans in American political history. Indeed, Jackson's failed quest for the presidency in 1824, and his success in 1828, would define a new era of U.S. politics, one that was defined by its unapologetic partisanship. And yet, this was the same man who lectured Monroe in 1816, "The chief magistrate of a great and powerful nation should never indulge in party feeling."[2] Why the about-face?

This sea change in American politics, embodied in the person of Jackson, is the story of this chapter. At its heart, it is a story about the destruction of the ideal of political harmony, an ideal that was so much on the minds of the Revolutionary generation. It is also a story of irony on top of irony on top of irony. Ultimately, while the revolutionary ideal of political harmony would die a quick death in the mid-1820s, it seemed to have emerged completely victorious only a few years before.

Harmony Stillborn

Unlike the right to rebel and the rights of women—as we have seen, issues that remained contested in the aftermath of the American Revolution—few Americans disagreed about partisanship, division, and faction. Faction was abhorrent, dangerous, subversive, and anti-republican. Faction was the antithesis of republican government. Republican politicians (small "r"—Federalists and Republicans were both republicans) were supposed to be virtuous and disinterested. They were supposed to be men who could rise above political infighting and backroom dealing and smoke-filled rooms, and instead unite as republicans to govern for the good of all. They were supposed to forgo partisanship.

So, too, were all Americans. As Tom Paine wrote in *Common Sense*, Americans had "the power to begin the world over again. A situation similar to the present hath not happened since the days of Noah until now."[3] In this new world, a new people would be united toward a harmonious destiny of liberty and opportunity. Unity was virtuous—and intoxicating.

To be clear, in this context unity meant something specific: national political unity. When men like Andrew Jackson and James Monroe talked of harmony, they were not going to emancipate their slaves, redistribute their wealth, or welcome Native people into the body politic with open arms. As wealthy white men, they dominated the United States' politics, economy, and society, and, in their minds, realizing national unity would do nothing to change this fact. When they talked of "amalgamation" and "harmony," they meant it for the white men who ran the country. To them, harmony was *national*, and it was *political*. The simmering economic and social divisions that crisscrossed the land (and crisscross this book) would remain—although, perhaps, national political unity would mitigate, even suppress, the social chaos.

But national unity was almost always near impossible, even at the time when Paine wrote, when revolutionary sentiments were at their height. While the Second Continental Congress maintained that the Declaration of Independence was "unanimous," agreed to by all thirteen states, this was a scarcely veiled fiction. These words disguised the fact that tens of thousands of Loyalists—*Americans* all—would take up arms against the Patriot cause. More than 85,000 would leave the new United States for Canada, Great Britain, and other parts of the British Empire at the conclusion of the war.

At least the Patriots knew where the Loyalists stood. Far more disturbing to the Patriots were the tens of thousands of what historians now deem "the disaffected."[4] These were the men and women who simply hoped to survive the brutal conflict, and they were willing to shift their allegiances depending on which way the winds of war blew. As the war continued seemingly without end in the late 1770s and early 1780s, the ranks of the disaffected only increased. They existed in every town and village throughout the Thirteen Colonies. In response to the ubiquitous presence of the disaffected, Patriots sought ways to figure out who was *really* on their side, and who was just acting. Their concern led them to pass the "Test Acts," which required everyone to publicly swear their allegiance to the new United States. If political harmony could not emerge by happenstance, it needed to be enforced.

Unity was no better in the years after the 1783 Treaty of Paris. In the midst of a dreadful economic depression, Americans were divided over whether the Articles of Confederation—and, for that matter, many state governments—needed to be altered or even thrown out. It was during these years that Shays's Rebellion erupted in western Massachusetts over the state's hard money policies and the domination of eastern elites. Although not as dramatic or violent, similar disagreements over monetary policy and east–west geographic divisions also emerged in other states.

The drafting of the Constitution hardly solved these rifts. Once the Federalists unveiled their new proposed government that they claimed would solve all these issues, they were immediately and vociferously opposed by thousands of Antifederalists, who comprised at the very least a substantial minority, and perhaps even a majority, of the U.S. population. The Federalists were able to secure the Constitution's ratification through the concentration of their numbers in cities, their control of most newspapers, and, as we have seen, their political savviness.

With ratification came the ascension of George Washington to the presidency. Here, it seemed, was real national political harmony, for the Electoral College's decision was unanimous, and it would be so again four years later—for the first and last times in the nation's history. Yet Alexander Hamilton's expansive financial program and the administration's Anglophilic international stance quickly angered thousands of Americans (including our Whiskey Rebels from chapter 2) who felt the new administration was betraying the republican ideals of the Revolution. Whatever political consensus Washington hoped to achieve evaporated seemingly overnight, with opposition even coming from within his own handpicked cabinet. Washington's secretary of state, Thomas Jefferson, along with James Madison, then serving in the House of Representatives, were horrified by Hamilton's policies and his personal sway over Washington himself.

In 1791, they hired editor Philip Freneau to publish the *National Gazette*, a newspaper whose sole purpose was to make the case against the administration's policies. It did so with language everyone could understand: the language of the American Revolution. Thus Alexander Hamilton and his allies were "monarchical" and "anti-republican"; they were trying to reinstall a "baneful monarchy in our country" and believed that the American people should practice "nothing but obedience" to their rulers.[5] Jefferson and Madison's role in this remained anonymous, and any articles they contributed were published under noms de plume. While the paper would go under by 1793, in retrospect the founding of this newspaper marked the birth of U.S. partisan politics.[6]

While the Republicans, as this fledgling opposition party was called, could not and did not challenge Washington's reelection in 1792, by 1796 the United States had entered what is now deemed the "First Party System," with Hamilton's Federalists battling Jefferson and Madison's Republicans for political control. This seemingly banal term obscures the paranoia and hostility between the two parties, each of which thought the other was undermining the country and betraying the American Revolution. Because partisanship was still deemed to be anti-republican and therefore vile, both parties constructed their arguments against the other using a tactic that one historian has called "partisan antipartisanship."[7] In this rendering, each faction deemed the other faction an illegitimate, dangerous minority that did not represent *real* Americans, but rather something sinister and conspiratorial. Elections, therefore, were not just contests over which party would control federal and state governments over the next two or four years, but whether the United States would even survive as an independent republic.

To be sure, it was not as if Americans did not try to overcome faction. The language American leaders employed consistently demonstrated their fervent hope that partisanship could be banished from the republic simply by pretending it did not exist. Thus, the Declaration of Independence was "unanimous" (it was not) and the Constitution was written by "We the People" (it was not). In 1796, Washington warned of the dangers of faction in his famous Farewell Address, reminding Americans that they were "one people" who "in a common cause fought and triumphed together" (they had not). Four years later, after his bitter victory over John Adams, newly elected president Thomas Jefferson famously proclaimed, "We are all Federalists.

We are all Republicans" (they were not). The seductive and soaring rhetoric of unity was always belied by the sour rancor of partisanship.

Perhaps if Americans squinted and looked hard enough, they saw actual moments of national unanimity in their past, although these moments were fleeting and imperfect. They may have looked to the response to the Stamp Act in 1765, which brought together future Patriots *and* future Loyalists, of all classes and backgrounds, against what was arguably the most loathed British measure of the entire Revolutionary struggle. Another was the response to the first battles of the Revolutionary War at Lexington and Concord in 1775, which witnessed a "*rage militaire*" throughout New England, during which everyday New Englanders (and many other Americans) eagerly joined the Patriot cause in righteous anger against British perfidy.[8] A third was embodied in the prestige of George Washington himself. As the "American Cincinnatus"—so named because his actions mirrored a legendary (and perhaps fictitious) ancient Roman leader—who led the United States to victory in war but then gave up his power in peace, Washington was trusted and beloved by Americans of all backgrounds and political persuasions. His presence alone at the Constitutional Convention lent the Framers enough gravitas to undertake their quasi-legal quasi-coup, and his twice-unanimous election as president demonstrated that it was he—and he alone—whom Americans trusted to ensure the United States' survival in a hostile world.

These moments of unity were exception to the rule of faction. However, after Jefferson's election in 1800, Republicans *finally* began to hope that perhaps the Federalist Party would soon disappear, for the Republican Party began to dominate much of the country. Only New England remained a Federalist bastion. Yet Jefferson's self-defeating 1807 Embargo Act that closed all U.S. ports to trade in order to hurt Great Britain and, to a much greater extent, Madison's disastrous War of 1812 revived Federalist hopes. Republicans had promised that the war would lead to the U.S. conquest of Canada, the end of the British practice of impressment, and the end of Native power in the Trans-Appalachian West. Instead, the United States experienced a series of unmitigated, humiliating disasters, which culminated with the British capture of Washington, DC, and the burning of the White House in August 1814.

It was immediately after these calamities that one Federalist in particular, Francis Scott Key, sought to craft a song that would once again unify Americans around a—as the revolutionaries of 1776 had termed it—"common cause." Key may have been a Federalist, but he still supported the war effort, and believed national victory was more important than party victory. As he famously watched Fort McHenry hold out against a day-long British bombardment, Key wrote the lyrics to what eventually became "The Star-Spangled Banner," which celebrated the United States as the "land of the free and the home of the brave." No partisanship here. *Everyone* was free, and *everyone* was brave.[9]

But not all Federalists were nationalists like Key. More stringent members of the unabashedly elitist party, particularly those from New England, hoped to capitalize on the disastrous war and regain their power and influence. Smelling blood in the water, these Federalists issued a call in October to convene in Hartford later that year, where they hoped to seize the initiative from the Republican Party, offer an alternative to Republican policies, and begin the road back to political dominance.

Good Feelings

Unfortunately for the Federalists, the Hartford Convention was a mistake from which they would never recover. It was not the convention itself that dealt them the fatal blow, but what happened thousands of miles to the south, on the outskirts of New Orleans. There, Andrew Jackson led a motley force of U.S. regular soldiers and militia to a stunning victory over an invading British army. It did not matter that, weeks before in the Netherlands, U.S. ambassadors had signed a treaty of peace with the British ending the war, nor did it matter that the delegates at the Hartford Convention did not actually endorse secession from the Union. Instead, what mattered was perception: The United States had not won the war, but now, with Jackson's victory, it *felt* like they did; the Federalists were not traitors, but now, with Jackson's victory, they *seemed* like they were. As Jackson became "the Hero," and as Americans throughout the Union sang the newly written popular ballad "The Hunters of Kentucky" (even if most of Jackson's militia hailed from Tennessee), the Federalist Party's support cratered. The famed song seemed to be almost mocking Federalists: "And 'twould have you done good, I think, / To see Kentuckians drop 'em." From then on, the Federalist Party began a period of precipitous—and permanent—decline. As the historian George Dangerfield memorably phrased it, in certain localities Federalists continued to cling to power in a "rather fungoid manner," but they were dead as a force in national politics.[10]

So it was that James Monroe was elected almost unanimously in 1816, with scant Federalist opposition. In the aftermath of his landslide victory, Monroe decided to go on a goodwill tour of the Northern states to ostensibly examine the state of national defenses, which were of particular concern after so many failures during the War of 1812. Yet behind this superficial purpose lay a deeper one that was lost on nobody: He hoped to reach out to the disillusioned Federalists who still wielded some power in New England. Here Monroe was deliberately echoing the precedent of George Washington, who himself had gone on a tour of the nation after his first presidential election in order foster national sentiment and national unity in the aftermath of the bitter debates over ratification.

It was not just Washington's actions that Monroe mimicked, but Washington's dress. Monroe typically wore knee breeches, a black coat, black silk hose, and white-topped boots, and continued to powder his hair and wear it in a ponytail, all choices that were decidedly out of fashion by 1816. To an observer, Monroe's sartorial choices must have appeared odd or even absurd, but at the same time also reassuring. Clearly this was a president who understood his place in U.S. history. He was the last president of the Virginia Dynasty, and the last president who served in the Revolutionary War—and he was unwilling to let current fashion trends blemish the role he planned to play.

Americans from all backgrounds also understood that he was playing this role. As his Northern tour proceeded, comparisons to Washington abounded, particularly when it came to Monroe's outreach toward disaffected Federalists. One newspaper noted that Monroe's nonpartisan stance "looked like a restoration of the policy of Washington."[11] Another paper claimed that Monroe, like Washington, seemed "to have united *all* hearts and *all* voices in his praise."[12] When Monroe traveled through Federalist

Boston, he was accompanied by famed Boston architect Charles Bulfinch, who explained to Monroe why he was greeted so enthusiastically. Wrote Bulfinch, "The visit, with which you are pleased to honor them, recalls to the recollection of many, their interview with your illustrious predecessor, the Father of his Country, on a similar occasion. They remember with great satisfaction, the hope, the confidence, and the fond anticipation of national prosperity which his presence inspired."[13]

Monroe himself hoped Americans would recall other moments of unity besides Washington's tour. While in Boston, he noted that he was "deeply affected" when approaching Bunker Hill, the site of the second major battle of the Revolutionary War. Monroe recalled how "the blood spilt here roused the whole American people, and united them in a common cause in defence of their rights—That union will never be broken."[14]

Such was the success of the Northern tour that one arch-Federalist Boston newspaper, the *Columbia Centinel*, claimed that Monroe had inaugurated an "ERA OF GOOD FEELINGS." Other newspapers quickly echoed this phrase, and historians have continued to use it to describe this seemingly unique era of one-party rule. Both contemporaries and historians, however, have employed it with a grain of salt, because whatever the Era of Good Feelings was, it was never an era of *actual* good feelings.[15] As one skeptical newspaper quipped, any American believing in future harmony may have a "good heart," but "there must be a defect in his head."[16]

Bad Feelings

James Monroe is often overlooked as the least talented (and least interesting) of the first generation of presidents, but his understated manner disguised an acute political mind and a deft political touch. His talents were sorely needed near the end of his first term, when the United States experienced twin crises that rocked the foundations of the still-precarious Union. There was the nation's first major economic depression, followed by the nation's first major political conflict over slavery.

The economic depression began in early 1819, when the U.S. economy entered a tailspin now known as the Panic of 1819. As with all economic depressions, the roots of the 1819 collapse are complicated, located in diminishing European demand for American crops in 1817, which in turn burst a four-year bubble of easy credit and rampant land speculation consuming most U.S. states, particularly those in the West. The roots and effects of the panic will be more fully detailed in chapter 6, but suffice it to say, the Panic essentially inaugurated the United States' entry into a modern(ish) capitalist economy, with periods of intoxicating boom and tragic bust that touched Americans of all backgrounds.

With unemployment reaching 50 percent in some eastern cities, and thousands of farmers unable to pay their loans, the panic devastated the livelihoods of tens of thousands of Americans.[17] The United States had seemed ascendant after the end of the War of 1812, but the depression now called into question whether it still promised economic prosperity to its citizens. It also called into question the United States' supposed ideological superiority. Republics were premised on virtue and "disinterestedness," on the need for the "better" citizens to behave with a certain sort of integrity, yet all the panic pointed to was a nation corrupt and a people "interested," devoid of any moral responsibility. As one of the directors of the Bank of the United States noted in the first months of the panic, "A long continuation of distresses in the commercial world has had a bad effect on the morality of the country."[18]

This economic crisis was compounded by a political (and, to some, moral) crisis the following year when Missourians sought statehood status from the federal government as a slave state. Few expected any serious issues—five slave states had been admitted since the ratification of the Constitution in 1789—but a Republican representative from New York named James Tallmadge proposed an amendment that would allow Missouri statehood only if it banned slavery. This amendment opened a debate that many had long thought closed, as other Northern Republicans joined with a rump contingent of New England Federalists to back Tallmadge's amendment and officially oppose the extension of slavery.

In response, Southern Republicans mounted a vehement defense of Missouri statehood and, less coherently, slavery itself, for proslavery arguments would not yet be fully formulated until the 1830s. The debates themselves took Americans back to the founding of the country and the intention of the Founders. Massachusetts congressman Timothy Fuller even mounted an argument that would over time become more prevalent: Slavery may be protected in the Constitution, but it was antithetical to the spirit of the Declaration of Independence.[19] Thomas Jefferson famously termed the Missouri Crisis a "fire bell in the night," for it awakened an issue that he and many other Americans had long thought dormant. A few of the more dramatic speeches in Congress even mentioned disunion as one possible outcome of the whole mess. Tallmadge himself suggested as much, saying, "If a dissolution of the Union must take place, let it be so! If civil war . . . must come, I can only say, let it come!"[20]

The stakes were very clear: The very future of the nation was in jeopardy.

With the depression and Missouri Crisis threatening the precarious social fabric of the fledgling republic, it was no surprise that Americans of all backgrounds and sections looked around for leaders who could provide reassurance for the future by bringing them back to the past, to the American Revolution. To a certain extent, Monroe was such a figure. After all, he had brought them back to the past in 1817 with his Northern tour. Yet Monroe was hardly charismatic or outspoken. On the contrary, he possessed a remarkable amount of self-control in public, and his contributions to the nation's politics often came behind the scenes, hidden from public view.

Such was the case with the Missouri Crisis, which Monroe helped steer from crisis to compromise, prodding and nudging congressional allies off the record to craft a deal that would be satisfactory to the moderate middle. When all was said and done, Missouri did enter the Union as a slave state, but statehood was paired with two antislavery measures: First, Maine, long a part of Massachusetts, entered the Union as a free state in order to maintain the free-slave state balance in the Senate; second, slavery would be barred from all future states lying north of 36°30″ line of latitude (Missouri's southern border). Considering that the United States officially claimed far more territory north of this line than south of it, this latter measure soothed moderate antislavery Northerners.

Like most Americans, Monroe himself was not entirely pleased with the compromise. A member of the Virginia slave-owning plantocracy like his presidential forebears Washington, Jefferson, and Madison, Monroe at first had hoped to keep all U.S. territory open to slavery. Not doing so, he fretted, would mean that the growing population of enslaved people in Virginia and its neighboring slave states would remain confined within those states, increasing the likelihood of slave rebellion. Monroe, of course, was Virginia's governor during Gabriel's Rebellion, so he knew all too well the risks that underlay a slave society that was based, at its heart, on the threat and use of violence to keep enslaved people enslaved. In Monroe's eyes, new slave territory would lead the slave population to peacefully "diffuse" in the West—and, of course, provide a market for Monroe and his fellow Virginia slave owners to sell their excess slaves.

As the crisis deepened, however, Monroe started to worry that the Federalists' staunch antislavery stance would lead to the party's resurgence in the North, which in turn increased the likelihood of the Union's disintegration. This disintegration could lead to two or even three American republics, in the North, the South, and, populated by Americans only tenuously tied to the Union, the West. A western republic was particularly concerning for Monroe, because at the time most U.S. western territory lay north of Missouri and most western Americans outside Missouri were hostile to slavery. This western republic, so Monroe's thinking went, could also abolish slavery in Missouri. And so, Monroe moderated his behind-the-scenes politicking, accepting the compromise line of latitude, reasoning—correctly, it would turn out—that eventually Spanish Texas would become U.S. slave territory.[21]

He was less integral when it came to a government response to the Panic of 1819—largely because there was not one, at least at the federal level. As we shall see in chapter 6, countless states enacted a range of relief measures, but policymakers at the federal level believed (and would continue to believe for another century) that it was not the federal government's job to further interfere with the economy in the case of a panic. On the contrary, Adam Smith's doctrine of laissez-faire argued that government interference would only exacerbate and lengthen a depression. Congress did intervene when it came to the sale of and payment for federal land, reducing the price of land in 1820 and giving debtors more time and options for repayment a year later, but neither the Land Act nor the Relief Act made a significant dent in the number of foreclosures. Besides this, the federal government simply tried to make sure its own finances were in order, and then wait out the crisis like the rest of the country. Monroe, never one to rock the boat, let the federal government ride the current of economic depression by cutting the federal budget in order to stay solvent. Nothing else was done.

The Five-Way Contest

By 1824, it had been quite a few years since presidential elections had really mattered. While James Madison's first election in 1812 was incredibly close, 1816 and 1820 were Republican routs—and yet, appearances were somewhat deceiving. Since 1796, every presidential election had seen between 20 and 40 percent of eligible voters cast a ballot; in 1820, it was an uninterested 10 percent. It was not that Americans had rejected Monroe: On the contrary, they largely agreed with his policies and they supported his desire to end partisan strife. Yet, with perhaps the exception of his 1817 tour, they never embraced him either. He may have had Revolutionary pedigree, but soon it became clear that he was not the man who would alleviate Americans' anxiety about the future of the country. Secretary of War John C. Calhoun, ever an astute political observer, aptly voiced the country's mood in a remark to his colleague Secretary of State John Quincy Adams, confiding in him that there were "Multitudes in deep distress; and a general mass of disaffection to the Government, not concentrated in any particular direction, but ready to seize upon any event, and looking out any where for a leader."[22]

But who would that leader be? The contest for Monroe's successor was on as soon as Monroe's reelection was official. Over the course of the next two years, five candidates emerged. Three were part of Monroe's cabinet: Secretary of State Adams, Secretary of War Calhoun, and Secretary of the Treasury William Crawford. The fourth, Henry Clay, was the Speaker of the House, and the only candidate who explicitly positioned himself against Monroe's policies. The fifth was none other than Andrew Jackson, the Hero of New Orleans himself.

All five candidates appealed to Americans in different ways. Clay and Calhoun, from Kentucky and South Carolina, respectively, represented a new generation of American leadership that did not have its roots in the American Revolution. Both had made names for themselves as leaders of the "War Hawks" who sought war with Great Britain in 1812, and in the early 1820s both advocated for measures that would knit together the U.S. economy and foster U.S. nationalism, such as federal spending on internal improvements and, at least for Clay, protective tariffs that would foster U.S. manufacturing.

Crawford, who was born in Virginia but spent all of his adult life in Georgia, was also of this second generation. First a state representative and then U.S. senator, Crawford was a member of the "Old Republicans," sometimes called the "Radicals," a loosely knit group of politicians who believed that the Republican Party under Madison and Monroe had deviated from its ideological origins of strict interpretation of the Constitution and support for states' rights. Old Republicans like Crawford were particularly displeased by their party's embrace of Federalist policies like a national bank and a high tariff. In 1824, he was by far the most partisan and political of the candidates. He had sought the presidency in 1816, only to get beaten out for the Republican nomination by Monroe, but he was angling to succeed Monroe the moment he agreed to serve as secretary of the treasury. Adams memorably noted in his diary that Crawford's "talent is intrigue," and his "ambition swallows up his principle."[23] There was good reason for his ambition: In the early 1820s, he was viewed by most Americans as the odds-on favorite to win the 1824 election.

As for John Quincy Adams himself, he was also of the second generation, although he was more directly connected to the first generation than any other candidate because he was the son of John Adams, the nation's second president and one of the great men of the American Revolution. Like his father, John Quincy possessed a deep moral sense of right and wrong, which, again like his father, he combined with sanctimoniousness and irritability. The historian George Dangerfield, ever one to offer a wonderful turn of phrase, memorably wrote that Adams's two great qualities were "wrath and vision": "wrath" because Adams picked frequent political fights and refused to play any sort of political game (and, therefore, openly admitted he had no political friends); "vision" because Adams was an astute observer and predictor of both national and international politics.

Adams's most lasting visionary moment came in 1823 when Monroe proclaimed that the United States would oppose all new European colonization in the Americas. Although the Monroe Doctrine, as it became known, still bears Monroe's name, it was largely the brainchild of Secretary of State Adams. Importantly, Adams also supported Monroe's party "amalgamation" policy wholeheartedly, and he believed himself to be above what he called "caballing" and "electioneering," by which he essentially meant politicians doing political things. As for his own political future, Adams believed he had "neither talent nor inclination for intrigue."[24] In all likelihood, he honestly believed this—but he was also lying to himself.

And then there was Andrew Jackson. To understand Jackson's appeal, it is necessary to ignore almost everything we know about how Jackson's two presidential terms eventually turned out. The Maysville Road Veto, the clash with Chief Justice John Marshall over Indian Removal, the Bank War, the Nullification Crisis, the Eaton Affair—these were all far in the future in 1824, conflicts that no one could have predicted. At the time, it was Jackson's illustrious—albeit controversial—military service that made him beloved among a wide sector of Americans. This service began during the Revolutionary War itself, making Jackson the only candidate directly connected to the founding.

Born on the Carolina frontier in 1767 to Scots-Irish parents who had recently immigrated to North America, Jackson's youth was one of family tragedy followed by family tragedy. Jackson's father was killed in a logging accident while he was clearing land only three weeks before Jackson was born. In 1779, his older brother died of heat exhaustion while fighting the British at the Battle of Stono Ferry. Jackson and his other brother then became couriers for the local Patriot militia during the final brutal years of the Revolutionary War in the South. In 1781, both were captured, with Jackson remembering that British soldiers "abused us very much" and threatened to "hang us all."[25]

Captivity led to the first of Jackson's many legendary military exploits. When ordered to shine a British officer's boots while in captivity, Jackson refused, at which point the officer slashed him with his sword, permanently scarring him on his left hand and head. While in captivity, Jackson and his brother both contracted smallpox. While their mother was able to secure their release, it did not save Jackson's brother, who died of the disease as soon as he arrived at home. After his brother's death, Jackson's mother volunteered to nurse Patriot prisoners of war on a British ship in Charleston Harbor, where she contracted cholera. She died a few weeks later and was buried in an unmarked grave. At age fourteen, Andrew Jackson was orphaned and alone, with three of the four members of his family dying in the Revolutionary War. For the rest of his life, Jackson bore an enduring hatred for all things British.

Jackson lived with several people over the next few years, including members of his extended family, with whom he did not get along. In 1788, he moved to the frontier town of Nashville, at which point his biography gets complicated. Over the next several decades Jackson worked as a lawyer, a merchant, a land speculator, and a planter. These latter two endeavors shaped his worldview: He would forever be committed to taking Indian land by whatever means necessary, and he would forever be committed to a proslavery ideology. In the 1790s, he was elected as first a U.S. representative from Tennessee, then a U.S. senator, and then a judge on the Tennessee Supreme Court. But the luster of this service was dimmed by controversy: He fought in multiple duels, and he lived with his wife, Rachel, before her divorce from a previous marriage was official. Neither of these acts was abnormal. On the contrary, dueling was widely practiced, and divorces often remained unofficial throughout the inaccessible frontier, where it was difficult to find judges to oversee divorce proceedings. Both acts, however, would be used by Jackson's political enemies down the road to prove that he was both uncouth and untrustworthy.

Yet, for many Americans, Jackson's military service made his controversial past irrelevant. During the War of 1812, he waged a brutal campaign against the British-allied Muscogee that culminated in the Battle of Horseshoe Bend, an overwhelming U.S. victory that made Jackson a national hero. Commissioned a major general thanks to his achievements, Jackson followed up this victory with his most famous one, this time over the British themselves at the Battle of New Orleans. He was now "the Hero."

Over the next several years, Jackson continued to wage war along the Florida frontier in what became known as the First Seminole War. At the time Florida was officially held by Spain but largely controlled by an alliance of Muscogee who had fled Georgia—soon named the Seminole—and the escaped slaves who joined them. Here, too, Jackson could not escape controversy. In 1818, he invaded Florida to crush Native resistance once and for all. When he found two British agents among the Seminole, he executed them after a hasty trial, causing an international incident. Some Americans were appalled, but others—likely a majority—were thrilled by Jackson's moxie. To them, he had stood up for white Americans against a perfidious combination of Native peoples, black people, and the British—the three groups who they believed most threatened the prosperity of white America.

It was this Jackson—the largely apolitical "Hero"—who was running for president in 1824. While Jackson had been a Democratic-Republican in the 1790s, so was nearly everyone in frontier Tennessee. Just like the frontier Pennsylvanians who rebelled against the Whiskey Excise during the same decade, Tennesseans fiercely defended their independence from what they perceived as an increasingly powerful federal government that cared little for their needs (of which, the primary one was expelling Native people from their land). Indeed, for most of his life, Jackson espoused few political principles. Certainly, there were some timeless Jackson qualities that would remain unchanged: He forever hated Great Britain, he forever supported the desires of white Americans over Native peoples, he was a fervent believer in slavery and an avowed slaveholder, he was not afraid to resort to violence to get his way, and he forever made politics personal. He was almost never spurred to anger over ideas, as he could be swayed in different directions. Instead, he was angry with *men* who took a stand against him personally and publicly. Only then would he seek restitution, and only then would he seek to crush this opposition. It was this quality in particular that would end up shaping the next decade of American politics.

If Jackson gave his support to few actual policies, what was the point of his candidacy? The most famous case was made by Jackson's friend and fellow Tennessean John Eaton, who would eventually serve as secretary of war in Jackson's cabinet. Eaton was an early Jackson supporter, and in 1823 he laid out the case for Jackson in a series of letters in a Philadelphia newspaper—Pennsylvania was a crucial electoral battleground—that he signed with the pseudonym "Wyoming." The "Wyoming Letters," as they became called, were published in pamphlet form and read by thousands.

There was nothing subtle or complicated in Eaton's argument. On the contrary, it was quite simple—and, over the course of twelve letters, quite repetitive. Eaton began with a premise all Americans agreed upon: The United States' greatness was due to its glorious and noble revolutionary founding. Yet, in recent years, American leaders had failed to live up to their gallant heritage. As Eaton summarized, "The Patriots of the Revolution, and with them those elevated sentiments of the rights of man which characterized that period, have passed away, and intrigue is fast becoming that passport to office and preferment, which in former times was yielded to virtue and to faithful service."[26] To be clear, this was not the fault of the American people themselves. Instead, it was the country's current leaders who were petty and corrupt, and it was they who were failing the country's still virtuous citizens. What the people needed was a champion who could restore the United States to its revolutionary past and bring virtue back into its government. That leader, of course, was none other than Andrew Jackson.

Why Jackson? Once again, Eaton was not one for subtlety: "Remember he was of the Revolution!" He went on, "Even at the tender age of fifteen, was he found in the ranks of the Revolution fighting and bleeding for his country."[27] As he summarized Jackson's accomplishments, Eaton time and again came back to the same comparison: Jackson was a second George Washington. Just as Washington's virtue had laid the groundwork for American prosperity, so too would Jackson's virtue restore this prosperity from the corrupt politicians who were leading the country astray. Eaton knew there were some demons in Jackson's past, such as when he declared martial law in New Orleans on the eve of his great triumph, but even these moments could be defended because, Eaton asserted, "WASHINGTON would have done the same."[28]

Jackson's appeal was not that he was someone new, but that he was someone old, the last of the Revolutionary generation, as Eaton made all too clear in his "finale": "He is the last of that high-minded, and proud corps, who stood upon the tossed battlements of the country, and fearlessly rocked the cradle of the Revolution. Like the avaricious miner, in quest of gold, as long as a view of those precious materials can be found, I will love it, pursue it, and cleave to it."[29] The Revolutionary generation may have been disappearing, but to Jackson fans like Eaton, there was no need to move on just yet. Jackson was the hope of the future precisely because he was a figure of the past.

Most Americans agreed with Monroe, Adams, and Jackson and detested political parties, but not *every* American. If there was one man in the United States most outraged with—and disturbed by—Monroe's (and Jackson's and Adams's) goal of party amalgamation, it was Martin Van Buren. Van Buren was of Dutch descent and hailed from Kinderhook, a town twenty miles south of the state capital of Albany, where his father had owned and operated a local tavern. Although Van Buren's education was modest—he attended a local academy intermittently until he was fourteen—he was clearly brilliant. His first profession was technically law, but it was clear from the outset that politics was his true calling, and both his allies and enemies knew it, deeming him the "Little Magician" and the "Red Fox of Kinderhook" for his political prowess ("red" because of his hair color). He was, in the words of his biographer, America's "first politician," a man who embraced political horse trading, dealmaking, and smoke-filled back rooms, whereas everyone before him had abhorred such practices as unseemly (or, at the least, they *claimed* to). To Van Buren, by contrast, politics, when practiced democratically, prevented wealthy men from manipulating the government to enrich themselves, and it kept regular citizens engaged.[30]

Elected to the New York State Senate in 1812, Van Buren and his allies eventually united to oppose New York governor DeWitt Clinton, once one of their allies but now rejected for his flirtations with New York Federalists. So successful were they in taking over New York politics that Van Buren's coalition came to be known as the "Albany Regency." At the heart of the Albany Regency's success lay two crucial political principles: party unity and patronage. Party unity meant that politicians were not free to vote their personal opinion but instead needed to vote the way the party directed. Patronage meant that prominent party supporters would be rewarded with various local and state offices once the party achieved victory. The two principles reinforced one another: It was much easier to follow the party line, even if it was personally distasteful at times, if a politician (or one of his family members) would be handsomely compensated with a political appointment, a form of patronage that would then reinforce the benefits of voting the party line. Neither Van Buren nor his allies, most of whom were self-made middle-class men like him, spelled out these principles in any sort of coherent ideological program or document, at least not at first. Rather, they acted first and thought later, eventually developing an ideology that buttressed their actions. Yet, even if developed after the fact, this ideology marked a profound caesura in the political thought of the early republic. It held that *the political party was a positive good.* Party united people across a wide geographic spectrum, and, once that party was in power, it provided a direction for government action.

By itself, this guiding principle was nothing too radical. At times, prominent Americans like Jefferson had stated that a political party could be a tool for good, if only to defeat the evils of Federalism.[31] Rather, it was the additional corollary to this principle that marked a true sea change in American political thought: Not only was the political party a positive good, *but so too was partisan opposition.* Only a second antagonistic—and robust—political party would ensure that the first political party maintained coherence and unity. And so, while most Republicans like Monroe celebrated the disintegration of the Federalist Party and sought party amalgamation, Van Buren mourned it. Without Federalist opposition, he would later write, "the Republican party, so long in the ascendant, and apparently omnipotent, was literally shattered into fragments."[32] That this state of affairs had occurred despite any sort of national emergency or crisis, when supposedly everything was "good feelings," only further strengthened Van Buren's stance. In fact, it helped *create* a national crisis over Missouri statehood. As Van Buren noted, partisanship had once acted as the "antidote for sectional prejudices," but during the Missouri Crisis, Northerners and Southerners retreated to their respective geographies.[33] And, when not replaced by sectionalism, partisanship was instead supplanted by "personal factions" that were just as disastrous, which led to unfortunate outcomes like a five-man presidential race—and the mess that would soon emerge after all the votes were counted.[34]

Van Buren's practical innovations and developing ideology flew in the face of classic Republicanism, the dominant ideology of the Revolution and the one espoused by the likes of Monroe, Adams, and Jackson, in which politicians were *supposed* to vote their personal preference, regardless of what their party or even their constituents wanted. They were *supposed* to be both virtuous and disinterested. They were *supposed* to be *above* politics. However, for Van Buren, elected to the U.S. Senate in 1820, interestedness and politics were two peas in a pod. A politician without interests was either hopelessly naive or criminally arrogant, putting his own reputation and self-righteousness above the needs of his constituents and his political party, and it was to these whom his loyalties lay.

Van Buren and his allies waged a curious political battle during Monroe's second term, in which they opposed all of Monroe's efforts at party amalgamation, but none of the policies—the national bank, tariffs, internal improvements—that were the most discussed political issues of the day. This led them to wage all-out battles on seemingly unimportant political appointments, most notably that of Federalist and War of 1812 veteran Solomon Van Rensselaer to the position of Albany postmaster. To Van Buren, it mattered little that this position was largely apolitical and mostly inconsequential: Monroe was using the power of patronage to further erode Republican unity, when he should have been using it to strengthen it.

In this light, Van Buren's support for William Crawford's candidacy in 1824 made sense. When John Quincy Adams lamented in his diary that Crawford's "talent is intrigue," and that his "ambition swallows up his principle," Van Buren thought: *Exactly right.* Here was a man—a *politician*—he could work with. It helped that Crawford and Van Buren shared some ideological beliefs about the importance of states' rights and a wariness of federal power. Crawford's candidacy was also attractive to Van Buren because, in the early 1820s, he was widely regarded as the odds-on favorite to win the election. If Crawford became president, then partisanship and patronage would emerge victorious, and all would be right in American politics.

Not-So-Corrupt Bargains

It did not work out as Crawford and Van Buren hoped. For starters, all four of Crawford's opponents also knew he was the odds-on favorite to win the presidency, so they all directed their primary political attacks against him—or, more accurately, their allies did, for in the 1820s candidates were still supposed to stay above the petty fray of "electioneering." Key to their strategy was their attack on the caucus nominating system that had been in place since 1800, in which Republican politicians throughout the country convened in Washington to vote on their choice for president. Their choice would then be put on the ballot against the Federalist opponent. In the past, the caucus system had allowed the party to unite around a single presidential candidate, a method that Van Buren of course favored. For the 1824 election, it was clear that Crawford would win any caucus, so supporters of the other four candidates united against holding it. Ultimately a caucus was held, but supporters of the other four candidates refused to attend, leaving only 64 attendees. Crawford won their votes—62 to 2—but it was clear to everyone that the sparsely attended convention did not impart any sort of extra legitimacy on his candidacy. As one comic verse in the press quipped, "*Sixty two / Won't Do.*"[35]

Even more disastrously for Crawford, he suffered a stroke in 1823. For months afterward he was largely incapacitated, and some wondered whether he would ever fully recover. In this case it helped that he was not supposed to campaign for himself, for his allies simply continued what they had been doing before, hoping and calculating—accurately, as it turned out—that Crawford would mostly recover by the time of the election (although he would never be fully the same). Yet Crawford's ill health nevertheless took the wind out of the sails of his campaign. He was unable to attend cabinet meetings or meet with allies to discuss political strategy, causing many to consider other possible candidates. Crawford would eventually finish third.

Yet he would still run ahead of both Henry Clay and John C. Calhoun, both of whom underestimated how much Andrew Jackson's candidacy would sink their own. Both candidates had counted on support from certain constituencies. The South Carolinian Calhoun had long cultivated ties to Pennsylvania's leading men, and he believed that support from Pennsylvania, combined with that of his home state (which was one of six states whose state legislature still awarded electoral votes), would demonstrate powerful cross-sectional appeal, building momentum for his candidacy throughout the Union. Clay, meanwhile, believed his Kentucky background would make him the candidate to beat throughout the western states.

Jackson's candidacy shattered both men's plans. Calhoun *was* popular in Pennsylvania, but Jackson was even more so. To everyone's surprise outside of Pennsylvania, he won the support of the state's Republicans at their nominating convention in 1823, which was the first signal to the rest of the country that Jackson was a serious contender. Calhoun saw the writing on the wall. He promptly abandoned his presidential hopes for the moment, choosing instead to run for vice president. Still in his early forties, respected and popular throughout the Union, Calhoun reasoned he would have another chance to win the presidency. He would be wrong, as much would change about American politics over the next decade—as would Calhoun himself.

Unlike Calhoun's chances, the bottom did not fall out of Clay's candidacy entirely, but Jackson's popularity in the West nevertheless weakened it severely. When all the votes were counted, Clay held on to his home state of Kentucky, as well Ohio, the most populous western state with 16 electoral votes, and tiny Missouri, with only 3 electoral votes. This gave him 33 electoral votes from the West to Jackson's 29, yet Jackson had national appeal that Clay did not, taking 70 votes in the East (including all of Pennsylvania's crucial 28 votes) to only 4 for Clay. Clay had never believed he would finish first, and he did not believe he needed to. If no single candidate received an Electoral College majority—as Clay and many others predicted—then the House of Representatives would decide the winner among the top three vote-getters. In the case of this "contingent election," Clay, as Speaker of that body, held a distinct advantage. The problem for Clay was that he narrowly finished behind Crawford, putting him in fourth place. Clay had a consolation prize, however: He would now play kingmaker, and would be able to extract concessions from whomever he chose to anoint.

In the end, it all came down to Andrew Jackson and John Quincy Adams. Uncoincidentally, these were the two men who best embodied the legacy of the American Revolution, who most vocally supported an end to political parties, and who celebrated the seeming consummation of political harmony. In 1824, nostalgia drove politics, and only Jackson and Adams were able to tap into this throughout the entire Union. Jackson won electoral votes in every region save New England. Adams, meanwhile, dominated in New England, but also won most of New York's electoral votes, as well as a smattering of votes in Maryland, Delaware, Louisiana, and Illinois. When all the electoral votes were counted, Jackson won 99 electoral votes, Adams 84. Crawford finished a distant third with 41 electoral votes, narrowly edging Clay's 37. As Clay predicted, no candidate won 50 percent of the vote, so the election went to the House.

The stage was set for what is now known to posterity as the "Corrupt Bargain," in which Henry Clay delivered the presidency to John Quincy Adams, and in exchange Adams made Clay his secretary of state, the traditional stepping-stone position for the presidency. While clearly a *bargain* between the two men, there was nothing *corrupt* about it, at least in the modern definition of the word. No money was exchanged, and there was nothing fraudulent or dishonest about what Adams and Clay did. Indeed, Clay had good policy reasons to support Adams. Adams was in favor of Clay's "American System"—high tariffs to foster American industries, federal spending on internal improvements, and a national bank to hold the whole system together. And, while Clay did not oppose Jackson's political policies (largely because he failed to express any policy positions whatsoever), he thought Jackson uneducated, impulsive, and, quite simply, unfit for such a high office. A president "must be a STATESMAN," he wrote, and Jackson "has [not] exhibited the qualities of a statesman."[36] He shared the sentiments of many other Jackson detractors throughout the Union.

Clay's decision for Adams, and Adams's gift to Clay, was simply politics—but, in 1824, there lay the rub. Neither man exhibited the virtue nor the disinterestedness that the Revolutionary generation had supposedly embodied. This was not a problem for Clay, but Adams's whole appeal was his refusal to "electioneer," and here he was betraying his own raison d'être—and Adams was almost certainly aware he was doing it. We see this best in his diary. Adams's cantankerousness, combined with his verbosity and dedication to making an entry every single day (for sixty-nine years!), makes his diary one of the most entertaining and informative of historical sources, yet, on the night he made his bargain with Clay, he wrote almost nothing. While he mentioned Clay coming over to his house, there is nothing about what was said, or how Adams felt about it. Perhaps he felt ashamed. With the presidency so tantalizingly close, even the righteous Adams could not help himself. For perhaps the first and only time in his life, he "electioneered."

The End of Political Harmony

Andrew Jackson, meanwhile, had no problem voicing his own opinion about the outcome. Adams had once been one of Jackson's most valuable political allies. In 1817, when Jackson had caused the international stir in British West Florida by sentencing two British "spies" to death, it was Secretary of State Adams who was his lone defender in Monroe's cabinet, arguably saving Jackson's career. This no longer mattered to Jackson, whose own raison d'être was anger and vengeance. He had been denied what he felt was rightfully his, and he was predictably furious. Jackson and Adams would never speak to each other again.

Jackson reserved much more rage for Clay, whom he already disliked and now blamed as villain number one in the whole affair (to Jackson, a very sordid one). Of Clay, Jackson immortalized, "The Judas of the West has closed the contract and will receive his thirty pieces of silver. His end will be the same."[37] He was only half right: Despite Jackson's enduring hatred, Henry Clay would serve in the federal government for another quarter century, solidifying his legacy as one of the United States' most accomplished legislators. However, his ultimate goal was always the presidency, and this would remain forever just out of reach. He would become the Tantalus of American political history.

Jackson and his supporters argued that Jackson had been denied his rightful victory, but so too had the American people. While Jackson may not have received a majority of electoral votes, he still received both more electoral and popular votes than anyone else. Thus, Adams and Clay had failed to follow the will of the people. Here Jackson and his political allies tapped into an ideology that had been growing for quite some time in American politics: democracy.

There had been numerous signs and trends in the Monroe years that pointed to a growing belief among many Americans—meaning, in this case, *white* and *male* Americans—that widespread political participation by all white men, not just the elite, was both a cause for celebration and a trend that ought to continue. We can see this in countless areas, beginning with the death of the Federalist Party, which partially stemmed from the Federalists' outright embrace of their own elitism and their vocal opposition to expanded political participation. We can see this in states expanding the eligible electorate to include non-property-holding white men, such as New Jersey did in 1807, in the same law that prohibited women and black men from voting. We can see this in the Marquis de Lafayette's tour of the United States in 1824, when common people throughout the Union demanded upfront, often personal access to Lafayette, taking down physical barriers that elites had put up to separate the great hero from his celebrators.[38] Likewise, this trend was evident in the lead-up to the 1824 presidential election. While the candidates themselves were still supposed to avoid the appearance of campaigning, their supporters employed the use of political rallies and campaign ditties for the first time, in an attempt to appeal to the common man. Of course, politicians weaponized this trend for their own advantage, such as when Clay, Calhoun, Adams, and Jackson all preemptively attacked the caucus nominating system that lent its support to Crawford in 1824, thereby tainting his nomination as elitist and undemocratic. We can see this in the growing trend to let voters, not state legislators, decide the presidential electors. In 1816, ten of nineteen states held popular votes for president; in 1820, it was fifteen of twenty-four, and in 1824, eighteen of twenty-four, with only six states leaving the decision in the hands of the state legislature.

One of these six was New York, which had awarded 26 of its 36 electoral votes to Adams in 1824, with Crawford receiving 5, Clay 4, and Jackson 1. As we have seen in the rise of Martin Van Buren, the state's politics were far more complicated and sophisticated than politics at the federal level. Consequently, the political maneuvering and complicated reasons for the legislature's ultimate decision are far too byzantine to be detailed here. Yet, after wading through the clutter, one thing is ultimately clear: The results were an utter disaster for Van Buren. He had thought he could deliver the state to Crawford, but his intrigues utterly failed, and he and everyone else knew it. "Van B.," wrote one observer, "looks like a wilted cabbage."[39]

Van Buren believed that the root of his failure lay in the collapse of the two-party system. Without either the carrot of party patronage or the stick of partisan opposition, New York legislators felt little incentive to coalesce around Van Buren's choice. To the Little Magician, the solution was obvious: Revive the old party system, once again bringing together Republicans against a common enemy. Of course, to do so, he needed a new standard-bearer for the party, for Van Buren, while skilled, was hardly a national force—but Andrew Jackson was.

And so began the forging of a political coalition that would eventually become the Democratic Party, or, in the parlance of the time, simply "the Democracy." It did not happen overnight. At first Jackson did not trust Van Buren because of his former support for Crawford. It took the third key member of the coalition, Vice President John C. Calhoun, to bring them together. Although part of the Adams administration, Calhoun disliked Clay and detested his backroom deal with Adams.[40] From the perspective of someone mindful of his own political future, he also recognized that Clay was now the heir apparent to Adams in a partisan coalition, which soon became known as the National Republicans. Calhoun needed to find a different political future—and Van Buren offered one.

It took a while to come together, but once this alliance was finally made, it was an effective one indeed. The coalition united a candidate from the West (Jackson) with leaders from the North (Van Buren) and South (Calhoun), creating a truly national party. Van Buren and Calhoun effectively brought most former Crawford supporters into Jackson's camp. While Jackson's early supporters had united behind him simply because he was "the Hero of New Orleans" who could curb corruption in politics, the addition of the mostly Southern Crawfordites made the expanded coalition more explicitly one in support of slavery, Indian removal, and states' rights—policies that would be permanently welded to the Jacksonian Democrats until the Civil War.[41] In a famous letter to Thomas Ritchie, editor of the *Richmond Enquirer* and political kingmaker in Virginia, Van Buren discussed how Jackson's coalition brought together a "natural and beneficial" alliance between the "planters of the South and the plain Republicans of the North."[42] The letter was, in the words of Van Buren's biographer, "one of the essential political documents of the early republic."[43]

Much less often quoted from this letter, but just as important to the future of the United States, was *how* Van Buren wanted to get Jackson elected, which was the real purpose behind his letter to Ritchie. The situation for Jackson supporters, particularly in the North, would be greatly improved "by substituting *party principle* for *personal preference* as one of the leading parts of the contest." The goal of the 1828 presidential election was not to elect Jackson *the person*—general, statesman, hero—but Jackson *the head of the Democratic Party* (although the party name itself was not yet coined).[44] Because Jackson had "been so little in public life" and had very few actual policy positions, Van Buren made the case to Ritchie that they—Van Buren, Ritchie, and other influential Jackson supporters—would need to supply these positions in the pro-Jackson press. This strategy, Van Buren believed, would transform a personal victory of Jackson over Adams into a victory of one party over another, thereby reigniting partisanship throughout the country. To Van Buren, of course, this was the way American politics should work. Indeed, it was the way it *must* work.

A New Political World

As for Jackson himself, he quietly and effectively managed the ins and outs of the 1828 campaign from the Hermitage, his plantation in Nashville, but publicly he made no effort to "electioneer" or push any specific policies. He offered himself up as the champion of the American people, one who could cleanse the government of its insidious elements for good. To show that he himself was not corrupt, Jackson resigned from the Senate, arguing that running for president and serving in the Senate at the same time was a conflict of interest. He then blasted the Adams administration for its depraved corruption—a stance he wholeheartedly believed was true. At one point, Jackson wrote a friend, "The patronage of the government of the last three years has been wielded to corrupt every thing that comes within its influence, and was capable of being corrupted, and it would seem, that virtue and truth, has fled from its embrace."[45] The ills of society lay at the feet of Adams, Clay, and their minions.

In fact, none of these allegations were true. John Quincy Adams was neither corrupt as we define the term today, nor was he corrupt as Jackson (and Adams himself) defined it, by which Jackson meant, essentially, *being political*. But perhaps Adams should have been, if only to save his presidency. He refused to engage in any sort of political patronage, keeping many of Monroe's former appointees in power even after it became obvious that they were Jackson supporters and were actively working against Adams's own administration. He also explicitly refused to consider what the American people would think of his policies. In his First Annual Message to Congress, he proposed a vast expansion of the reach of the federal government through funding projects such as a national university and a national observatory. These ideas were, as one historian wrote, "bold, courageous, statesmanlike, and politically inept."[46] Americans long wary of a too-powerful central government had tolerated Monroe's co-opting of Federalist policies like the Bank of the United States, but this was another level entirely, one that most Americans could not countenance.

Neither did Americans appreciate Adams's desire to send delegates to an international conference in Panama consisting of the newly independent nations of Central and South America. To many—including Andrew Jackson—such a move would mark the first step on a slippery slope into the entangling alliances that George Washington had warned about in his famous Farewell Address. These would be alliances, it is important to add, with countries inhabited by people of, in the eyes of white Americans, concerning racial and ethnic backgrounds. Adams knew all too well that his proposals did not command widespread support but, as he infamously lectured in the same disastrous First Annual Message, Congress should not be "palsied by the will of our constituents."[47] The line between the candidates could not have been drawn any clearer.

The result of the 1828 presidential election was never in doubt. Jackson was able to have it both ways: He was a military hero portraying himself above politics, while simultaneously the nascent—thoroughly partisan—Democratic Party worked for his election. Party operatives employed methods—mudslinging, political evasion, the use of symbols—that represented the first modern presidential campaign in U.S. history. Adams, meanwhile, had it neither way. He was an unpopular president who not only did not have much of a constituency outside of New England, but actively disdained trying to get one. When all the votes were counted, Jackson won 55 percent of the popular vote, which translated into an easy 178–83 victory in the Electoral College. Outside of New England, Adams received electoral votes from only Maryland, Delaware, and a portion of New York.

To be clear, despite Jackson's victory and Van Buren's deep-laid plans for restoring partisanship, the Second Party System, as it is now called, had not yet fully crystallized. Even in 1828, both candidates attached "Republican" to their name. Jackson was the Democratic-Republican candidate, Adams the National Republican. Only in 1832 did Jackson run explicitly as the candidate of the Democratic Party, and it was not until the mid-1830s that the opposition Whig Party fully coalesced—"Whig" because, like their Revolutionary ancestors, Whigs were opposed to the policies of a seemingly all-powerful king: "King Andrew the First."

Yet even if the final form of the party system had not yet crystallized, all the conditions were there. These conditions included a vicious partisan campaign from both sides that witnessed various forms of mudslinging, most notably salacious attacks on Jackson's wife Rachel regarding her marriage to Jackson before her divorce with another man had been finalized. Called an adulterer by the pro-Adams press and thus under severe stress throughout the presidential campaign, Rachel Jackson died of a heart attack three weeks after Jackson was declared the winner. Although Rachel had health issues for a long time, Jackson blamed his political opponents. When he eulogized Rachel at her funeral, Jackson stated that he could never "forget or forgive" those who slandered her. He then memorialized the attacks on her tombstone, which read, "A being so gentle and virtuous, slander might wound but could not dishonor."[48]

With Jackson vowing revenge against his political enemies, it was all but certain: The Second Party System—and with it, the triumph of partisanship over political harmony—was here to stay. For almost a half century after the American Revolution, Americans dreamed a dream of political unity and harmony. It died in the 1820s, returning ever so briefly during moments of national triumph or tragedy. But this has not kept Americans from still dreaming of a day when unity can become more permanent. Fourth of July fireworks and Memorial Day parades may seem trite, but they point to a desire among Americans of all backgrounds and political persuasions to find refuge from the cacophony of division. This desire is rooted in the American Revolution itself. These ceremonies remind us that we are all Americans.

We forget that at our peril.

6

Economic Equality: The Relief War in Kentucky, 1818–28

In early 1825, the attorney general of Kentucky, Solomon Porcius Sharp, ordered his clerk Francis Preston Blair to break into the house of the clerk of the Kentucky Court of Appeals Achilles Sneed. Sharp could argue that, legally, it was not actually a break-in, for Sneed was in illegal possession of court documents, and twice he had refused to hand them over. Blair found the door locked, so he went in through a window, found the documents, and delivered them to Sharp. To the casual observer, however, it sure *looked* like a break-in. The thirty-six-year-old Sharp had already publicly taken Sneed to task for his intransigence, asking sixteen pointed questions that challenged the respected fifty-two-year-old Sneed's integrity and honesty, all of which were printed in Kentucky newspapers. Between the imperious questioning and the break-in, Sharp's image took a hit, and his actions allowed his partisan enemies to attack him vociferously. The *Kentucky Reporter*, for example, called Sharp's questions "truly revolting to a republican mind."[1]

At some point in this affair Sharp must have asked himself how he got into this mess. After all, he was a highly respected Kentucky lawyer, landowner, and politician. Between 1809 and 1812, he had served several terms in the Kentucky General Assembly. After the United States declared war on Great Britain in 1812, he volunteered with the state militia. In only forty-two days, he was promoted from private to major to colonel. Considering that his militia unit never saw real action, his rise was all thanks to his background and influence. He then parlayed his rapid military promotion into two terms in the U.S. House of Representatives. In 1821, Kentucky governor John Adair appointed Sharp the state's attorney general.

Sharp's professional rise was matched by his economic and social accomplishments. By the time of his appointment to attorney general, he owned twelve thousand acres and enslaved thirteen people, and his prestige allowed him to marry Eliza Scott, the daughter of John Scott, one of the wealthiest and most influential men in the Kentucky capital of Frankfort.[2] Most impressively, he had achieved all this as largely a self-made man, the son of a Virginia migrant who had traveled to Kentucky looking for a modest amount of land. His father had found it, which allowed him to provide Solomon and his siblings with a rudimentary education—but little else. Most of Solomon Sharp's success, therefore, was due to his own impressive abilities.

Perhaps it was his modest upbringing that made Solomon Sharp an advocate of what Americans at the time called "relief," or more often capitalized, "Relief." As we have seen, in the aftermath of the devastating Panic of 1819, the federal government did little to ease the economic suffering of everyday Americans. Instead, it was up to various states to step in—and some did. Many states, particularly western states, passed measures that protected debtors and expanded the money supply, measures that Americans all grouped under "relief." Yet every state that passed relief measures received intense partisan backlash, as conservative opponents attacked these laws for destroying the sanctity of contracts. It was in Kentucky where the most heated, complicated, and strangest "Relief War" took place, which saw not only two parties emerge ("Relief" and "Anti-Relief"), but two entirely separate state supreme courts.

In 1825, Solomon Sharp was at the forefront of this political battle. Despite the Anti-Relief attacks on his actions as attorney general, his political ascendancy was still in its early stages. Indeed, in May of that year, he was given the honor of welcoming the Revolutionary War hero the Marquis de Lafayette to Kentucky on his American tour. Soon after that, Sharp resigned as attorney general to once again run for a seat in the state legislature, the General Assembly. He won his seat, which was a testament to his popularity, for he defeated the respected John J. Crittenden in an election that saw his Relief Party suffer defeat statewide. It would be up to Solomon Sharp to restore the fortunes of the Relief Party and reinvigorate the state's attempt to provide economic support for Kentuckians still in need.

Solomon Sharp would never get the chance. On November 7, 1825, only days before the General Assembly would convene, he was shockingly murdered. His murder would spell the end of the Relief program—and with it the American Revolution's promise of economic equality.

Competing Economic Legacies

What was the economic ideology of the American Revolution? The question itself is anachronistic. Revolutionary-era Americans simply did not think in the terms of "economics" and all the modern terms grouped under the field's enormous umbrella of analysis—class, supply and demand, capital, fiscal policy, surplus and deficit, and so on. There was good reason for this. The field of economics was in its infancy. Adam Smith published *The Wealth of Nations* in 1776, only a few months before the Declaration of Independence, and it would take time to gain a wide readership in the United States. Other influential economists, such as Thomas Malthus and David Ricardo, were still decades away from fame, and Karl Marx had not yet been born. Therefore, when Americans thought about economics, they combined it with politics and society into a single organic whole, and they conceived of economics more in terms of what today we call "political economy."[3] To them, economic problems were, at their core, political problems. Indeed, the historian James Huston contended that revolutionaries wrote about economics constantly, but these statements were "seldom more than one or two sentences long." Instead, economic insights "were tucked away in speeches and treatises about governments, congresses, branches of government, attributes of a republican people, principles of justice, and the failings of European society. No pamphlets or speeches were devoted solely to an examination of the distribution of wealth. The topic was always an appendage to some other subject."[4]

Of course, Americans could not help but live and breathe economics, and economic historians can analyze their economic viewpoints and decision-making, even if Americans themselves did not put it in those terms. For most Americans at the time of the Revolution, there were three bedrock economic principles. First, free men were entitled to the "fruits of their labor," meaning whatever work a man did, he should receive equal value in return. In an agricultural world, as the early United States overwhelmingly was, this concept was easy enough to understand: A farmer worked the fields and was entitled to the crops that were grown and the profits he received if they were sold.[5] Herein lay Americans' profound dislike and fear of aristocracy. Unlike independent yeoman farmers, aristocrats did not labor themselves, but took the fruits of labor from their tenants, leaving tenants "dependent." Politically, "dependent" men could not be trusted to participate in politics, for they would only vote the way in which their patron dictated, which is why most states restricted the franchise to property holders in the early years of independence.

This first principle led to a second: At its core, the "fruits of labor" meant a man's property, and, because all men were entitled to the fruits of their own labor, this meant that private property was sacrosanct.[6] It was a natural right, and no outside entity, person or government, had a right to interfere with it. No wonder so many Americans of *all* classes were so disturbed by British taxes. Even if a person owned a small amount of property, that property was their own by virtue of the fruits of their labor, and now Parliament was seizing it.[7] Importantly, this belief was not simply a full-throated embrace of laissez-faire capitalism (even if Americans at the time would not have used this terminology). At the time of the Revolution, there remained a "moral economy" that allowed for measures like price controls that would alleviate the hardships of the "lower sort."[8] Usually, however, price controls were a result of "crowd action"—meaning targeted rioting—and were haphazardly implemented, meaning that, even if the early United States was not necessarily fully capitalist, it was certainly not socialist (another term Americans would not have used). This fact is borne out in the various states' bills of rights, all of which protected private property, almost none of which endorsed any sort of redistribution of that property. The one exception was radical Vermont, whose bill of rights stated that "private property ought to be subservient to public uses, when necessity requires it"—but, if taken, the owner needed to be compensated.[9]

However, running alongside the sanctity of private property was a third principle, one that explicitly intersected with politics and seemed to run at cross-purposes with the protection of private property: a celebration of economic equality. Americans saw themselves as different—*better*—than Europeans because wealth was relatively well distributed throughout the

Thirteen Colonies, and this belief only intensified during and after the Revolution. The viewpoint of J. Hector St. John Crèvecour's famous *Letters from an American Farmer* was typical. "[American society] is not composed, as in Europe, of great lords who possess everything, and of a herd of people who have nothing," Crèvecour wrote. "Here are no aristocratical families, no courts, no kings, no bishops, no ecclesiastical dominion, no invisible power giving to a few a very visible one; no great manufacturers employing thousands, no great refinements of luxury. The rich and the poor are not so far removed from each other as they are in Europe."[10] Noah Webster (the same Noah Webster who would publish his famous dictionary) contrasted the United States with England, asserting that England would never have enough property "sufficiently distributed . . . to give the powers of the government wholly into the hands of the people." He then argued, "A general and tolerably equal distribution of landed property is the whole basis of national freedom"—which, he believed, described the young United States to a tee.[11]

Before we go any further, it is important to point out the obvious caveats that belie statements like these. Commenters like Webster and Crèvecour were obviously ignoring a huge swath of the American population, namely married women and the enslaved, neither of whom could legally own property. They were also ignoring where all this landed property originally came from: the conquest of Native peoples and the confiscation of their land. When they argued that *Americans* were all equal, what they really meant was *white men*. White American men had erected borders around a vision of participatory citizenship that only grew more fixed in the decades after the Revolution, in which they were the in-group while women, black people, and Native peoples were perpetually out-groups. According to white American men, things were relatively equal within their group—and this equality was both praiseworthy and unique on the world stage.

If private property was inviolable, then how could Americans ensure economic equality? In the decades after the Revolution, they did not try to resolve this question, and legislators passed laws and judges made rulings that failed to resolve the contradiction. During the 1780s, when many states were issuing bank notes to inflate their state currencies so it was easier for debtors to repay their debts, conservatives cried foul. Their solution was the Constitution, which supposedly made contracts ironclad. The Contract Clause said it explicitly: no state could pass "a Law impairing the Obligation of Contracts."[12] This law and the classical liberal ideology that undergirded it helped realize a U.S. economy that became increasingly capitalist. On the other hand, states routinely violated this clause to help debtors, passing laws that gave them more time to repay their loans (called "replevin" or "stay" laws), that spread out repayment over time ("installment" laws), or gave debtors the ability to declare bankruptcy. State legislatures justified these laws because they had been common before the Constitution, during the hard economic times of the 1780s, so they believed they could keep passing them.[13] No court told them they could not do this—at least not thus far. A capitalist economy was growing, but the moral economy was not dead just yet.

Were commenters like Webster and Crèvecour right? Was income really that evenly distributed during the Revolutionary era? It depends on how the question is answered. By one estimate, at the time of the Revolution the wealthiest 10 percent of Americans possessed half of the republic's wealth.[14] Yet, in comparison to Europe, the United States really was a much more equal society. In the United States, the average farmer owned 150 acres and few farmers owned less than 50 acres, whereas in Europe the average farmer owned only 5 acres.[15] Importantly, when Americans discussed economic equality, they never meant *absolute* equality, but *relative* economic equality undergirded by equal economic *opportunity*—which, by these numbers, they had largely achieved.

This economic equality translated into political rights. At the time of the Revolution, only 20 percent of English men owned enough land to vote in local elections, which marked a stark contrast with the United States, where 90 percent of men on the frontier, 70 percent in settled farming communities, and 50 percent in coastal towns and cities could vote.[16] Indeed, Americans who traveled to Europe were stunned at the destitution and squalor of the laboring classes (again, conveniently ignoring the plight of the enslaved at home).

Not only did Americans believe there was more equality in the United States than in Europe, but they also believed there was more economic opportunity—and, once again, here they were largely correct, if considering only white men. The leveling influence of the Revolution eroded many of the old forms of patronage that forced would-be entrepreneurs to find men of the "better sort" to take them under their wing to achieve a modest rise in social and economic standing. Now, business opportunities were available for everyone, allowing a class of what Americans called "new men" to advance in wealth and prestige, Solomon Sharp being but one example. The rise of "new men" did not entirely erase the importance of personal connections, but overall, the possibilities for white men were much wider after the Revolution than before it. Or, to put it another way, the Revolution opened up the positive economic opportunities of capitalism without its negative excesses.[17]

For Americans, economic equality was not just a point of distinction between the virtuous, republican United States and a corrupt, aristocratic Europe. It was a necessary precondition—perhaps *the* necessary precondition—for the success of their republican experiment. To Americans, both the lessons of history and political theorists taught that republics required relative economic equality to function effectively. "An equality of property," Noah Webster claimed, "is the very *soul of a republic*."[18] Once property was consolidated in the hands of the few, those few could and would invariably corrupt the republic and establish an oligarchy or aristocracy. How, then, could Americans balance the inviolability of property—in essence, economic *liberty*—with the need for economic *equality*? If a man were free to accrue vast sums of wealth, and this wealth was fundamentally untouchable, then how could the young republic ensure that property remain relatively evenly distributed?

One small but important way was to abolish not only aristocratic titles, as the Constitution did, but the means by which aristocracy was preserved in property law, via primogeniture and entail. The former guaranteed that the oldest son received all the property of his father, the latter ensured large estates stayed intact over generations, and both worked toward maintaining a wealthy landed nobility, as England had at the time of the Revolution. Therefore, all states abolished both primogeniture and entail during or just after the Revolution. Many soon went further, mandating that inheritance was equally divided among all sons and—revealing the Revolution's radicalism—daughters.[19]

The First Great Depression

For nearly a half century, Americans celebrated their relative economic equality. To be sure, there were severe economic downturns. The postwar 1780s, a credit crisis in 1792, and the Jefferson embargo years of 1807 to 1809 were particularly hard on many Americans. Yet several factors mitigated the economic hardship: First, much of the hardship was localized to certain regions, and the continued practice of subsistence farming meant that, even if Americans lost money during these "hard times," they did not necessarily starve; second, politics did the work of explaining economic disasters. To New Englanders, for example, it was quite easy to blame Thomas Jefferson for their hardships between 1807 and 1809. *Of course* shutting down nearly all international shipping to and from New England ports would ravage the region's economy.

The Panic of 1819 was an economic shock of an entirely different sort. In the decades since the Revolution, but particularly after the War of 1812 as the "Market Revolution" (to use the historians' label) picked up steam, the United States economy became nationalized. The economy boomed in the years immediately following the War of 1812, which led to rampant speculation throughout the country. Banks, including the once-conservative Bank of the United States, provided sketchy loans to thousands of Americans, many of whom used the money to buy land in the West. However, a downturn in international trade, due partially to changing British trade policy, caused the Bank of the United States to begin demanding payments from other banks, and these banks then demanded payments from their debtors, most of whom could not afford to pay. Just before the Panic, many banks' liabilities outweighed assets by more than ten to one, so when Americans could not pay back their loans, banks simply closed, taking Americans' money with them.[20] As would happen again and again in U.S. history, boom rapidly turned to bust.

A few telling statistics provide perspective on just how bad the United States' first great depression really was. The percentage drop in U.S. GDP was the third worst in all American history, trailing only the Great Depression and the Panic of 1893.[21] More than 20 percent of wage-earning Americans became unemployed, and this number reached perhaps

50 percent in some East Coast cities.[22] No wonder that the 1820 census was the one and only census in all U.S. history that reported a decrease in the urban population.[23] Meanwhile, outside the cities, public land sales dropped from nearly $14 million to $2 million.[24] Of course, this massive decline did not mean Americans simply stopped farming. Rather, they stopped farming *legally*, as thousands fled their debts and moved to find unclaimed land where they could become squatters. Thousands more left the United States entirely, mostly to Mexican Texas, where the Mexican government offered land practically for free.

Americans at the time were stunned by the scale and depth of the crisis. It was not just the real-world suffering and hardship that alarmed them, however. The Panic of 1819 called into question the moral foundations of the United States itself. Since the Revolution, Americans had been able to believe in both of those two seemingly incompatible economic ideas: first, property was inviolable, and every man could do with his own property as he wished; and second, relative economic equality had been achieved—which was not just a good outcome but a vital one, for it was one of the most important preconditions for a functioning, virtuous republic. The former had fostered the growth of a fledgling, flourishing capitalist economy (even though Americans did not yet use the word "capitalist"), but now that this capitalist economy was in freefall, it was destroying the latter. Economic *liberty* and economic *equality* no longer went hand in hand.

For those Americans who valued equality more than liberty, something had gone wrong in the decades since the founding of the United States. Americans' obsessions with business, capital, profit, and property had taken the country to a place that no longer represented the economic ideals of the Revolution. An editorial signed with the unsubtle nom de plume "Franklin" made this explicit, arguing that Americans' full-throated embrace of the market betrayed the Revolution's promises. Wrote "Franklin," "We indignantly threw aside the homespun and republican virtues by which our fathers prospered, to ape the manners, the fashions and the follies of European courts."[25] In 1819, damning the United States as European was just about the biggest insult one could make.

This editorial appeared in the *Argus of Western America*, published in Frankfort, Kentucky, under the purview of editor in chief Amos Kendall.

Kentucky became ground zero in the battle for economic equality for a variety of reasons. Although the state had once promised free, fertile land for would-be white settlers that spurred rapid settlement (once again, Kentuckians did not consider Native people), by the time of the 1819 depression much of this land had been snatched up by wealthy landowners and speculators (the historian Stephen Aron appropriately titled his book on the subject *How the West Was Lost*).[26] Wealthy landowners required lawyers and judges to consolidate their landholdings, creating a hated triumvirate for those thousands of Kentuckians who lost their property or were kicked off land they were squatting on.[27] Crucially, however, the propertyless held real power, for, like most western states at the time, Kentucky granted suffrage to all white men over the age of twenty-one, regardless of their property-owning status (free black men could vote in 1792, but their suffrage was rescinded in 1799). Therefore, poor white Kentuckians, if united, could wield political power against their perceived elitist enemies.

Kentucky was a slave state, with a quarter of the population enslaved. Like Virginia slaveholders, Kentucky slaveholders would profit from slavery by participating in the internal trade of slaves, selling their slaves south and west. Henry Clay, Kentucky's most famous son during the early republic, was typical of Kentucky slaveholders: He profited from slavery, but he was not an ardent defender of it, and he was one of the founders of the American Colonization Society, the well-intentioned but fundamentally racist antislavery organization that sought to end slavery by sending black Americans "back" to Africa. His stance foreshadowed his state's actions during the Civil War: Kentucky remained in the Union, and more than twice as many Kentuckians fought for the Union than fought for the Confederacy. Slavery would play its part in the story that follows, but it was never the driving factor.

The best lens for viewing the convulsions that would rock Kentucky society for most of the 1820s is through the eyes of Amos Kendall. Like many in the state, Kendall was a migrant from the east, but unlike most Kentuckians who had traveled directly west from Virginia, Kendall was from New England. He was born in 1789, the year George Washington was inaugurated president, in the small town of Dunstable, Massachusetts, close to the New Hampshire border. His parents were middling farmers, and they had the means to provide him with just enough intermittent education that he was able to get accepted to Dartmouth.

After graduating from Dartmouth in 1811, the soft-spoken, bookish Kendall considered teaching, but he was persuaded to go into law by William Richardson, a prominent Massachusetts lawyer and newly elected member of the House of Representatives. Richardson even suggested Kendall could become his apprentice, but then he decided to move his practice to Portsmouth, New Hampshire. At this point, with New England suffering an economic downturn caused by the War of 1812 and with no definitive career prospects, Kendall made the same choice as thousands of other Americans: he left his home for good. First he traveled to Washington, where Richardson introduced him to influential politicians, including Kentucky senator Jesse Bledsoe. Bledsoe hired Kendall to tutor his children in Kentucky—or so Kendall later claimed—but when Kendall arrived in Lexington, he found Bledsoe's offer had been rescinded. He later recalled that during this time he "suffered more mortification than ever at any period of my life."[28] Luckily, he was quickly hired by Lucretia Hart Clay, wife of Henry Clay, to tutor her children, offering six times what Bledsoe had offered. Kendall accepted.

Kendall taught the Clay children for a year, and then moved into other ventures—law, land speculation, newspaper publishing, teaching; he even considered running a post office—but, for a time, nothing stuck. It was during these shiftless years that Kendall studied how to navigate the rough-and-tumble world of Kentucky society, which was marked by frequent dueling, drinking, and gambling. At one point he recorded, "I have learnt the way to be popular in Kentucky. . . . Drink whiskey and talk loud, with the fullest confidence, and you will hardly fail to be called a clever fellow."[29] Crucially, Kendall himself did *not* "talk loud," but as he immersed himself in the local culture, he later recalled that, even if he could not "out-speak" most Kentuckians, he could "out-write . . . all of them."[30]

And so it was that, after dabbling briefly with editing a few local newspapers, Kendall became the part owner and editor in chief of the *Argus of Western America*. Soon the *Argus* had a respectable circulation of 1,500, and Kendall was rewarded with a printing contract by the Kentucky legislature.[31] On the face of it, Kendall's embrace of journalism and its inundation with politics was a surprising career move. He had never been a particularly political person, and newspaper editing meant an inundation into local politics. In New England, last bastion of the Federalists, Kendall had stood out for his penchant for the Republican Party, but his party devotion was always modest and his republicanism moderate. It was not that he lacked political opinions of his own, but these opinions never got significantly out of step with majority opinion. Combined with his accomplished, pointed writing style, Kendall's ability to seamlessly tack in the face of changing public attitudes would prove a crucial skill in the years that followed.

It was just as Kendall was making the *Argus* an influential regional newspaper that the effects of the Panic of 1819 arrived in Kentucky. Thousands of indebted Kentuckians demanded relief from the state government. Thousands of creditors cried foul. The Relief War, as it would come to be called, was about to begin—and, at times, the *Argus* would drive its course.

The Relief War

In 1819, Kentuckians, like all Americans, tried to make sense of the national depression and why it happened. An "Old Resident" of Kentucky summarized its effects on thousands of the state's indebted residents, writing, "[The debtor] must be taken by order of the relentless creditor and shut up in prison, until he pays the uttermost farthing, or give up his little hard earned property to be sacrificed, at perhaps one fiftieth part of its real intrinsic value, leave his helpless family to suffer with hunger, cold and nakedness, and finally take the oath of insolvency." Could it get worse than this? Yes! "Nine tenths of his creditors yet unpaid, he loses all hope of ever being able to discharge his just debts, and his family ruined. He languishes, takes to drink, and dies a miserable death."[32]

Many Kentuckians, like many Americans more generally, considered the depression a sign of a sort of national moral failure—a sharp decline since the American Revolution. Back then, everyone (i.e., white men) had been (relatively) equal. A half century later, speculation, the market, banking, corporations—in essence, capitalism—had destroyed the equality upon which the United States was built.

As the 1820 gubernatorial election approached, Kentucky became officially divided into two newly created, bitterly opposed political parties, called simply "Relief" and "Anti-Relief." Before this, nearly everyone in Kentucky was a Republican to such an extent that the moniker "Federalist" had simply become a pejorative detached from any actual party. "Federalist" simply meant everything from eastern and elitist to antidemocratic and anti-American.[33] The "Relief War," as it would soon be called, represented a new partisan realignment that broke the state's Republicans into two. The initial schism revolved around debates about contracts, debt, and relief that had been going on since the 1780s, when the infant United States experienced its first economic downturn. On one side were those who held that, while states could not simply cancel contracts outright, they could pass legislation that eased the burden on the debtor, such as "stay" laws that gave debtors more time to pay their debts and inflationary money policies that made that debt less difficult to pay off. On the other were more conservative Americans who held that contracts were inviolable, full stop, and *any* state interference in the terms of the contract was both illegal and ineffective.

As he surveyed the scene, Amos Kendall was torn. On the one hand, ideologically he was in the latter camp, opposing extensive relief policies that he believed not only violated contracts, but also were simply ineffective or even made the situation worse. As he wrote in the *Argus* in 1821: "The people must pay their own debts at last."[34] However, whatever his personal beliefs about the limitations of relief as an economic tool, the Relief Party was politically ascendant in 1820, and, as an ambitious editor living in the state capital, it made abundant sense for Kendall to hitch his wagon to what he perceived to be the winning team, no matter how flawed its economic stance. From a career standpoint, Kendall made the right choice. Thanks to his talents as a writer and editor, by supporting the Relief Party, Kendall's *Argus* quickly became the most influential newspaper in the entire state.

In the 1820 election for Kentucky governor, four candidates from the Relief Party faced off against a single Anti-Relief candidate, which showed how the Relief Party had not yet fully cohered into a tightly run political organization. Still, John Adair, the most popular Relief candidate, won the election, although by fewer than a thousand votes. This slim plurality, however, did not accurately represent the overwhelming popularity of the Relief Party, which received almost 43,000 votes between the four contenders, compared with a little less than 20,000 for the Anti-Relief candidate.[35] Relief candidates also won control of the Kentucky General Assembly and Senate. When Kendall wrote in the *Argus* that Relief had "sprung from the great mass of the community," he was not wrong.[36] A remarkable 74 percent of eligible voters cast votes in the election.[37]

In the first half of 1820, the now dominant Relief Party responded to its overwhelming mandate by passing several relief measures designed to help suffering Kentuckians. First, legislatures created a new "republican" bank, called the Bank of the Commonwealth. Unlike any other bank in the state, including the conservative, state-created Bank of Kentucky, this people's bank would have no wealthy stockholders to worry about. Instead, it would be managed by a committee chosen by the Kentucky legislature. It would place bank notes totaling $3 million into circulation and would lend $1,000 to any debtor who asked. Crucially, these bank notes would not be backed up by any specie. Second, the legislature passed a new stay law that allowed debtors to postpone payment of their debts, but the postponement varied depending on how those debts would be paid. If the creditor accepted Bank of the Commonwealth bank notes, he could demand payment in three months. If he accepted Bank of Kentucky bank notes, the debtor had a year. If, however, he accepted neither and wanted payment in the soundest currency—read: Bank of the United States bank notes—the debtor had *two* years.

Next, to restore true economic equality and real economic opportunity, Relief leaders tried to restore the "Spirit of '76"—a phrase they invoked often—by implementing a program of "moral justice." They would, in one congressman's words, restore "an original republicanism" to the Kentucky commonwealth.[38] This program involved several pieces of legislation. First, Kentucky became the first state in the Union to abolish debtors' prison. Then, the legislature implemented a "three-quarters" property law, which meant that bidders could not purchase foreclosures for anything less than three-quarters of the valuation of the property. The valuation would be determined by a group of commissioners from "the neighborhood," who could then postpone foreclosure indefinitely if the three-quarter purchase amount was not met.[39] To inculcate morality in the state's residents, the legislature established a literary fund to pay for public education, and then passed a variety of measures that established various poorhouses, asylums, internal improvements, penitentiaries, and hospitals.[40]

The Court War

As soon as the 1820 stay law was passed, it was challenged in court by creditors claiming that the state did not have legal authority to interfere with private contracts between individuals. The Relief Party countered that, although it could not *cancel* contracts, it could *alter* them, which is exactly what the stay law did. Eventually, after several circuit court rulings, the challenge to the stay law wound up in front of the Kentucky Court of Appeals, the highest court in the commonwealth. There, in 1823, in two separate but overlapping cases (*Blair v. Williams* and *Lapsley v. Brashears*), the court declared the stay law unconstitutional. By interfering in private contracts, the court claimed, the stay law violated both the Kentucky and U.S. Constitutions.

Bedlam followed. Already Kentuckians had been frustrated with courts, but this took their frustration to new levels. A majority of voters were outraged. By what right was the court allowed to overturn a law passed by the Kentucky legislature? Was not the legislature popularly elected and therefore an embodiment of the people? And did not *the people* govern Kentucky rather than a few elitist, unaccountable judges?

Amos Kendall welcomed the changing nature of the debate. He had always been wary of the Relief Party's actual economic policies, in terms of both their effectiveness and the economic philosophy that undergirded them (although he would not have understood "economic philosophy" as a category). Now, however, policy took a backseat to political principle. To him, in the United States, the people governed, not the courts. As Kendall argued, "The law must be supreme until the people choose to abrogate it. . . . Monarchy is banished to no purpose, if judges can constitute themselves dictators. . . . The judges will be driven back. They will be obliged to repass the Rubicon, and remain within their own bounds."[41] The court decision also entirely reinvigorated the Relief Party as a political force. Many echoed Kendall. One writer even claimed that the "Spirit of 1824" echoed the Spirit of '76, claiming, like Kendall, that judges could not overturn laws. "Why is it that it is only to the general assembly to legislate?" this writer asked rhetorically. "Is it not because, that general assembly is yourselves, the people by representation, and that there is not any other way by which laws could be made without a government ceasing to be republican?"[42]

But how, exactly, to drive the judges back? One way was to create an elected judiciary, but that would require a new constitution and therefore a new constitutional convention. Legislators had discussed this in 1821, after the Kentucky Court of Appeals had already made several decisions that favored the Bank of the United States. Here is where slavery entered the discussion. In 1799, when Kentuckians had first written a constitution, emancipation had become a heated topic. Now, less than a year after the Missouri Compromise, legislators feared opening that Pandora's box.[43] So, instead of a new constitution, they turned to removing the judges, which required two-thirds support in the General Assembly. After all votes were counted, the motion failed—by one vote. The court remained in power.

Relief Party leaders then turned to a third method. While they needed two-thirds of the vote to remove judges, they only needed a majority to create a new court—and that is exactly what they did. The Reorganization Act of 1824 was passed by both the General Assembly and the Senate, and then signed by the new governor, Joseph Desha, who had been elected on the Relief Party ticket in a landslide. The New Court was then filled with four pro-Relief judges, and the act also prohibited the overruling of any law without the unanimous consent of all four. According to Relief partisans, all of this was constitutional because the legislature had been tasked with creating courts, and, much more importantly, the legislature reflected the will of the people of Kentucky. Solomon Sharp, the state's attorney general, was somewhat disturbed by the extremes the Relief Party had gone to but, like Kendall, he would not betray the majority. Without any rhetorical flourish, he simply claimed the new law was constitutional. Anti-Relief Party critics pounced. Wrote one Anti-Relief newspaper, "We trust Mr. Sharp was not also in danger of being *politely legislated out of office*."[44]

If the stakes for democracy, law, and Kentucky's constitution had not been so high, what happened next could almost be seen as a farcical comedy. In response to the Reorganization Act, the judges on the original Court of Appeals—the "Old Court," as they would soon be called—refused to step down, and they refused to hand over any court documents to what was soon called the "New Court." This is what led Sharp to send Francis Blair to break into the house of the Old Court's clerk. The young Blair had already been writing pro-Relief editorials for Kendall's *Argus*, and he would go on to have a colorful career of his own. For the next several years, Kentucky had essentially two dueling supreme courts, both of which claimed legitimacy and denied the other court's right to exist.

Almost overnight, the Relief Party changed its name to the New Court Party, and the Anti-Relief Party became the Old Court Party. For the next year, the "Court War," as it would come to be called, took over Kentucky politics. The term was used hyperbolically. No civil war or partisan violence ever erupted—although many people thought it would. Observing from his home in Tennessee, Andrew Jackson reportedly said that "forty thousand muskets would be required to rectify the politics of Kentucky."[45] The daughter of John Crittenden, Sharp's political rival, later remembered that "public feeling . . . was only less violent than civil war," and another Kentucky resident recalled how everyone congratulated each other after election day because violence did *not* occur.[46] The concern was justified, for Kentucky society remained one in which dueling was still common.

More importantly, Kentuckians believed 1776 was being fought again. To New Court partisans, unelected Kentucky judges were acting like King George III and ignoring the will of the people, which they argued was channeled through the popularly elected legislature. The question was "whether the people shall govern, or be governed by the few, or a still smaller number."[47] Seemingly channeling the ideas of philosopher Jean-Jacques Rousseau and his theory of the General Will, they claimed minority rights were irrelevant, for elected leaders needed to pass measures "only conducive to the general good."[48] To Old Court adherents, by contrast, the

Kentucky legislature had become, in one writer's eyes, an "*omnipotent parliament*" akin to the British Parliament during the Revolution, passing anything it wanted due to majority rule, constitutions and minority rights be damned.[49] When New Court supporters heard cries of constitutions, they responded by arguing that the people were quite capable of understanding both the Kentucky and U.S. Constitutions, thank you very much.[50] According to one partisan, in fact, "the will of the people is the constitution—the Legislature expresses the people's will."[51]

As much as anyone, Amos Kendall was responsible for amplifying the political rhetoric and maintaining popular support for the New Court Party, not only in the *Argus*, but in a new pro–New Court paper, *The Patriot*.[52] In both papers, his rhetoric generally focused on several main themes. First, he argued again and again for the sovereignty of the people, and how this sovereignty was being thwarted by unelected aristocratic conspirators. In one of his more inspired comparisons, he compared Kentucky to Europe, which was currently under the thumb of the conservative, antidemocratic "Holy Alliance" of Russia, Prussia, and Austria. He argued that Kentuckians, too, were being held down by "the Holy Alliance of America," which was composed of the Bank of the United States, the U.S. Supreme Court, and the Kentucky Court of Appeals.[53] He also routinely employed the language of class, for it was clear that the Old Court Party was dominated by more established Kentuckians (by one count, 530 of the 580 lawyers in Kentucky supported the Old Court Party).[54] Judges, like speculators, bankers, and the "pliant . . . poor profession of lawyers," "produce nothing," and instead "prey upon the productions of others."[55] Kendall was hardly a proto–Karl Marx, but in phrases like this, he could sound Marx-*ish*.[56] As he attacked the rich, he also maintained that it was a government's duty to look out for the destitute. How could any government not offer relief to the poor? "Hell is the only place where relief never comes," Kendall concluded.[57]

But time was not on the side of the New Court Party. Its radicalism required the public's belief that Kentucky remained in economic crisis. By 1825, however, Kentucky, along with most other U.S. states, had weathered the worst effects of the Panic. To many Kentuckians, it was time to move on and, quite simply, to get back to normal—and the New Court Party's rhetoric was anything but normal. When Kentuckians went to the polls in the summer of 1825, therefore, a majority turned against the New Court Party. The Old Court Party won control of the General Assembly, and it gained back seats in the state senate (only one-third of the senate seats were at stake). The New Court Party was not dead just yet, though, for Desha remained governor, and the New Court Party still controlled the senate. It was at this point that its leaders put their hopes into Solomon Sharp, who had resigned from the position of attorney general to get elected to the General Assembly, narrowly defeating the Old Court nominee John J. Crittenden. That Sharp won the election over Crittenden was a testament to his political abilities, for not only were the winds blowing against the New Court Party, but Crittenden was one of the state's most illustrious figures, having already served six terms in the General Assembly and one as a U.S. senator.[58] There was a reason New Court leaders had put Sharp in charge of welcoming the Marquis de Lafayette to Kentucky on his American tour. New Court leaders now looked to Sharp, who had been hesitant about the Reorganization Act from the very beginning, to broker some sort of compromise with the newly ascendant Old Court Party.

He would never get the chance. On the night of November 7, 1825, just before he took his seat in the General Assembly, Sharp was brutally stabbed to death in his home by the remarkably named Jereboam Orville Beauchamp. Beauchamp was a twenty-three-year-old lawyer who was described by everyone—including himself—as possessing a "volatile, idle, and wild disposition."[59] He was also an ardent supporter of the Old Court Party, and therefore, after he was quickly apprehended, everyone assumed the murder was political. After all, Beauchamp himself described Sharp as the "leader, orator, and saviour" of the New Court Party, so it made sense that Beauchamp's partisan leanings led him to cut down the only man who could resuscitate New Court fortunes. More than anyone else, Amos Kendall made this point again and again in the *Argus*, claiming that Old Court partisans had put Beauchamp up to it. Without Sharp, Kendall claimed, the New Court Party was "destitute" and "paralyzed."[60]

It turned out Sharp's murder had absolutely nothing to do with politics; Beauchamp's motivations were entirely personal. In the summer of 1824, Beauchamp had married Ann Cooke. The daughter of a wealthy Virginia transplant, Cooke was thirty-eight at the time, had made a name for herself as a stubborn, nonconforming recluse, and was described as an "avowed disciple of Mary Wollstonecraft."[61] Beauchamp was only twenty-one, which made the marriage strange by the standards of the time, but he was captivated by someone so willing to cast aside the confining norms of wealthy Kentucky society. He was so captivated, in fact, that he overlooked what, at the time, would normally have disqualified Cooke for marriage at all. In 1820, she had given birth to a stillborn child, and she claimed the father was Solomon Sharp.

Rumors about an affair between Sharp and Cooke had circulated since the birth of the child, but they had dissipated when Sharp was attorney general and out of the electoral limelight. Once he ran for election again, however, Sharp's Old Court enemies resurrected the rumor to attack his reputation. He had always maintained he was not the father of the baby, but now he added insult to injury: He claimed the child was half-black and therefore had a black father. In Kentucky's racist, slave-owning society, this accusation was likely the final straw for Beauchamp.[62]

After an extensive trial, Beauchamp was found guilty and sentenced to hang. Once in jail, he appealed for a pardon from Governor Desha, tried to escape by bribing the guard, and wrote a lengthy confession to garner sympathy. What happened next immortalized what already was a sad, sordid, but nevertheless enthralling story. On the night before Beauchamp's execution, Cooke visited and brought with her a bottle of laudanum. Together, they tried to poison themselves, but the laudanum failed to kill them. Once the guard discovered their attempted suicide, they were watched carefully, but Cooke had still managed to sneak a knife into the jail cell undetected. On the morning of the execution, both Cooke and Beauchamp stabbed themselves. Cooke soon died of her wounds, with Beauchamp by her side. He, however, was well enough to still go to the gallows. After he was hanged, the two were buried in the same coffin. The epitaph on the grave was a poem written by Cooke.

The "Kentucky Tragedy," as it quickly became known, has maintained cultural resonance for two centuries, its melodramatic plot the subject of various retellings in plays and novels, including works by Edgar Allan Poe and Robert Penn Warren. Often lost in the melodrama, however, was the fact that Sharp's death did indeed spell the end of the New Court Party.

By 1826, the Old Court Party won the state senate, which allowed the legislature to repeal the Reorganization Act over Governor Desha's veto. The only legislation that remained from the era of Relief was the prohibition of debtors' prison. Here, at least, Kentucky would prove to be at the vanguard, with many other states following suit in the late 1820s and 1830s, and the federal government itself ending debtors' prison in 1833. By the late 1820s, most Kentuckians were embarrassed by the entire Relief War and Court War. In 1828, the state's newly elected governor, Thomas Metcalfe, gave a fitting epitaph on the era. "The conflict," he said, "has left but little worth to be remembered."[63]

Legacies

The Relief War *should* be remembered, however, because the events in Kentucky, more than any other state, represented the final attempt to realize the economic goals of the American Revolution on the terms of the revolutionaries. They had sought to bring together two seemingly incompatible ideologies: the absolute protection of private property and a society that was (relatively) economically egalitarian. Without modern financial and economic tools, the Relief Party's attempts failed.

As relief failed in Kentucky, so did it fail across the country. Other state supreme courts followed the trend of the U.S. Supreme Court and the Kentucky Court of Appeals, declaring contracts inviolable and relief measures therefore illegal. There was some anger at these rulings, but the country had largely recovered from the Panic of 1819, so there was no concerted movement to challenge them. For all intents and purposes, economic liberty was permanently ascendent, while government efforts at realizing economic equality were largely dead. During the next nationwide depression, the Panic of 1837, no state would attempt to pass a stay law or make it easier for debtors to stay solvent. Indeed, there would not be a significant challenge to the inviolability of property (other than, momentously but uniquely, *enslaved* property) until the Progressive Era in the early years of the twentieth century.

How, then, did Americans call the decades after the Panic of 1819 the era of the "common man"? Here, Amos Kendall's trajectory is illustrative.

Kendall had felt most at home defending the populism of the Relief Party, and it was on this ground where his talents as an editor were most clearly on display. On financial matters, however, Kendall was relatively conservative. This combination was tailor-made to get the attention of Andrew Jackson, who himself was both a populist and, as a wealthy slaveholder, a financial conservative. In Tennessee, Jackson was a strident opponent of all the legislature's relief measures, but, wary of relief's temporary popularity, he never made anti-relief a key plank of his politics.[64]

In 1827, Kendall, at the nadir of his influence, sent a letter to Andrew Jackson with information about his old employer Henry Clay. Jackson, desperate for any dirt on Clay since the Corrupt Bargain between Clay and John Quincy Adams that denied Jackson the presidency, responded favorably, telling Kendall that he was an "able writer."[65] Soon the two men became stalwart allies. After Jackson's election in 1828, Kendall moved to Washington, where he became an auditor in the Treasury Department and eventually postmaster general. Kendall was also responsible for bringing Francis Blair to Washington, where Blair became editor in chief of the Jackson organ the *Washington Globe.* Blair had written pro-Relief articles for the *Argus* and, of course, had helped oversee the infamous break-in to obtain the Old Court records. For his part, Kendall eventually became arguably the most influential member of Jackson's informal "Kitchen Cabinet," where he helped craft populist messages for Jackson that rallied Americans against corrupt bankers taking advantage of hardworking yeoman farmers—but, crucially, never called for any economic measures focused on redistribution or relief. The trade-off was implicit: Jackson would fight for the *political* equality of all white men, but neither he nor Kendall would ever attempt to realize *economic* equality.

The death of Relief did not mean the end of calls for economic equality, of course—but it was the end of calls for economic equality on the terms of the American Revolution's republicanism, which saw relative equality as a necessary condition for a republic to thrive, and which maintained that economic equality and economic liberty could coincide. Under these terms, people of all classes were able to call for relative economic equality. However, by the 1820s, with the rise of the Market Revolution and the apparent victory of economic liberty and defeat of economic equality, those who continued to argue for economic equality changed the terms of the debate. No longer were all Americans working together, they said. Instead, Americans were divided by class, and for the poor to prosper, the wealthy needed to pay.

Calls for redistribution and the acceptance of class conflict began where Karl Marx would later predict: in the cities, where a growing number of men and women were forced to take low-paying jobs that gave them no prospect for advancing. In New York City, for example, the pro-labor Working Men's Party gained more than 30 percent of the vote in the 1829 elections, and Thomas Skidmore, its most radical leader, published "The Rights of Man to Property!" that same year. The treatise's subtitle put economic equality at the forefront: "Being a Proposition to Make it Equal Among the Adults of the Present Generation: And to Provide for its Equal Transmission to Every Individual of Each Succeeding Generation." On the cover page, below the subtitle, Skidmore quoted the Declaration of Independence but replaced "pursuit of happiness" with "property."[66] The struggle for economic equality had entered a new era. This class-based attack on inequality also occurred in rural areas, notably during the Anti-Rent Wars of the late 1830s and 1840s in upstate New York and the rise of the Farmers' Alliance and creation of the People's Party in the 1880s, both of which still employed rhetoric that echoed the Revolution, but now this rhetoric fully and explicitly merged with that of class conflict. Even after the Populists, it would take another half century for the New Deal to actually make a dent in inequality, using different tools but under the same ideological umbrella as Kentucky's Relief Party in the 1820s. (Indeed, one New Deal policymaker and amateur historian from Kentucky even deemed the Relief War "Kentucky's New Deal of the 1820's.")[67]

Why did it take so long? And, according to some Americans, why is it *still* taking so long, and *still* so difficult to gain widespread American support for wealth redistribution? The answer, once again, goes back to the Panic of 1819 and the failures of Relief. To accept that the United States was and would forever be a land of economic inequality, Americans needed to find a satisfactory explanation, for few actually *wanted* increasing inequality—even if they did not believe they should do anything about it. The answer lay in what one historian termed the "moralization of economic disaster."[68] Poverty was not the result of larger societal forces, but personal failure. As part of this ideological shift, debtors' prisons disappeared, replaced by "workhouses," in which the destitute were given food and shelter in return for their manual labor, conducted under constant supervision by their supposed moral (and financial) superiors. Providing for the poor was no longer seen as a community responsibility, as it had been during the American Revolution and its ideas about a "moral economy." Government spending on poor relief collapsed, replaced by private charities that tried—but usually failed—to fill the void.

As the debates over the causes for and solutions to economic inequality have changed over time, and as the American Revolution has faded into the past, Americans have largely remembered its one economic legacy—a struggle for economic liberty—at the expense of its other economic legacy: a struggle for economic equality. Indeed, some conservatives celebrate the Revolution as a fundamentally anti-tax libertarian revolt, and thus they deem any measure that would raise taxes in the present day quintessentially anti-American.

On the contrary, celebrations of both economic liberty *and* economic equality were present at the dawn of the United States. If cutting taxes represents one legacy of the Revolution, providing food, housing, and medical care for those who cannot afford it—what is, in reality, modern "Relief"—is equally a legacy. That neither the Founders nor their children could resolve the impossible contradictions embedded where liberty and equality overlap scarcely discredits the economic legacy of the Revolution. We still live with those contradictions.

7

Indigenous Rights: The Cherokees' Fight to Remain, 1830–38

In January 1838, John Ross traveled to Washington, DC, alone. Ross was the elected leader of the twenty-thousand-strong Cherokee Nation; his isolation reflected the Cherokees' dire circumstances for, come May 1838, the U.S. government would force them to evacuate their homeland and travel west, to what was then U.S. Indian Territory and is today Oklahoma. All other Cherokee leaders—at least the leaders who hoped to remain in the East—were busy preparing themselves and their families for what everyone knew would be a brutal, perhaps catastrophic journey. Yet Ross held out hope that his editorials, his letters, and his meetings with prominent politicians could somehow forestall what most believed was now inevitable.

In speech after speech to sympathetic Northern whites, Ross asked the United States to live up to its many treaties with the Cherokee Nation. In the immediate term, Ross also wanted the federal government to curb the excesses of Georgia's government and its white residents. For decades, Georgians had coveted the lands of the Cherokee Nation that they believed were rightfully theirs. In 1828, Georgia's legislature followed through on their wish. It officially extended its laws over the Cherokee Nation, including a statute that stated Indians could not provide testimony in court, and then opened Cherokee lands to all Georgians via a land lottery. By the early 1830s, with the Cherokees unable to testify in their own defense in Georgia courts, white Georgians were encroaching on, invading, and confiscating Cherokee land with impunity, frequently unleashing violence on any Cherokee person who got in their way.

According to the 1832 Supreme Court case *Worcester v. Georgia*, all of this was illegal, but President Andrew Jackson and his administration refused to lift a finger for the Cherokees. John Ross's message to white

Americans was simple: *Live up to your half century of treaty commitments to the Cherokee Nation.* These treaties were still the law, even though the Cherokee Nation was by far the weaker party and, in reality, the United States could do as it wished without fear of Cherokee reprisal. As Ross wrote, "You can expel us by force, we grant; but you cannot make us call it fairness."[1] If Jackson would not live up to these treaties, then Ross placed his final hopes in "the magnanimity of the American people" and the "American character."[2]

Ross questioned whether Americans could live up to the American Revolution's ideals of justice and equality and apply them without prejudice to the Cherokee Nation. He asked, What type of country was the United States? What sort of nation did the American Revolution create? Did the ideals of the Declaration of Independence apply to Native peoples, or were these ideals just for white Americans? If the latter was true, then the entire Revolution was a sham. Instead of an inspiring turning point in world history, it was simply a power grab by disgruntled white elites bent on confiscating Native land—unless, Ross argued, Americans could once again live up to their founding.

The United States and Native Nations

Americans read and recite the opening sentences of the Declaration of Independence obsessively, for good reason. "Self-evident truths" and "life, liberty, and the pursuit of happiness"—these are inspiring phrases. They were inspiring two hundred years ago, and they remain so today.

Americans do not have the same obsession with the lengthy middle section, also for good reason. This expansive list of grievances against King George III is rooted in a place and time, explaining what, exactly, the king and his ministers had done that necessitated U.S. independence. This list mattered greatly in 1776, however. Indeed, revolutionary Americans likely cared more about these grievances than they did about the soaring opening paragraph, for the grievances spelled out in concrete terms the evils of the British crown, including the following:

> He has excited domestic insurrections amongst us, and has endeavored to bring on the inhabitants of our frontiers, the merciless Indian Savages, whose known rule of warfare, is an undistinguished destruction of all ages, sexes and conditions.

The description of Native peoples as "merciless Indian savages" may have been racist, but it also inadvertently acknowledged a truth about Natives that few white Americans wanted to admit, but all knew to be true: In 1776, Native people possessed real power. From the Abenaki in Maine to the Muscogee in Georgia, Native nations conducted diplomacy, raised armies, and traded across their borders as independent, sovereign nations—as their choosing of sides during the Revolutionary War made all too clear. Certainly, they were not dependent wards of the United States. The Constitution eventually acknowledged this fact. In describing how to apportion representation, the Constitution specified that the census would exclude "Indians not taxed" in the counting of a state's population—because, quite simply, Native people were not U.S. citizens, but instead citizens of their own independent nations.

More importantly, the Constitution gave Congress the power to "regulate commerce with foreign nations, and among several states, and with the Indian tribes." At the time, "commerce" referred to something more than simply economics; it was more akin to "affairs" or "relations."[3] (Indeed, early drafts of the Constitution used the word "affairs.") From an ideological perspective, that the Framers did not simply fold Native peoples into "foreign nations" reveals that these men did not necessarily consider Native nations as being equal to European nations, for they did not consider the individual citizens of those nations on an equal plain. This treatment went back to the Treaty of Paris itself. No Native nation participated in the discussions that made U.S. victory in the Revolutionary War official, even as that treaty awarded the United States thousands of miles in the Trans-Appalachian West that were very much controlled by Native nations. In the words of the historian Samantha Seeley, "Native sovereignty was undermined at the very moment the new United States gained international recognition."[4]

When it came to *action*, however, the U.S. government certainly treated Native nations like European nations, particularly regional powers such as the Muscogee and the Haudenosaunee (who still are incorrectly labeled as the "Iroquois" in many textbooks). The U.S. government routinely sent diplomatic missions to Native nations, just as it sent diplomatic missions to European states—indeed, one scholar has argued that Indian treaties were really the first instances of U.S. statecraft.[5] The separation of "several states" from "Indian tribes" in the Constitution, moreover, made all too clear that Native peoples were not part of the United States.

For this reason, the Constitution did not ask for Native votes in the ratification process. *Americans* needed to ratify the document—and Native peoples were not Americans. Yet because Native nations were independent, powerful, and right next door, U.S. leaders did send diplomats to these nations explaining the parameters of the Constitution and asking for Native approval. When Federalists argued their case about the benefits of the Constitution to skeptical white people, they argued that the newly empowered central government would finally be able to expel Indians from the frontier. As the historian Maggie Blackhawk argued, it was "a constitution for colonialism."[6]

Yet, when talking to Native people, Federalists made the exact opposite argument: the newly empowered central government would finally be able to restrain white frontiersmen from attacking Native people with impunity. For this reason, some Native leaders gave the Constitution their blessing. Others, meanwhile, realized that a stronger, better governed United States would only pose greater problems down the road. Would the federal government really side with Indians over white Americans when both groups desired the same land? After all, as one Native leader, Big Cat (Mkhequeh Posees) of the Delaware, argued, "The white people have taken all our lands from us, from time to time, until this time, and that they will continue the same way."[7]

Big Cat proved correct. What followed in the generation after the Revolution was an assault on Native independence. While the federal government signed treaties guaranteeing Native sovereignty in exchange for significant portions of their land, these treaties were wholly ineffective at restraining covetous white Americans on the ground. Although the Constitution proved far more effective than the Articles of Confederation as an instrument of state power, in most cases the federal government was still both unable and unwilling to prevent whites on the frontier from making incursions into Native land. Native peoples fought back to preserve their independence, and when violence escalated, whites demanded the federal government send military aid—which, invariably, the federal government did.[8]

Time and again, Native peoples were blamed for nearly everything. Violence between Americans and Indians? The Indians' fault. Failure to become fully Christian? The Indians' fault. Poverty and destitution in Native communities? The Indians' fault. The Mohegan Samson Occom was a devoted convert to Christianity, an ardent defender of Native sovereignty, and the most prolific Native writer of the Revolutionary era. In 1791, he called for Native teachers for Native peoples, for they had "very great" prejudice against white people, and had "good reason for it." Occom continued, "When there is any Mischief . . . then there is an out Cry against them . . . Vulgar Language is; Kill kill 'em, Damn em."[9]

A half century later, nothing had changed. The words of William Apess, a mixed-race Pequot activist who wrote in the 1830s, were little different from Occum's: Native peoples were treated "as beasts of prey," for "prejudice stung every white man, from the oldest to the youngest, to the very centre of the heart."[10] It did not matter that the United States had signed treaties with Native nations. It did not matter that, in the cases of nations like the Oneida, assaults against Native independence were visited upon people who had fought and died alongside white Americans during the Revolutionary War. Ultimately, Americans wanted land that Natives held, and therefore Natives needed to be—in the parlance of the time—"removed."

Very few white Americans believed that the natural rights proclaimed in the Declaration of Independence applied to Indians. On the contrary, on the frontier the surest way to hero status was to kill as many Indians as possible, which became essentially the frontier definition of American patriotism.[11] This violence, too, was a dark promise of the American Revolution. The Revolution was fought to get rid of Britain's Proclamation Line, meaning violence against Native peoples was built into the Revolution from the outset. In the 1790s and early 1800s, Trans-Appalachian Native peoples had a good recourse: They could fight back. The United States remained weak and vulnerable, the British continued to ally with many Native peoples, and Native peoples themselves could bring substantial military force to bear on any encroaching U.S. force—particularly when they formed alliances among one another, as they did under the chiefs Little Turtle and Blue Jacket in 1795, and Tecumseh and Tenskwatawa a decade later.

This all changed during and after the War of 1812. In 1813, Tecumseh was killed at the Battle of the Thames. A year later, Great Britain abandoned its Native allies when it signed the Treaty of Ghent with the United States. Tens of thousands of white Americans then swarmed west, creating a demographic tsunami no Native nation could withstand. Native peoples were left with no good options: They could fight back and be killed; they could leave their homes and flee farther west; or they could acquiesce to the American presence and try to make the best of it, trusting that perpetually untrustworthy, racist white Americans would somehow change their ways and allow Native peoples to maintain their sovereignty. This, of course, almost never happened.

There was only one small silver lining that ever so slightly—*very* slightly—mitigated the United States' ruthless treatment of Native peoples. Most educated revolutionaries, men like Thomas Jefferson and George Washington, did not believe Native peoples were entirely irredeemable. To them, Indians represented a lower state of "degenerated" humanity, but they were humans nonetheless, and therefore, with time, they could eventually ascend to the level of white people, which would then allow them to live as equals in the United States.[12] This would happen in two ways: first, intermarriage with whites, which would eventually lead to a single, thoroughly civilized race of people, neither white nor Indian, simply American. Addressing a delegation of Mohicans and Delaware visiting the capital in 1808, President Thomas Jefferson laid out this vision, saying, "You will mix with us by marriage. Your blood will run in our veins, and will spread with us over this great island." The end was the kicker: "We shall all be Americans."[13]

Second, Native peoples would also culturally assimilate through what became known as the "civilization program." First implemented by

Henry Knox and Timothy Pickering, the first two secretaries of war, this policy sought to "civilize" Native peoples by sending them U.S. officials and providing them with U.S.-made goods like plows and other farming tools. With these goods and guidance, Indians would "become herdsmen and cultivators, instead of remaining in a state of hunters," as one U.S. treaty stated.[14] By becoming a sedentary agricultural community whose settlements looked just like those of white American settlements, Indians would also presumably convert to Christianity, learn to read and write English, and eventually adopt American culture wholesale.

From the modern perspective, we can name this plainly: Bias. Bigotry. Prejudice. This view held out hope that Native people could one day be equal to white Americans, but it also acknowledged that, in terms of their current status, they were decidedly inferior—and therefore barbaric. However, from the perspective of the much less tolerant late eighteenth century, this policy was also well intentioned and well meaning, as the historian Nicholas Guyatt has argued.[15] At the least, the civilization program was designed so Native people could live alongside whites in peace, even if they had to change how they lived. It was *something*—which, considering Europeans' and Americans' brutal treatment of Native peoples since the sixteenth century, was better than *nothing*.

When it came down to the details, both the intermarriage and civilization goals were lazy, ill-thought policy, crafted in the minds of daydreaming American elites instead of hammered out by officials on the ground. Intermarriage was a fine goal, but Thomas Jefferson and George Washington were not going to marry Native women. The people who would, presumably, were those white Americans actually living on the frontier, in close proximity to Native nations. The problem was, these were the Americans who hated Indians the most. They wanted Indians gone—killed, subjugated, or expelled, it did not matter—so they could get Indian land. Under very few circumstances did white men want to marry Native women and treat them as family members.

The civilization program was also unrealistic. If a Native nation did fully embrace American cultural and economic norms, would these same frontier whites simply acquiesce to permanent Native sovereignty over lands they had long coveted? It was not as if the colonists hated the Proclamation of 1763 because of the *way* Native peoples lived, but because it prevented them from moving west and confiscating even more Native land. And who would define what "civilized" really meant? After all, countless Native peoples had long been sedentary farmers, just like white Americans. Indeed, the problem for would-be frontier settlers who wanted to obtain land in the Trans-Appalachian West was not that there were scattered bands of roaming Indian hunters and gatherers who might interfere with Americans as they built farms, villages, and towns. Rather, the problem was that these farms, villages, and towns already existed—they just had been built by tens of thousands of Native people. By one estimate, what was called the "Ohio country"—today's Rust Belt—contained Native towns that rivaled the population of any U.S. city.[16] Many Native people not only practiced settled agriculture, but also had adopted various aspects of American culture, picking and choosing what they liked and what benefited them, and discarding the rest. When the Prophet Tenskwatawa sought to forge an alliance of Native peoples in the early 1800s, he preached to Natives the radical doctrine that they needed to cast off white culture entirely, demonstrating just how much cultural blending had already occurred.

For elites like Washington, Jefferson, Henry Knox, and Timothy Pickering in the 1790s, none of this mattered, for what the civilization policy really did was allow them to kick the can down the road and buy time. By claiming that Native peoples would be welcomed as equals once they were civilized—in two or three or four decades—they kept all U.S. options on the table when it came to Native relations. If Native peoples did not "civilize" over the next generation? Then it was their own fault, and the United States had every right to confiscate land that was supposedly not being used properly. And if they did "civilize"? Well, then it was for a future administration to deal with the backlash from frontier whites who would be shut out of land ownership. But this was for another day and time.

By the 1830s, for those Native peoples who had been able to resist white encroachment for half a century, time had run out.

The Cherokees

If the proponents of white–Native intermarriage and the civilization program were looking for the perfect person to demonstrate that both ideas could be realized, then John Ross was their man.

Born in 1790, Ross was the product of several generations of intermarriage. Technically only one-eighth of his ancestry was Cherokee. Not only was his father Scottish, but so was his mother's father and his maternal grandmother's father, all of whom had married Cherokee or mixed-race Cherokee-Scottish women while profiting from the lucrative deerskin trade that dominated the eighteenth-century Cherokee economy. Ross's heritage reflected several generations of strategic marriage: By marrying high-ranking Cherokee women, Scottish traders gained permanent access to the strategically located Cherokee homeland, which in the mid-eighteenth century ran from what is now western North Carolina and western Georgia to the western edge of Tennessee, including parts of northern Mississippi and Alabama. By marrying relatively prosperous Scottish traders, Cherokee women ensured their mixed-race children would have access to many more opportunities in the British colonial world than if they were—in the parlance of the time—"full-blooded" Cherokee.

At home Ross spoke English, and his father first hired him a private tutor and then sent him to an academy in Tennessee, where Ross also began to engage in various business ventures. By the time he reached adulthood, Ross was more educated than a vast majority of his Southern neighbors, both Cherokee and American—including his future nemesis Andrew Jackson, who wrote with none of Ross's eloquence. Despite his predominantly Scottish ancestry, his American-style education, and his lifelong struggles with the Cherokee language, Ross identified as Cherokee—and, indeed, he *was* 100 percent Cherokee by the standards of the Cherokees themselves. The Cherokees organized themselves through matrilineal clans, in which every child was a member of the clan of his or her mother, and thus John Ross was a member of the Bird Clan, regardless of the status of his father. He also married a Cherokee woman, Elizabeth "Quatie" Brown Henley, about whom little is known. This was Quatie's second marriage, her previous husband having died during the War of 1812. His name, Robert Henley, suggests he too was of biracial descent, meaning he too would have had an advantaged upbringing that most Cherokees lacked, which suggests that Quatie herself had significant social standing within the Cherokee Nation. Yet Ross never mentioned her in any of the nearly one thousand letters he wrote during more than fifty years of correspondence, and no correspondence exists between the two. Perhaps Quatie was illiterate, or perhaps their marriage was one of convenience for two members of the Cherokee elite, or perhaps both.[17] Whatever their relationship, John Ross and Quatie would have six children, with one dying in infancy and another stillborn.

The combination of Ross's bicultural upbringing and his many talents led to his rapid ascension in Cherokee politics. This began with his appointment as an adjutant in a Cherokee regiment that served under Andrew Jackson in the Creek War of 1812–13—which, considering that Ross and Jackson would later become bitter nemeses, was ironic indeed. He then clerked for two Cherokee chiefs, Pathkiller and Charles Hicks, who valued him for his ability to speak and write English. In 1816 he was named a Cherokee delegate to Washington, where he was the only appointee fluent in English, making him the de facto leader. A year later the Cherokees elected Ross to the thirteen-member National Council. Two years after that he became its president, and in 1827 he was elected the Principal Chief of the Cherokee Nation. Remarkably, the Cherokees would continuously elect him for thirty-nine consecutive years.

Ross was clearly an exceptional individual, but he was not wholly unique. There were other elite, biracial Cherokee men—usually, like Ross, the sons of Cherokee women who had married Scottish traders—and they too were raised in a world that embraced English-style education and culture while remaining dedicated to the interests of the Cherokee Nation. These men—among them James Vann, Charles Hicks, Major Ridge and his son John, and John Ridge's cousin Elias Boudinot—were the leaders responsible for what one historian has labeled the "Cherokee Renascence."[18]

Beginning in the early nineteenth century, these men began to remake the Cherokee Nation from its "traditional" orientation to one that embraced American political, economic, social, and cultural norms. As they wrote to President Monroe in 1819, "We have long since been induced to believe that civilized life was preferable to that of the hunters."[19] In reality, the Cherokees had only recently turned to being "hunters" in the eighteenth century, for it was the growth of Britain's North American colonies that fueled the European desire for deerskins. Turning to agriculture in the early nineteenth century represented, in some ways, a return to older Cherokee practices from the seventeenth century and earlier.

Yet it was not looking back, but forward—and outward—that represented the goals of the Cherokee elite. Not only did they hope to replace the deerskin trade with settled agriculture, but they hoped to replace the Cherokees' matrilineal clan system with a government modeled on the U.S. Constitution, and they hoped to replace the Cherokees' traditional religious beliefs with Christianity. Judging by their own writings and the writings of Christian missionaries who visited the Cherokee Nation, they were spectacularly successful. Over time, the Cherokee economy increasingly resembled that of the U.S. South, while the Cherokee government increasingly resembled the U.S. federal government. These transformations culminated in 1827, when the Cherokees wrote their own constitution and modeled it on the U.S. Constitution. Like the U.S. Constitution, the Cherokee constitution divided the government into three branches, with an executive led by the Principal Chief and a bicameral legislature divided into a General Council and Committee. The imitation was not subtle. "We the Representatives of the people of the Cherokee Nation," the constitution's preamble began, "in Convention assembled, in order to establish justice, ensure tranquility, promote our common welfare . . . ," and so on, in words that mirrored the U.S. Constitution's famous preamble.[20] The only major difference was in regard to land ownership: The Cherokee Nation's land remained "common property" that no Cherokee citizen could own, thereby preventing individuals from selling Cherokee lands piecemeal to covetous whites.[21] Like many other Native peoples, the Cherokees saw communal landholding as the backstop that would prevent Americans from negating their precarious sovereignty.

Both before and after he was elected Principal Chief, Ross performed his political duties while operating a store, a warehouse, a ferry crossing, and, eventually, a plantation—worked by roughly ten enslaved people. Here lay the great contradiction of the reconstituted Cherokee Nation. Embracing the practices of the United States, particularly the practices of the U.S. South, included embracing the enslavement of black people. Scattered evidence suggests that enslaved black people living in the Cherokee Nation enjoyed greater rights and privileges than those living in the U.S. South. Notably, Cherokee–black marriages were largely accepted although still uncommon. Yet here too was something the Cherokee elite wanted to change, and over time they instituted a series of slave codes that further racialized the Cherokee Nation. At the same time, they also began to curb the traditional power of Cherokee women, who had long held significant sway in the Cherokees' matrilineal clans. Remaking oneself in the image of the U.S. early republic had material benefits—and it also had its moral costs.

To the Cherokee male elite, the benefits were twofold. First, there was the political benefit: By embracing the U.S. civilization program—albeit on Cherokee terms—the Cherokees would be allowed to remain on their land in the East. Indeed, as they saw it, their success in Americanization made them exceptional among Native peoples. As Cherokee leaders proclaimed in one of their many memorial letters to Congress, "While we deplore the fate of thousands of our complexion and kind, we rejoice that our nation stands and grows a lasting monument of God's mercy, and a durable contradiction to the misconceived opinion that the aborigines are incapable of civilization."[22] Second, of course, there were personal benefits: By being at the vanguard of the Cherokee Nation's economic and political transformation, these men would reap the economic and political benefits, accruing money, land, power, and prestige, as they led the Cherokee Nation toward something they believed no other Native people had yet done. Interests seamlessly merged with ideology.

The Cherokee elite represented at most 10 percent of the Cherokee Nation's roughly twenty thousand people, but more likely even less. Most Cherokees did not speak English, did not own slaves, were not Christian, practiced subsistence farming, and still lived by the traditions of clan and kinship that long shaped Cherokee history. While many of these people did learn to read Cherokee, 39 percent remained illiterate.[23] As one missionary reported after living for two years in the Cherokee Nation, most

Cherokees "cling to their old customs as much as possible, and on many occasions, exhibit the original character of the tribe."[24]

But while we do not know the specific worldviews and motivations of most of the Cherokee Nation, we can say one thing for certain: Nearly the entire nation fully trusted John Ross to lead for more than forty years. He never lost an election.

Ross's popularity would prove to be a serious problem for U.S. policymakers, for if he chose to defy U.S. authority, so too would a vast majority of the Cherokee Nation.

Questions Asked

By 1830, the Cherokee Nation's sovereignty was under assault. White Americans had always wanted Cherokee land; now, however, they also wanted the Cherokees' gold, which was discovered within Cherokee borders in 1829. Andrew Jackson, Indian fighter and Indian hater extraordinaire, was president. One of his key campaign planks in 1828 was the "removal" of all Native nations from the East to the West, which he justified as a means to save Native nations from extinction. In reality, as critics of Jackson argued, it was the reverse: Removal in fact paved the way for extinction.[25]

In the early 1830s, the Cherokees sought redress from Congress and the Supreme Court. They began with Congress. In his 1829 State of the Union Address, Jackson had called for a removal bill from Congress, and his allies in Congress quickly obliged, introducing the Indian Removal Act later that year, which authorized the president to conduct negotiations with not just the Cherokees but all Native nations in the eastern United States to "remove" themselves from their homelands and travel west, to U.S. Indian Territory.

As early as 1824, John Ross and other Cherokee leaders had sent a petition to Congress that demanded Congress honor its treaty obligations and the right to Cherokee self-government. "We expect it from them under that *memorable* declaration," the petition stated, "'that all men are created equal, that they are endowed by their Creator with certain unalienable rights, that among these are Life, Liberty, and the pursuit of Happiness.'"[26] There was no subtlety here. Considering the Cherokees' increasingly desperate circumstances, there was no need for any.

The Cherokees were asking Jacksonian Americans a simple question: Could they live up to the legacy of the American Revolution and the supposed righteousness of the American Founding by stopping removal? It is a testament to the Cherokees' strategy and messaging that thousands of white Americans heard their pleas and responded with vigor. They believed the United States stood for liberty and self-government, which the Cherokees had every right to also enjoy. Most of these sympathizers were from the North, and among that group most were Whigs, evangelicals, or both. Even so, there were also some Southerners, even Georgians, who supported the Cherokees.[27]

Most notable among these sympathizers was the Vermont-born Jeremiah Evarts, an evangelical who edited the influential religious magazine *The Panoplist*, in which he published twenty-four essays under the pen name "William Penn" that argued against Indian removal. (Again, no subtlety here—William Penn had founded Pennsylvania under Quaker principles, which included the peaceful tolerance of Native peoples.) What nation is responsible for Indian removal? Evarts asked. "Is it some rotten Asiatic despotism, sinking under the crimes and corruptions of by-gone centuries . . . ? Not so. It is a government, which sprung into existence with the declaration 'that all men are created equal.'"[28] His reference to the Declaration was not only political but personal: His wife, Mehitable Sherman Barnes, was the daughter of Roger Sherman, signer of the Declaration and delegate to the Constitutional Convention. Other allies of the Cherokees made similar references to the American past, sometimes broadening the argument beyond U.S. borders to the reputation the United States enjoyed throughout the world. As another anonymous memorial letter noted, "As illustrating the benefits of democracy, the reputation of our government is pre-eminently important to the human family," and it needed to maintain its reputation for the "eyes of the friends of liberty."[29]

The activism of Cherokee leaders and white allies like Evarts generated the first widespread civil rights campaign in U.S. history, which included, significantly, the widespread involvement of women. Evarts's William Penn essays were the most widely distributed pamphlets since Tom Paine's *Common Sense*. The Cherokees' message resonated particularly with young American evangelicals growing up in the middle of the Second Great Awakening. At the time, evangelical periodicals reached a wider audience than secular and partisan ones. Thirty religious magazines had over three thousand subscribers, at a time when secular magazines rarely reached half that readership, and, for several years, anti-removal essays dominated their content.[30] Throughout the Union, particularly but not exclusively in the North, Cherokee emissaries and their white allies spoke to packed churches and meetinghouses. Martin Van Buren, at the time Jackson's vice president, later remembered, "A more persevering opposition to a public measure had scarcely ever been made."[31]

We should give Evarts and the thousands of Americans who supported the Cherokees some credit: Their innumerable petitions, meetings, and voting records in opposition to removal were sincere and effective, and their campaign reverberated beyond just the Cherokees. Many of the anti-removal activists would soon become the first generation of radical white abolitionists. Yet their stance was also one of convenience: As Northerners, their focus lay largely on the five large Southern Native nations—the Cherokee, Choctaw, Chickasaw, Muscogee (until recently, referred to as the Creek), and Seminole, whom sympathetic Americans often referred to as the "Five Civilized Tribes," a term that implicitly argued for their right to remain in the South. Of course, unlike many white Southerners, Northerners would gain nothing if these Indians were expelled, so it was easy to support these distant peoples. However, many smaller Northern Native nations would also be affected by the Indian Removal Act, and Northern activists had little to say about them. On a national level, Northern Indian removal would be ignored at the time—and would continue to be ignored by most historians, until only very recently.[32]

Congress took the fateful vote on the Indian Removal Act in late May 1830. The vote in the Senate was not close: twenty-eight senators voted for the act, nineteen against. The vote in the House, however, thoroughly demonstrated just how successful the Cherokees' public outreach had been. Ninety-seven congressmen voted against the bill, including the famed Tennessean David Crockett of later Walt Disney fame, who declared that this bill betrayed "the foundation of the government."[33] While it was to be expected that Northern Whigs would vote against the bill, some Northern Jacksonian Democrats did as well, clearly uncomfortable with a measure they perceived as immoral or, at the very least, unnecessary.

Tragically for the Cherokees, however, Crockett was among only a handful of Southern representatives who were willing to take such a stand, and there were simply not enough Northern Democrats who were willing to buck their own party, demonstrating the hardening of partisan lines that had been developing since the mid-1820s. In the vote for removal, there were 101 yays, defeating the nays by just four votes. Many often assume that Indian removal was a foregone conclusion, one that fit seamlessly into centuries of injustice and persecution of countless Native nations, and yet, in the end: a margin of only four votes. The decisions of only four men triggered the beginning of "removal"—a term that hides the horrors of what the yay votes really wanted: violent expulsion and ethnic cleansing.[34] Here was a hinge upon which history turned, one that was hardly baked in but instead was subject to the in-the-moment whims of a handful of individuals.

These narrow numbers mask another tragic irony: Without the Three-Fifths Clause, the removal bill would have gone down to defeat. Thus, white Americans used the oppression of one people to dispossess another. No wonder Evarts lamented, "Nothing like it ever before stained the annals of this country."[35]

With the legislative branch having sided with Jackson, the Cherokees turned to their final hope: the judicial branch, helmed by the U.S. Supreme Court and its renowned chief justice John Marshall, the very same justice who had time and again blunted any redistribution of private property in the 1820s. Marshall was far more sympathetic to the Cherokees. The two Cherokee court cases he presided over remain the most famous cases involving Native peoples in the Supreme Court's history, and arguably sit in the top ten most famous and important Supreme Court cases in all of U.S. history. The first, *Cherokee Nation v. Georgia*, was a defeat for the Cherokees, as Marshall and the majority of the court ruled that the Cherokee Nation did not have standing to sue Georgia for its violation of Cherokee sovereignty because it was not a foreign nation, and thus was not sovereign. Instead, the Cherokee Nation was, in the words of Marshall, a "domestic dependent nation," akin to a "ward to its guardian"—the guardian, of course, being the United States.[36] But there was hope for the Cherokees: If a proper party *did* sue, the court majority noted, then it might rule in favor of the Cherokees.

Georgia officials soon obliged. In 1830, the state passed a law that mandated all white men obtain a state license if they wanted to live on Cherokee land. Superficially, the law appeared to protect the Cherokees from white encroachment; in reality, it was another attempt by Georgia officials to wrest sovereignty from the Cherokee Nation by mandating that Georgia, not the Cherokees, could pick and choose the inhabitants of Cherokee lands. After the law's passage, the Georgia militia arrested eleven white missionaries in the Cherokee Nation for violating the new law, though these missionaries had been welcomed by Cherokee leaders and were present for legitimate educational and religious outreach. Those arrested included Samuel Worcester, a confidant of Elias Boudinot who had been integral in obtaining the printing press first used to print the *Cherokee Phoenix*. All eleven men were then convicted and sentenced to four years of hard labor. Nine quickly obtained a pardon from Georgia's governor, but Worcester and one other missionary refused to accept it, believing—correctly—their imprisonment to be the vehicle by which the Cherokee Nation could win at the Supreme Court. Worcester, after all, was a U.S. citizen. He clearly had standing to sue.

The Supreme Court's decision in *Worcester v. Georgia* was an equivocal victory for the Cherokee Nation and for tribal sovereignty more generally. Native nations, Marshall maintained, were "distinct, independent political communities retaining their original natural rights, as the undisputed possessors of the soil."[37] Therefore, all diplomatic relations between Native nations and the United States needed to be conducted via the federal government. States had no jurisdiction to interfere, meaning all of Georgia's increasingly aggressive legislation that aimed at expelling the Cherokees was illegal and unconstitutional.

John Ross and his allies were ecstatic. Writing from the Cherokee Nation to the three Cherokee delegates currently in Washington, Ross reported "great rejoicings throughout the nation on the decision of the supreme court upon the Cherokee case."[38] But other Cherokee leaders sensed that their victory would prove to be pyrrhic. How would the Supreme Court enforce its ruling? Would President Jackson change his tune and agree to the court's ruling? Would Georgia authorities actually back down? Considering Andrew Jackson and his Georgia allies had proven they were Indian haters without peer, these unanswered questions led only to troubling answers. Boudinot, one of the Cherokee Nation's political leaders and the editor of the *Cherokee Phoenix*, proclaimed "GOOD NEWS" in English in the pages of the paper, but in Cherokee he warned his readers, "Now it is dangerous."[39]

Georgia officials were not going to back down, and neither was Andrew Jackson. According to a later account, Jackson reportedly proclaimed, "John Marshall has made his decision; now let him enforce it." Never quippy or eloquent, often halting and wordy, Jackson actually wrote something more convoluted and less memorable, but historians still quote the apocryphal statement because it best exemplifies his uncompromising, cynical position: The law be damned.[40] To Jackson and his allies, the Cherokees would be expelled one way or another.

Questions Answered

Soon after he published his secret warning to his fellow Cherokees, Elias Boudinot broke decisively with John Ross. His decision came after meeting with his cousin and fellow Cherokee leader John Ridge, who had just returned from Washington. There, Ridge had met with President Jackson, who had just been reelected, and Jackson coldly informed Ridge that he would not send federal forces to Georgia to enforce the Supreme Court's ruling. The Cherokees were on their own.

In despair, Ridge decided that removal was now the best of all the bad options, and he was able to persuade Boudinot, as well as his father, Major Ridge; Boudinot's brother Stand Watie; and several other influential Cherokee leaders. They would become known as the "Treaty Party," for it was these men who sat down with U.S. authorities in 1835 and negotiated the infamous Treaty of New Echota. Claiming to speak for the Cherokee

Nation, the Treaty Party agreed to move west, giving up for good the long-held goal of remaining on their lands in the East. The terms of the treaty stated that the Cherokee would be removed "comfortably," but it remained unclear exactly how thousands and thousands of families could be forcibly moved thousands of miles in "comfort."[41]

It is easy to blast these men for what was, in many ways, a betrayal of the Cherokee Nation. They knew full well that they did not speak for a majority of Cherokees. At the same time, they believed they were doing the best for their people. Better to move the entire Cherokee Nation west, peacefully and all together, than to be violently destroyed piecemeal by their white neighbors in Georgia, who had no compunction about killing Indians with impunity.

Andrew Jackson finally had his treaty, no matter how fraudulent. John Ross, however, remained undaunted. From 1835 through nearly a day before removal commenced, Ross crisscrossed the country, writing countless editorials and making countless speeches, trying to rally Americans against removal. In the spring of 1836, Ross delivered sixteen thousand Cherokee signatures to Congress protesting the treaty. In all likelihood, Ross simply hoped to buy more time until a new president or a new Congress would step into the breach and reverse the tragic events of the past decade. His strategy failed: The Senate ratified the Treaty of New Echota by one vote in May 1836. The terms of the treaty gave the Cherokees two years to leave their homeland. If they refused, they would be forcibly expelled.

And so in 1838 John Ross and his Cherokee allies found themselves pleading with Americans to *do something*: *What sort of country is this? What sort of people are you?* These were the questions posed to an American public still struggling to understand the United States' place in the world. Supporters of the Cherokees—Northerners, Whigs, evangelicals, reformers—believed that the United States, as a nation founded on the moral righteousness of the American Revolution, needed to uphold its original treaties with the Cherokees from the late eighteenth century. Thousands petitioned Congress, asserting that the very soul of the republic was at stake. "If our national faith is abandoned," one petition stated, "nothing of our vaunted republicanism worth contending for is left, and the days of our republic numbered."[42] After all, to Americans at the time, republics were precariously held together by the virtuousness of its citizens. A republic without virtue was no republic at all.

Throughout the 1830s, Americans who opposed removal arrived at a disturbing realization: The United States, founded in glory and virtue during the American Revolution, was now in the process of moral decay. Jeremiah Evarts felt this keenly. In his last, futile protest, he lamented Americans' "apathy" toward Cherokee removal, which pointed to a deeper issue: If the Cherokees were expelled, "the character of the country will be out, before the country is aware of it."[43] Only in hindsight, Evarts argued, would Americans realize how far their vaunted republic had fallen. Exhausted by his failed campaign against Indian removal, Evarts died of tuberculosis one year later.

Tragedy and Ruin

Even if U.S. authorities and their state allies had acted in good faith, the process of the euphemistically termed "Indian removal" still would have claimed hundreds of lives. Thousands of people traveling in large groups for months at time was a recipe for a range of disasters—outbreaks of cholera and dysentery, starvation, food poisoning, bad weather, and difficult river crossings—that no nineteenth-century state could overcome. But, for the most part, neither U.S. authorities nor the state militias who aided them acted in good faith. On the contrary, many preyed on the plight of Native peoples—stealing from them or extorting their supplies for a pittance, providing unsanitary food and water, and murdering, raping, and torturing Native people who did not comply with their orders fast enough.[44] Numbers may not capture the depth of the horror as Native peoples experienced it in the moment, but they do capture its scale: in the South, 3,500 Muscogee deaths out of 23,000 total people, 3,000 Choctaw deaths out of 20,000, and 650 Chickasaw deaths out of 5,000. Indian removal in the North is less well known simply because smaller numbers of people were expelled, but deaths reached similar percentages among the Wyandot, Delaware, Shawnee, Seneca, Cayuga, Miami, and Potawatomi.

As the second-to-last Native nation holding out in the East (the Seminoles would fight to remain in Florida until 1842), the Cherokees knew what was coming. They knew that, even if Major General Winfield Scott, who was in charge of facilitating removal, was acting in good faith, he had no ability to control the 3,500 militiamen under his control. Simply put, the Cherokees knew removal meant death. As John Ross's brother Lewis wrote to him in the final months before the journey, the Cherokees were preparing for their "final doom."[45]

It was not, in fact, the Cherokees' "final doom," but it was still a tragedy of horrific proportions. In the end, more than sixteen thousand Cherokees and more than a thousand enslaved black people were forced west. Of these, more than four thousand never arrived in U.S. Indian Territory. The brutal journey claimed the lives of one in every four Cherokees. Not all were removed, however: Ensconced in the mountains of North Carolina, approximately 1,500 Cherokees remained, eventually becoming the Eastern Band of the Cherokee Nation, who live there to this day.

Amid this nearly unfathomable death and desolation, the Cherokees were not destroyed as a people. Once in Indian Territory, they would go on to reconstruct the Cherokee Nation and reassert its vibrancy. However, they would first have to deal with even more horror, as the Ross Party and the Treaty Party waged a low-level civil war for control of the Cherokee Nation in the immediate aftermath of removal. During this war, Ross Party members murdered Elias Boudinot, Boudinot's uncle Major Ridge, and his cousin John Ridge for signing the Treaty of New Echota. These murders still haunt Cherokee history—although in the end, responsibility should be placed at the feet of the United States, which had put leaders of the Cherokee Nation in an impossible position and then washed its hands, leaving the Cherokees to cope with the political consequences.

Despite tragedy piled upon tragedy, nearly four hundred thousand people today claim Cherokee heritage, which is a testament to the Cherokees' tenacity. They are four hundred thousand of the nearly 10 million Indigenous people, comprising nearly 3 percent of the U.S. population, who live in every state in the country, divided into 574 federally recognized tribal nations and dozens more recognized by individual states.[46] Native people are still here, resilient and increasingly resurgent.[47]

The Cherokees' story, and the story of Indian removal more generally, deserves to live in infamy, a permanent and hideous scar on the idea of American exceptionalism, on the premise that the founding of the United States was something uniquely noble and virtuous. Historians, rightfully, have argued just as much.[48] Unlike many such academic arguments, this portrayal has thankfully broken through to the American public. Millions of schoolchildren, even at the elementary level, now learn the general outline of the Trail of Tears, the story is recounted in every single American history textbook (not always paradigms of inclusivity), and the National Park Service has designated 2,200 miles of roads and waterways, in nine states, part of the Trail of Tears National Historic Trail. That most Americans can name this singular moment of injustice toward Indigenous people at the expense of others is a result of many factors—the Cherokees' large population and influence (more than 1.5 million people reported to be full or part Cherokee on the 2020 census, the largest of any Native nation), the century-length efforts of scholars who have recounted the horrors of Indian removal, and the awful poetic resonance of the term "Trail of Tears"—but it is also due to Ross and his allies' ability to generate document after document, and speech after speech, protesting their removal as it happened. Their efforts meant white Americans, too, knew the facts of Cherokee removal as it happened.[49] Unlike many other attacks on Native sovereignty, the U.S. government was unable to downplay its complicity in the terrible events that followed.

The Cherokees' ability to make their message resonate with vast swaths of the American public also reveals how the founding narrative continued to endure among Americans more than half a century after its supposed denouement. Ostensibly, the Cherokees' campaign should never have gotten as far as it did. Most Americans were intolerant of Native peoples, and most believed Native land was theirs for the taking—and yet tens of thousands of these racist and covetous Americans rallied to Ross and his allies just the same. They did so because they believed the American Revolution was more than just a naked quest for power. To them, the Revolution was a noble, righteous endeavor that portended a better, more just world. Their fervent support for the Cherokees showed that they still believed it was not too late for the United States to live up to that vision. The Revolution's meaning had dimmed—but it had not disappeared.

And so, many of these same anti-removal activists now cast their eyes toward other issues that they believed betrayed the promise of the Revolution. One clearly stood out from the rest: slavery.

The campaign for abolition was about to begin again.

8

Declarations of Independence: The Right to Found a New Nation, 1835–48

Hear Americans declare their independence!

"We, the people of Oregon Territory, for purposes of mutual protection, and to secure peace and prosperity among ourselves, agree to the following laws and regulations."[1]

Or maybe this one:

"The good people of Texas, availing themselves of their natural rights, solemnly declare, 1st. That they have taken up arms in defence of their rights and liberties, which are threatened by the encroachments of military despots."[2]

Or this one:

"[The Commander in Chief at Sonoma] invites all good and patriotic citizens in California to assist him—to establish and perpetuate a liberal, a just and honourable Government, which shall secure to all, civil, religious, and personal liberty; which shall insure the security of life and property."[3]

Or even this one:

"We, the People of the Kingdom of God, knowing that all power emanates from God . . . and knowing also that no government, which has thus originated, has the disposition and power to grant that protection to the persons and rights of man, viz., *life*, *liberty*, *possession* of *property*, and *pursuit* of *happiness*." After a lot more preamble, the document finally got down to business. Its writers would found a "Realm of liberty" that was meant "to establish a pure government, to lift up an ensign to all nations, and to establish a standard for all people."[4]

It is impossible to miss how these declarations echo the language of the Declaration of Independence and the U.S. Constitution. All were written more than a half century after the Revolution, authored by, respectively, Americans in Oregon Territory (1843), the Republic of Texas (1835), the Republic of California (1846), and finally leaders of the Church of Latter-day Saints, commonly referred to as Mormons (1844). The first three were public declarations, while the LDS constitution was kept secret and eventually scrapped, although its general goals were not.

For students of American history, these dates and declarations may seem strange. The 1840s is not typically portrayed as a decade of U.S. weakness, of Americans leaving U.S. borders and declaring independence from their home country. On the contrary, most textbooks define the decade, during which the United States defeated Mexico and annexed the southern half of Oregon Territory, as the era of "U.S. expansion" and "Manifest Destiny." It was the decade when the United States finally became the dominant power in the Western Hemisphere and a player on the world stage. It was the decade when the map of the contiguous United States, the one that is permanently etched in the brains of most Americans, mostly came to fruition (the 1854 Gadsden Purchase added a small sliver of southern Arizona and New Mexico). This map is so famous and so well known that it has often been reproduced in textbooks and history books, on T-shirts, bumper stickers, and other pieces of Americana, as an image unto itself, as if neither Canada nor Mexico exists (or Alaska, Hawaii, Puerto Rico, or the other U.S. territories, for that matter).

Yet defining the decade as one of "expansion" and "destiny," while not necessarily wrong, hides half of the story. *Something* must have been happening if Americans were declaring their independence in three different places, with the fourth, Texas, already independent since 1836. That *something* was, at the same time, both the most successful attempt and the last gasp at establishing one of the core principles of the American Revolution: the right to found a new nation.

This was a principle that two men, the focus of this chapter, spent much of their adult lives trying to fulfill. Their names were Lansford Hastings and Lyman Wight. Born and raised in Ohio, Hastings eventually became an overland trail leader for the route to California and Oregon, and he is credited with writing the key overland guide that spurred the first significant wave of Americans to California. Wight, meanwhile, was a New Yorker who became a devout member of the Church of Jesus Christ of Latter-day Saints, which was founded by Joseph Smith and is colloquially known as Mormonism. He eventually ascended into the ranks of LDS leadership. As persecutions of the Mormons heightened in the late 1830s and early 1840s, Wight was a key confidant of Joseph Smith. Eventually, Smith and Wight looked for a solution to their hardships in the independent Republic of Texas.

In the end, both Hastings and Wight failed to achieve their dreams of political independence—thanks to the United States' growing hostility to that very dream.

The Many Destinies of the American West

The Northwest Ordinance, approved by the Confederation Congress in 1787 (at the same time that delegates were meeting in Philadelphia for the Constitutional Convention), established the means through which U.S. territories would become states. The process was threefold: First, a territory with fewer than five thousand "free male inhabitants" would be overseen by a governor appointed by the U.S. Congress; second, once a territory had five thousand inhabitants, it could elect a territorial legislature that could pass laws and send a representative to Congress, though the federally appointed governor could still veto the laws and the congressional representative could not vote; finally, once a territory had sixty thousand inhabitants, it could petition Congress for full statehood (which, importantly, Congress did not automatically need to grant).

To its great credit, the Northwest Ordinance ensured that what happened with the Thirteen Colonies and the British Empire would not repeat itself with the western territories and the United States. Eventually, Americans living in the western territories would become full and equal citizens of the United States. While territorial status was anathema to Americans who lived there because it denied them representation (James Monroe described territorial government, accurately, as "Colonial government"), it was nevertheless temporary. A guarantee of full political equality was a crucial carrot that made white Americans in the West less willing to give loyalty to a European power. As the historian Jessica Roney has argued, the measure also ensured that future states looked very similar to the ones that already existed—states of landowning white men represented through a republican government—thereby creating what she terms a "unitary empire." The Northwest Ordinance thereby also foreclosed a United States of diverse states that encompassed different peoples and forms of government.[5] There would no equivalent to a British India or South Africa, or even a Wales or Scotland. In other words, the Northwest Ordinance benefited those people whom U.S. leaders saw as quintessentially American—free, landowning, white, and male.

Despite the success of the Northwest Ordinance, however, the future of the American West was still not certain. To see the American West as Americans did in 1844 requires engaging in a difficult mental exercise: You must abandon the mental map of the lower forty-eight states that is so embedded in Americans' minds today. At the time, official U.S. sovereignty excluded Texas, which was an independent republic, and the entire American Southwest and California, which were both under Mexican sovereignty. The Pacific Northwest, including today's states of Washington, Oregon, and Idaho, as well as the Canadian province of British Columbia, was under the "joint occupation" of the United States and Great Britain, which they agreed to in an 1818 treaty, meaning the future of "Oregon Country" remained ambiguous. Of course, most of this land, upward of 90 percent, remained under the actual control of Indigenous peoples, some of whom—the Comanche, the Lakota, the Diné (formerly referred to as the Navajo)—commanded formidable military power. These peoples not only were able to defend their own territory; they were expanding outward, creating empires of their own.[6]

Amid this swath of Native nations lay four regions controlled by people of European descent, three of which involved Americans. The oldest European settlement, New Mexico and its capital of Santa Fe, founded by Spain in the early seventeenth century, was that one exception. Although there was a robust trade between the United States and New Mexico via the Santa Fe Trail, few Americans actually lived in New Mexico. This was not the case with the three other regions.

The Republic of Texas was the region most populated by Americans, the result of two different moments of extensive migration and expatriation from the United States. The first began in the early 1820s, when newly independent Mexico decided that its northern regions were dangerously underpopulated and thus ripe for conquest by the United States, another European power, or Native peoples. With few Mexicans wanting to make the lengthy journey north, the Mexican government decided to offer vast amounts of nearly free land to American migrants if they became loyal Mexican citizens. In the devastating aftermath of the Panic of 1819, roughly twenty thousand Americans eagerly accepted the offer, most famously Moses Austin and his son Stephen. The Austins, like so many Americans, lost nearly everything during the depression. As Moses Austin wrote, "I am ruined in this country."[7] As economic opportunity dwindled in the United States, it beckoned in nearby Mexico, where Stephen Austin, working alone after his father died, and many other Americans became *empresarios*, essentially landed magnates tasked with recruiting more migrants and overseeing vast swaths of Mexican *Tejas*. They soon outnumbered the Tejano population, the roughly four thousand migrants from New Spain who had arrived during the century before.

Historians have long assumed that the loyalty of Americans in Texas to Mexico was essentially a lie. Empresarios like Austin were simply playing the long game, it has been argued, and were really bent on, first, expanding slavery in Texas even though it was illegal, and second, seeking eventual U.S. annexation—largely to protect slavery. Yet recently the picture has become more muddled. As historians Sarah Rodriguez and Eric Schlereth have shown, empresarios like Austin deeply appreciated the decentralized system that was Mexican federalism, in which Mexican states were largely left to themselves—more to themselves, certainly, than states under the U.S. federal system.[8] In these early years of migration, enslaved people were categorized as laborers, and while Mexican authorities knew full well what was going on, they willingly turned a blind eye. Largely left to their own devices, Austin and many other empresarios learned Spanish, converted to Catholicism, and generally got along with their Tejano neighbors. They even put down a small American rebellion in 1826 to uphold Mexican sovereignty. Their actions made sense, for Mexican federalism provided

"Texians"—as Americans in Texas referred to themselves—with, in Austin's words, "Freedom, Happiness, and Prosperity."[9]

This tranquility began to wane in the early 1830s, however, as Mexican officials became increasingly concerned about the preponderance of American migrants, but it was only in 1835 that real conflict began. That year, centralists overthrew federalists in Mexico City (in Mexico, what were termed "federalists" were ironically more akin to U.S. Antifederalists) and implemented a constitution that stripped power from all states and territories. Texas, along with several other regions, revolted. The efforts of longtime residents like Austin were at first halting and tentative, as they sought to restore the old Mexican constitution, not establish independence or join the United States. Yet this was not the case for the thousands of Americans who crossed the border to join the so-called Texas Revolution (a very Texas-centric term that slightly overstates the revolutionary aspects of the conflict). These men felt no loyalty toward the old Mexican constitution. Soon their faction gained control of the revolution's course, and quickly declared Texas an independent republic in 1835—in language that mimicked 1776. They experienced setbacks, some legendary, such as the famous last stand at the Alamo. The following year, a Texas army led by Sam Houston defeated an invading Mexican army at the Battle of San Jacinto, capturing Mexican president Antonia Lopéz de Santa Anna in the process. With victory at hand, the fledgling Texas government requested annexation from the United States.

Yet the United States rejected Texas as a suitor. President Martin Van Buren was concerned that adding slaveholding Texas would upset the United States' precarious balance between free and slave states, which would destroy the delicate alliance between Northern and Southern Democrats that held the party together. He was also uncomfortable with so easily shredding a peace treaty the United States had signed with Mexico. In Texas, U.S. rejection immediately activated the sentiment, long dormant, that Americans had every right to declare independence, wherever and whenever they could. After Sam Houston served a short term as Texas president, Texans elected Mirabeau Lamar, a migrant from Georgia who rejected U.S. annexation and embraced Texas independence.

But why did he reject annexation? Because, for Lamar and an increasing number of Texans, it was their *new* republic, not the United States, that could reopen some of the possibilities of the American Revolution that had long seemed foreclosed in the United States itself. Lamar made this abundantly clear in his inaugural address, in which he held up the "perfect" Texas Constitution next to its flawed predecessor the U.S. Constitution, which Lamar disparaged as having many "serious and alarming errors." The United States was riven by partisanship, but Texas had "union amongst the people," and, channeling George Washington, Lamar warned Texas to avoid "factious dissensions." The United States was beset by class conflict, but in Texas Lamar promised "equality of taxation, bur[d]ening none of the branches of industry for the benefit of others." In the United States, a very distant federal government imposed unjust laws that the people did not want, but Texas would have no "Governors and judges and excise men appointed from abroad to administer laws." (Notice the reference to "excise men," alluding at least loosely to the Whiskey Excise.) For all these reasons, Lamar maintained, Texas was better off independent. Indeed, he believed that Texas, not the United States, would soon take possession of lands all the way to the Pacific. If the country did join the United States, it would be "disastrous to our liberty and hopes."[10]

Not all of Lamar's visions hold up so well. He also obliquely referenced two other promises of the American Revolution in his speech that were far darker. These were promises that were explicitly for the benefit of white people: First, he believed in the total expulsion of Native peoples from Texas, by any means necessary. Here, he attacked his predecessor Sam Houston's sincere but futile attempts to ensure lasting peace between Texans and Indians. He also promised that, in Texas, slavery would be forever protected—unlike in the United States, where it was increasingly being challenged. Protections for slavery in the U.S. Constitution were, in Lamar's words, "feeble and inefficient."[11] These words appear in a draft for his speech that he later abandoned, almost certainly because Lamar realized that an explicitly proslavery stance was not helpful for securing diplomatic recognition from antislavery Great Britain.

The obvious retort to Lamar's vision, both then and now, was that, quite simply, his assessment of Texas was a near-total lie. In 1839, the Republic of Texas was a mess. Its economy was in shambles, its treasury was bankrupt, its army was nonexistent, and Mexico planned to reconquer it—and certainly had the means to do so, if its domestic politics could be resolved. But Lamar and his allies who embarked on Texas independence had an obvious counter: Was not the early United States just as much of a mess? It, too, had been bankrupt, divided, disorganized, and weak, but it was now a very real (albeit not particularly powerful) geopolitical player in the Western Hemisphere. Once again, the legacy of the American Revolution loomed large. Furthermore, just as the United States continued to be buttressed by immigrants from Europe, Texas was buttressed by immigrants from the United States. As Lamar spoke, the United States was suffering its second major depression, the Panic of 1837. Just as Americans had swarmed into Mexican Texas in the early 1820s, they were swarming in again, but this time in even greater numbers. In 1836, the republic's population was 40,000. Eight years later, it was 125,000.[12]

By 1844, eight years of Texas independence, even though they were often disastrous, reverberated throughout the rest of the American West. Texas mattered particularly in the two other regions where Americans could be found in substantial numbers: California and Oregon. California was claimed by Mexico, but the country's actual control of the vast region was spotty. Roughly 5,500 "Californios" lived along the coast, alongside a handful of New England and British merchants who had come to trade and decided to stay. Californios were migrants of Spanish descent who arrived in the eighteenth century and claimed vast tracts of land, which first coexisted with and eventually supplanted the extensive series of missions first built by Catholic missionaries. The interior, however, was under the control of roughly a quarter million Indigenous people, broken up into dozens and dozens of small native nations.

With California such a long journey from Mexico City, Californios were generally on their own. From an economic standpoint, they owned vast estates worked by Native laborers, many of whom were treated little better than enslaved people. From a political standpoint, they generally ran California as an autonomous territory, for Mexico had neither the means nor desire to establish a permanent foothold. By the early 1840s, small numbers of Americans began to arrive overland from Missouri, having learned of California from recently published travelogues. At first mostly single young men, these migrants settled in the Sacramento Valley, which was under the unofficial oversight of John Sutter. Sutter—originally Johann Sutter—was a Swiss migrant who had established a commanding fort in the valley. Sutter was talented and ambitious—but also egomaniacal and ruthless. His fort was the entrepôt for the Indian slave trade in the region, and he was the most prominent enslaver.[13]

North of California lay "Oregon Country," which referred to the huge swath of territory in the Pacific Northwest that today encompasses the U.S. states of Oregon, Washington, and Idaho, as well as the Canadian province of British Columbia. At the time, the region was under the "joint occupation" of Great Britain and the United States. The treaty the two countries had signed in 1818 essentially was an agreement to let the passage of time sort out the region's ultimate future. In 1842, Oregon Country was largely under Indigenous control, with one crucial exception: the fertile Willamette Valley that runs 150 miles north to south from what is present-day Portland to Eugene. There, two groups coexisted—a bit precariously—alongside each other, one of them comprising the employees of the Hudson's Bay Company (HBC), a massive British fur outfit that bestrode most of British North America. In Oregon, the HBC was managed by a domineering Scot named John McLoughlin, and most of its employees were French Canadians. The HBC's arrival was what depopulated the Willamette Valley of Native peoples, not because of violence—the HBC wanted to partner with Native peoples to expand the fur trade, not kill them—but because its employees brought disease, which decimated the valley's Indigenous population in 1831. They were soon joined by Protestant missionaries from the United States, who began traveling to Oregon in 1834 to convert Native peoples.[14] McLoughlin was not thrilled by their arrival, but he let them stay.

In 1839, a missionary in Oregon named Jason Lee returned to the United States, and his tales of Oregon began awakening Americans to the economic potential of the region. Land in the Willamette Valley was reportedly both fertile and available. Missouri senator Lewis Linn churned up further enthusiasm by urging Congress to pass a law that gave all migrants to Oregon 640 acres for free if they made the journey. The law was never passed—and, indeed, the United States had no right to pass it because Oregon was shared with the British—but it still helped get the word out about Oregon's potential. This news coincided with the effects of the Panic of 1837 that threw thousands of Americans into debt and thousands more off their land. "Oregon Fever," as it was called, soon took hold throughout the western states, as hundreds and eventually thousands of migrants left U.S. borders and set out for Oregon. Unlike the young men traveling to lesser-known California, Oregon migrants were largely made up of nuclear families, and their numbers were consistently larger than those traveling to California. In many ways, Oregon in the early 1840s acted as a Northern counterpart to Texas in the 1820s—but with one crucial difference. Most Oregon migrants rejected slavery, and indeed chose Oregon *because* it was supposedly "free soil." Free soil, however, did not mean Oregon pioneers believed in racial equality. Like the Whiskey Rebels decades before, they believed slavery hurt poor *white* men, because the institution allowed plantation owners to continuously expand their holdings at the expense of white yeomen farmers, who simply could not compete with slave labor's economy of scale. Once in Oregon they would make moves to explicitly prohibit all black migrants.

The Republic of Texas. Mexican California. Oregon Country. All three existed outside U.S. borders, but all three were places where Americans increasingly lived. The question was: How would this American presence affect local, national, and regional politics? The answer may be surprising.

The Continental Dreams of Lansford Hastings

Lansford Warren Hastings was born in 1819 in central Ohio. He could trace his roots back all the way back to Thomas Hastings, one of the early leaders of the Massachusetts Bay Colony. Little is known of Hastings's early life, other than that he was trained as a lawyer, meaning his parents had some, but likely not substantial, means. Clearly, however, he did not see a future for himself as a lawyer in Ohio, because, in 1842, he made the fateful decision to join a company of mostly Missourians bound for Oregon.[15]

This journey, which came in the very early years of the establishment of the Oregon Trail, was extremely difficult and uncertain, and it would become the most formative moment in the twenty-three-year-old Hastings's life. It began in early May in Independence, Missouri, the typical jumping-off point for most overland parties, with 114 people (although Hastings later claimed it was 160), half of whom were adult men. This was the largest group to undertake the journey to Oregon thus far.

During the first several days of the journey, Hastings recalled that everyone was in "high glee," but this feeling quickly dissipated. The problem, Hastings later recorded, was that every man began exhibiting the "'American Character.' . . . All appeared to be determined to govern, not to be governed." Thoroughly representative of Jacksonian America, the company soon decided to put all decisions to a vote. Direct democracy, however, caused its own problems when a slight majority voted for the "immediate and indiscriminate extermination" of every dog accompanying the party. The feeling among non-dog owners was that no dog could possibly make it to Oregon, and barking would give away the presence of the camp to hostile Indians. (This fear was constant on the trail, but in fact Native attacks on overland parties almost never happened.) Dog owners pushed back, and nearly revolted after the first several dogs were slain. Hastings laconically concluded this story, "This was our first and last effort at legislation."[16]

Clearly, the overland party needed *someone* to make decisions. Direct democracy was unfeasible, but representative democracy, American style, would do just fine. Once again, the men put this to a vote—and elected Lansford Hastings to take charge of what he later described as "our infant *republic*."[17] Why, exactly, they chose Hastings is uncertain. He was young and had no experience (as far as we know) with traveling across half a continent and all the massive difficulties that entailed. Throughout the rest of his life, however, Hastings would exhibit relentless energy, immense ambition, and clearly some sort of charisma that would lead people to follow him again and again, even after the failures of many of his schemes and dreams, and even though he does not seem to be a particularly likable figure, both at the time and in hindsight. Something about Hastings made people trust him. Something about him was captivating.

After nearly six months, Hastings's party arrived in Oregon without any major disasters, which was no small feat. Once in Oregon, most pioneers found places to shelter for the winter, after which point they would stake out new land claims. Hastings did no such thing. Instead, he provided legal services to HBC chief factor John McLoughlin, who was in a land dispute with some Oregon missionaries. This decision was revealing, demonstrating that Hastings had hitched himself to a man regarded by American pioneers as a threat, a man who embodied British power in the region and was seen as the chief obstacle to total American control of the Willamette Valley. Yet Hastings clearly admired McLoughlin's power and influence and saw him as a potential ally.

But an ally for what, exactly? Hastings likely made this clear at what are known in Oregon lore as the "Champoeg Meetings." In March 1843, Oregon residents, both Americans and the French Canadian employees of the HBC, met at the small village of Champoeg to discuss what to do about a series of wolf attacks on livestock. Soon, however, the talk turned to governance. How should this conglomerate of farmers, traders, and missionaries govern themselves? The sources are exceedingly murky: No minutes have survived, nearly all accounts were written decades later, and the village itself was washed away in a flood in 1861. Yet it seems clear that the hundred-odd attendees (all men) divided into two camps: One side wanted to create a token government that could manage things "until such time as the United States of America extend their jurisdiction over us."[18] The other side, which included Hastings, wanted no part of eventual U.S. annexation. They wanted to declare independence.[19]

Hastings believed that now was the time to establish an independent republic, before the United States had a chance to gain a foothold. This was extremely ambitious, perhaps even foolhardy, but not entirely illogical. After all, Americans would keep coming to Oregon, and they would depend on the Oregon government to provide them with free land. The United States, meanwhile, still had no official jurisdiction over the distant region. By doling out land to migrants, the Oregon government would gain the loyalty and buy-in of increasing numbers of people. Perhaps Hastings even saw John McLoughlin as an ally in such an endeavor. As a British agent, he definitively opposed U.S. annexation, but McLoughlin had largely been on his own for more than a decade, governing independently, even if not actually politically independent. Oregon was his home, and the British government seemed relatively uninterested in the local politics of the region. Why not use his local influence to push for total independence?

Yet a majority clearly felt different from Hastings. Ultimately, the pro-annexation, weak-government side won by two votes. The main reason was clear: Despite increased American immigration, the British, through the HBC, still had a major presence in the region, and the only way to counter one powerful—and rival—country was by attaching to another. American migrants, as Americans, were naturally wary of the British and looked to the United States to ease their anxieties.

After Champoeg, Hastings was done with Oregon. To him, Oregon pioneers were simply too moderate. They wanted land and economic opportunity, not independence. They had no desire to create a new nation. So he set off south, for Mexican California, alongside about fifty other people dissatisfied with their prospects in Oregon. Once again, he was chosen as trail leader.

What he found in California was much more to his liking. The American population in California was smaller and more ambitious, largely composed of risk-taking young men who Hastings believed would further his dreams of an independent republic. But more men were needed if they were going to declare California's independence from Mexico. Hastings estimated that he would need "15 to 20 thousand" to make his dreams a reality.

To induce emigration, Hastings returned to the United States and published *The Emigrants' Guide to Oregon and California* in 1845, which ostensibly sought to provide American migrants with routes, landmarks, and general advice for making the difficult journey west. At the same time, it was a form of California boosterism. In California, Hastings predicted, there would be "a Boston, a New York, a Philadelphia and a Baltimore growing up in a day," creating a land of "genuine *republicanism* and unsophisticated *democracy*."[20] The rhetoric worked. The year after Hastings published the *Emigrants' Guide*, roughly 1,500 Americans left for California, a sixfold increase from the year before, and the first year more traveled to California than Oregon.[21]

The guidebook was coy about Hastings's ambitious political plans. California was officially part of Mexico, after all. Yet the scattered evidence reveals that Hastings had made his goal clear to many, urging them to be ready for the arrival of more migrants—and a declaration of independence. One American in California predicted what would happen with Hastings's return: "The 'Republic of California' shall arise. Neither Europe nor the United States are prepared for that event."[22]

But there was another group of Americans who not only desired political independence but required it for their own safety. In 1844, the Mormons, too, looked west.

The Continental Dreams of Lyman Wight

Lyman Wight was born in 1796 in upstate New York. By 1844, he had already lived an eventful life. He had fought in the War of 1812, afterward supported himself as a farmer, married a woman named Harriet Benton in 1823, and together they moved to Cuyahoga County, Ohio, to what is today the suburbs of Cleveland. In 1829, he joined the congregation of Sidney Rigdon, an ex-Baptist minister who oversaw a communitarian, self-contained, "common-stock" church, in which all possessions were shared equally. Rigdon and Wight soon met Joseph Smith Jr., who had founded the Church of Christ in 1830, which would eventually become the Church of Jesus Christ of Latter-day Saints. In 1830, Smith published the Book of Mormon, which he and his followers claimed was an authentic revelation from God. Set in North America, the Book of Mormon describes Jesus's appearance in the Americas after his resurrection and the subsequent history of the Native people of the continent. Rigdon's entire community, including Lyman and Harriet, quickly converted to the LDS Church.

From the outset, Americans attacked the Mormons, both rhetorically and—with an increasing frequency—violently. Why Mormonism, in particular, was the target of such viciousness is the subject of a long debate among historians. After all, the LDS Church was just one of many denominations founded during the Second Great Awakening that confounded and disturbed more mainstream Americans. One assumed reason is the Mormons' embrace of what they called "plural marriage," and what other Americans attacked as polygamy. Yet Smith did not promulgate plural marriage until 1843, and it was not until the 1850s that a majority of the American public learned of the practice.

Instead, the problem was the LDS Church's continued and explicit embrace of politics. Most of the Second Great Awakening's more radical religious movements, such as the Shakers, Owenites, and Rappites, sought to remove congregants from the wider world to fulfill communitarian and utopian visions. To mainstream Americans, these beliefs were *strange*, but they were usually not *threatening*. By contrast, the Latter-day Saints refused to withdraw from the world. Instead, they sent missionaries out to convert—and ally with—Native people, based upon the teachings of the Book of Mormon. They often voted as a bloc, ensuring that they, with thousands of converts, became political players in whatever state they lived. They sought to found Zion, a gathering place for all Mormons that would eventually become a major geopolitical player on the world stage. In proslavery Missouri, they were even accused of being abolitionists—although this final accusation was not quite true. And so, wherever the Mormons went, they met unrelenting hostility.

Lyman Wight soon became one of the religion's fiercest defenders. He was charismatic, inspirational, and clearly a talented leader of men. He also became a trusted confidant of Joseph Smith personally, who called Wight "the Wild Ram of the Mountains." Tasked with preparing a gathering place for all Latter-day Saints in Jackson County, Missouri, Wight quickly emerged as the commander of the Mormon militia, known as the Danites. As conflict escalated between the Latter-day Saints and Missourians, which became known as the "Mormon War," Wight inspired Mormon forces with magnetic speeches. According to one militia member, Wight declared that the Mormons "would fight, and they would die upon the ground, and they would not give up their rights."[23] Eventually, Missourians ramped up attacks on the outnumbered Mormons, most infamously at Haun's Mill, where they murdered eighteen Mormon men and boys. The day after, Missouri officials arrested Smith, Wight, Rigdon, and several other Mormon leaders, accusing them of treason. Wight entered Latter-day Saint lore when he was asked to testify against Smith in exchange for his life, at which point he responded, "Shoot and be damned."[24] Eventually, the men all escaped, most likely with the help of some sympathetic guards. Afterward, Smith petitioned the federal government for redress. President Martin Van Buren, citing states' rights, said that nothing could be done.

The Latter-day Saints fled Missouri for Illinois, where they founded the city of Nauvoo, which Smith imagined as the new Zion. Wight's ascent continued when Smith appointed him a member of the Quorum of the Twelve in 1841, one of the most important leadership bodies of the church (it would eventually become the single most important body). At some point Smith revealed to Wight the doctrine of plural marriage, which Wight seems to have easily embraced. By all accounts, he was intensely patriarchal, and reportedly he openly criticized women who had trouble accepting polygamy. Eventually, he would have four wives.[25]

As Nauvoo grew, it needed lumber, so Smith tasked Wight with overseeing a Mormon logging operation in northern Wisconsin. In Wisconsin, Wight successfully built a community of several dozen Mormon families. Meanwhile, Nauvoo rapidly grew, becoming the second largest city in the state—but its size and influence, alongside Joseph Smith's growing political power, provoked fierce backlash from Nauvoo's non-Mormon neighbors. By early 1844, another Mormon War seemed imminent.

When Wight learned of this, he and several other leaders of the community wrote Joseph Smith with an idea. They recently had discussions with several local Native peoples—the Ho-Chunks, Ojibwes, and Menominees—who expressed frustration with American encroachments on their land, and thought about moving to the southwest. Asked Wight, could not the Mormons also move to the southwest, to "the table lands of Texas"? There they could convert Native peoples to Mormonism—a key part of LDS theology—and make their settlement a "gathering place for all the south."[26]

The letter clearly made an impression on Smith. After receiving it, he formed the Council of Fifty, a secretive body explicitly designed to further the Mormons' real-world political—as opposed to spiritual—goals. Although Lyman Wight was still in Wisconsin, Smith made him a part of the Council of Fifty, as he did with most of those already serving on the Quorum of the Twelve. In its early months of existence, the council formulated two plans simultaneously. First, it initiated a campaign to elect Joseph Smith as the U.S. president the 1844 election, perhaps hoping that he could take away enough votes from the Whig and Democratic candidates to play kingmaker (as Henry Clay had done in 1824). At the same time, the council hedged by planning a migration beyond U.S. borders, in case Smith's campaign failed. Either the Latter-day Saints would gain power in the United States—or outside of it. When it came to the latter plan, it is clear from these Council of Fifty meetings that its members quickly realized just how wide open North American geopolitics really were. Texas was one option—but there was talk about leaving for Oregon or California, trying to convert Native peoples to Mormonism in U.S. Indian Territory, or even guarding the Oregon Trail for overland migrants, presumably in exchange for some political favors from Washington.[27]

To further Mormon ambitions in Texas, Smith sent Council of Fifty member Lucien Woodworth to the young republic to negotiate with President Sam Houston. Houston believed there was no way annexation could make it through a divided U.S. Congress and, with Mexico hoping to reconquer Texas, welcomed the Mormons as "armed emigrants" who could help guard the Texas-Mexico border.[28] It seems Houston had little knowledge of LDS doctrine, for he requested, in Woodworth's words, "books on our religion," and therefore perhaps he did not calculate how Texas citizens themselves would receive the Mormons.[29] This issue, however, could be sorted out down the road. Meanwhile, the Council of Fifty got down to business trying to write a future constitution for their planned—in their words—"theo-democracy."

Woodworth's diplomatic mission—for that is what it really was—was the beginning of Mormon leaders' four-year quest to leave U.S. borders and establish an autonomous or fully independent country. Wherever Zion would be located, they believed it should exist alongside other world governments as an independent country. Through it, Smith and other leaders believed, the Mormons would convert more and more people, thereby laying the groundwork for the coming millennium, during which Jesus Christ would return to earth.

The Mormons and other American migrants shared one crucial belief: The United States had fallen away from the promises of the American Revolution. Joseph Smith's presidential platform listed all that had gone wrong in recent years, including the Nullification Crisis in South Carolina, the Dorr War in Rhode Island, and of course the Mormon expulsion from Missouri, along with general "hard times and distress" and "a thousand other difficulties." Lamented Smith, "The glory of American liberty is on the wane."[30]

Lyman Wight arrived in Nauvoo on the first of May, 1844, and immediately he took his place in the Council of Fifty, only a day before Lucien Woodworth returned from Texas to share with the council the results of his meeting with Sam Houston. Smith then made it clear that Wight should return home to prepare his community in Wisconsin for a migration to Texas. According to Wight's recollection, Smith told Wight that Wight would be the Mormon Moses, leading "the armys of Israel to Zion . . . out of Egypt."[31] It was the last time Wight would see Joseph Smith alive.

The Continental Dreams of James K. Polk

Formerly a congressman from Tennessee and two-time Speaker of the House, "Young Hickory," as James K. Polk was nicknamed (recall that Jackson was "Old Hickory"), had just lost his state's gubernatorial election twice in a row, and he appeared to be facing the end of his political career. A dour, humorless workaholic, Polk remains one of the least interesting personalities to ever win the presidency, but in the fall of 1844 he and his allies found—indeed, created—a winning political issue. They grafted Texas together with Oregon, calling for the "reoccupation" of Oregon (because American fur traders had lived there in the 1810s) and the "reannexation" of Texas (because they claimed Texas had once been a part of the United States, before the 1819 Adams-Onis Treaty with Spain). From sheerly an immediate political perspective, it was a brilliant move, for it called for the addition of both slave *and* free territory, thereby allowing Northern Democrats to get behind Texas annexation without appearing proslavery. In reality, few Northern Democrats (nor most national politicians in general) really cared all that much for annexing Oregon, at least immediately.[32] To them, Oregon mattered because it alleviated their interparty squabbles, not because they believed it was a vital piece of land for the United States to acquire.

At the Democratic Convention, Polk defeated former president Martin Van Buren to become the party nominee, and then he very narrowly defeated Henry Clay to win the 1844 presidential election. Elections have consequences, and Polk's election in particular reverberated across the North American continent. First, in the Democrats' view it was a mandate for Texas annexation—even though they still could not muster two-thirds in the Senate. Instead, with the lame duck John Tyler giving assent and Polk supervising things behind the scenes, Democrats in Congress approved Texas annexation via a joint resolution, which required only a simple majority. The measure was constitutionally dubious, but this political hardball nevertheless worked.

Once Polk became president, he demanded Great Britain cede all of Oregon Country (the famous slogan, citing the uppermost line of latitude, was "54°40' or Fight"), but he eventually backed down and settled on the current border between Washington and British Columbia. Even more consequentially and infamously, he provoked Mexico into a war by sending the U.S. Army into a region claimed by both Mexico and Texas. Although eventual U.S. victory was much more difficult and messier than is often assumed, the Treaty of Guadalupe Hidalgo that ended the war nevertheless gave the United States nearly half of Mexico's territory, including California and most of today's U.S. Southwest.

These consequential international events are well known, often grouped under the label "Manifest Destiny," a phrase coined by journalist John L. O'Sullivan in the pages of the *Democratic Review* in the summer of 1845. What historians treat as "destiny" in hindsight, however, was in fact anything but, for O'Sullivan was writing to persuade a very closely divided American public to support U.S. "expansion"—a euphemism akin to "removal" that obscured what was actually military conquest. Furthermore, these events were hardly preordained, with the supposedly prescient O'Sullivan predicting that Canada and California would join the United States "in the fast hastening year of the Lord 1945!"[33] Polk himself certainly knew that U.S. expansion would be a close-run thing, which explains his haste and aggression.

Yet Polk is responsible for one crucial, often unknown addition to the traditional story of U.S. expansion and Manifest Destiny. Publicly, Polk, like all presidents before him, supported Americans' right to found new nations on the continent. At his inauguration, for example, he asserted, "The people of this continent alone have the right to decide their own destiny."[34] And why shouldn't they have this right? It was a bedrock American principle, rooted in the American Revolution itself. Privately, however, he found the prospect of Americans declaring independence abhorrent, for two reasons: First, American migrants—who, legally, were expatriates—simply could not be trusted. Newspapers reported them to be shiftless ne'er-do-wells, "contemptible citizens," "restless citizens," and some—notably the Mormons—were "bitterly hostile" to the United States.[35]

Second, to Polk, Americans declaring independence outside U.S. borders robbed the United States of its negotiating power. This is exactly what happened during the negotiations with Texas, for it was Texas officials who were able to make demands on the United States: It would enter the United States as a state (thereby bypassing territorial "colonial" government, which Americans hated), and it would retain control of its public lands. Even under these generous terms, Polk's men on the ground in Texas informed him that Texas officials still did not want their "importance to be diminished," as they went from running a country to running a U.S. state.[36] In the end, most Texas citizens desired U.S. annexation, and Texan politicians decided not to buck their wishes.

A few years later, after Oregon was annexed, California conquered, and Mexico largely defeated, Polk could be more honest. No "inhabitants or foreigners," he declared—and Americans were of course inhabitants of the continent—could found "an independent revolutionary government" in North America. "Such a government," Polk continued, "would be too feeble to long maintain its separate independent existence, and would finally become annexed to or be a dependent colony of some powerful state."[37] Read from one perspective, these lines held up the tenets of the Monroe Doctrine to argue that foreign powers would interfere in newly established western republics. Read from another perspective, however, these lines clearly denied Americans the right to found new nations on the continent. Left unsaid was a profound irony: The "powerful state" annexing these "independent governments" was the United States itself.

Dreams Diminished

In the summer of 1844, neither Lansford Hastings nor Lyman Wight knew just what shape U.S. politics and continental geopolitics would take, so they continued to lay the groundwork for, respectively, establishing a republic of California and an autonomous Mormon settlement in the Texas borderlands. Both, however, were overtaken by international events and, also unexpectedly for both men, the loss of prestige in their local communities.

Hastings dreamed of founding a California republic under the auspices of American migrants. For all its seeming improbability (there were only a few hundred Americans in the Sacramento Valley), it actually happened. The moment was the famous Bear Flag Revolt that began in June 1846, when thirty-three Americans in the Sacramento Valley, having heard rumors that Californio leaders would expel them from the region, seized the sleepy village of Sonoma and proclaimed the "Bear Flag Republic." The rumors they heard emanated from escalating tensions between Californios and American settlers more generally, and these escalating tensions were entirely the result of U.S. actions. By 1846, two U.S. officials had made their way to California, albeit through very different means. The first, John C. Frémont, had crossed the continent with his exploring party, the U.S. Army Corps of Topographical Engineers. The other, Lieutenant Archibald Gillespie, arrived by ship. He was, according to Polk's diary, on a "secret mission."[38] The mission was almost certainly to be Polk's man in California, and Polk tasked him with trying his best to incorporate the distant Mexican territory into the American Union as fast and effectively as possible.

The Bear Flag Republic lasted less than a month (and never controlled much territory), for in early July the Bear Flaggers learned from a U.S. naval squadron that the United States and Mexico were at war, so they folded their very local struggle into the larger international conflict. Even so, in that short time the Bear Flaggers still behaved as typical Americans: They officially declared their independence and stated the reasons why their declaration was justified. Written by Vermont migrant William Ide, the Bear Flag declaration reads like someone tried to play the hits of the Declaration of Independence without having a copy in front of them or having read it in years—which, probably, was exactly what happened. "A Government to be prosperous and happyfying in its tendency must originate with its people who are friendly to its existence," the proclamation declared.[39] Ide was no Jefferson, but he was trying his best.

Few Bear Flaggers expressed regret at the rapid extinction of their republic. It was much easier to conquer California with U.S. support than without it. William Ide, however, did express some bitterness, attacking the United States for not negotiating with the Bear Flaggers as officials of a sovereign country. He desired "union with the land of our birth," achieved "honorably" and through "freedom of choice," but instead U.S. officials simply took control.[40]

Hastings, perhaps, would have wholeheartedly agreed with Ide, but he was not around to witness the raising or lowering of the Bear Flag. He was furthering his plan to bring thousands more emigrants to California, which would bolster his plans for independence. Now this independence had occurred much earlier than he had ever planned. By the time he arrived in California as part of another overland group, the United States was at war with Mexico, and the Bear Flag Republic was already defunct. It seems Hastings tried to make the best of things by enlisting in the California Battalion, a U.S. force composed of Americans who lived in California at the outbreak of war. For the next year, they fought the Californios for control of the huge territory. Although U.S. forces did suffer setbacks at the hands of a highly mobile and effective Californio cavalry, there were simply not enough Californios to win the war, and for its part Mexico never was able to send any additional forces. By 1847 it was clear that California had been conquered by the United States. The dream of a California republic was over.

While the Bear Flag Republic became a quaint local-interest story for most Americans in California, Lansford Hastings never gave up his dreams of an independent republic. Although the changing geopolitical situation was his main obstacle, it was not the only one. During the winter of 1846–47, the Donner Party, as it became known, tried to make the journey from Missouri to California, and it followed a new, supposedly shorter route that Hastings suggested in his guide. The party eventually became stranded in the Sierra Nevada, and nearly half of the party died while the rest resorted to cannibalism to survive. Hastings was blamed—perhaps somewhat unfairly, for although the route was not as easy as he portrayed, he personally had led a group of migrants on his route earlier in the year.

For a few years, Hastings still tried to make a name for himself in California. He married the daughter of a U.S. diplomat, and together they had three children, but circumstantial evidence points to him abandoning his family to partake in the California Gold Rush. Yet his culpability for the Donner Party followed him everywhere, and eventually his reputation in California was in tatters. Perhaps abandoning his family for good, Hastings moved to the town of Yuma in Arizona Territory, where he contacted the Latter-day Saints to create an independent government on the Colorado River. Superficially, this made some sense, for the Mormons still sought significant political autonomy within U.S. borders—but there is no reason why they would put their faith in someone like Hastings, a non-Mormon and a perceived ne'er-do-well. LDS leaders never responded. In 1862, he contacted Confederate president Jefferson Davis, proposing that he seize the Southwest for the Confederacy, a scheme that also went nowhere. Then, after the Civil War ended, he organized groups of Confederate slaveholders to migrate to Brazil where they could maintain their slaveholding, writing *The Emigrants' Guide to Brazil* to spur even more migration. Here, he did have some success, creating the most viable of all colonies of Confederados, as these slaveholding migrants in Brazil became known. Hastings died of yellow fever in 1870 on the island of St. Thomas, where he had stopped on a return journey from Brazil to the United States.

There is little reason to mourn Hastings. He was an ambitious schemer and a consummate self-promoter who supported the conquest of Native land and the subjugation of Native peoples, and, as his turn to the Confederacy makes clear, the enslavement of black people. Lyman Wight cut a more authentically sympathetic figure. After Joseph Smith sent him north, conflict in and around Nauvoo escalated. Wary of Smith's growing power and disturbed by increasing rumors of polygamy, some Mormons turned on Smith, which eventually led to his arrest and confinement in the neighboring town of Carthage. There, on June 27, 1844, an anti-Mormon mob stormed the jail and murdered Smith in cold blood. He was only thirty-eight.

The Mormons had long been torn between their innate American patriotism and their mounting and understandable aversion to U.S. policies and leaders. Smith's murder eliminated this tension. After the murder, one Council of Fifty member called the United States a "damned wrotten thing—, full of lice, moth eaten, corrupt, and there is nothing but meanness about it." No one disagreed.[41] It took some time, but eventually Brigham Young, with the support of the Quorum of the Twelve, emerged as Smith's successor. Knowing that the Mormons would soon have to flee Nauvoo for good, Young and the Twelve started exploring destinations throughout the continent where the Mormons could, after almost two decades of persecution, build Zion without American interference.

But that destination would not be Texas, to Lyman Wight's everlasting lament. Texas annexation in late 1845, seemingly improbable in 1844, made sure of that. Wherever the Mormons went, it would not be within U.S. borders. Instead, Young and other LDS leaders eagerly read the exploration reports of John Frémont, and they eventually decided their best hope lay in the Salt Lake Valley, a remote, isolated region in far northern Mexico. There, Young believed, they could found an independent country, particularly as they converted the region's Native peoples to the LDS Church. Even though Young and Mormon leaders now despised the United States, their right to self-determination—and, just as importantly, their right to practice their religion freely—was still rooted in the promises of the American Revolution. The problem was, to the Latter-day Saints, the United States had irrevocably betrayed those promises.

Continental events, however, once again destroyed Mormon plans. By the time Salt Lake City had been founded, it was not Mexican but U.S. territory, thanks to the Treaty of Guadalupe Hidalgo. President Polk once again played a role in this story, even before the treaty was signed. When he learned that the Mormons were leaving U.S. borders in the midst of the United States waging war against Mexico, he grew concerned. Here was an armed, united, and motivated group of people who were hostile to U.S. expansion, moving across the U.S.-Mexico border while the two countries were at war. His concern was valid, for at the time the Mormons were pulling for a Mexican victory, and one Mormon leader even contemplated joining with Mexico against the United States.[42] LDS leader Jesse Little made the threat explicit, writing Polk that the Mormons would not ally with another country "unless our government . . . will not help us, and compel us to be foreigners."[43] Polk got the not-so-subtle hint, writing in his diary that he needed to "conciliate" the Mormons to "prevent this singular sect from becoming hostile to the US."[44] A series of negotiations produced a truce: The United States would not interfere with Mormon emigration, and in return the Latter-day Saints would raise a battalion to fight for the United States. As he did with his emissaries in California, Polk's negotiations ensured that Americans who planned to form their own country would in fact be bound to U.S. interests.

Even as Brigham Young and Mormon leaders organized a trek of thousands to the Salt Lake Valley, Lyman Wight refused to give up on Joseph Smith's original Texas plans. Texas no longer made sense politically but, to Wight, it still made sense religiously and personally. Not only had Joseph Smith been Wight's spiritual leader, but he had been Wight's personal friend, and to the day he died he believed that the Mormons should follow Smith's original Texas plans. He had long distrusted most other Mormon leaders besides Smith, and the feeling was mutual. For their part, Mormon leaders like Brigham Young believed Wight was hotheaded and stubborn, and they were concerned about Wight's increasing tendency to drink. (Wight's biographer believes that by this point Wight was a functional alcoholic.) Wight had become, quite simply, a problem. One Council of Fifty member remarked memorably that, after Wight left Nauvoo, the city "had a mighty puke and it is the bad stuff that is thrown up."[45]

Ultimately, Brigham Young decided that he would allow Wight to go to Texas with his community from Wisconsin, but anyone else who went "will be damned and go to destruction."[46] Presumably, Young hoped his acquiescence and Wight's initial journey would sate him enough that he and his followers would eventually return to the fold. Wight and about 150 others then journeyed to Texas, where Wight claimed they would find "a land which the Lord will bless to us and our posterity; where we can build the city in peace."[47] In Texas, they eventually founded the community of Zodiac in the Texas Hill Country, located a few miles from what is today the town of Fredericksburg.

As time went on, Young and the Quorum of the Twelve urged Wight to return and join the Mormon community in the Salt Lake Valley, but Wight refused. He was expelled from the Council of Fifty and the Quorum of the Twelve, and in 1848 he was excommunicated from the LDS Church altogether. He and his community persisted in Texas, and at times their small settlements even thrived, but by 1858 the "Wightites" wanted to reunite with another break-off branch of Mormonism, Joseph Smith's son's community in Missouri. Wight died on the journey to Missouri of an epileptic fit and was buried in Zodiac, while the rest of his followers scattered—many to Missouri as planned, a few to Utah. Zodiac became a ghost town. Almost nothing remains of the community other than a cemetery and a small historical marker.

The End of an Era

Unlike most Americans in the late 1840s, Lansford Hastings and Lyman Wight were unwilling to abandon their dreams of independence. Hastings's Confederado colony in Brazil and Wight's small settlement in Texas are curious, obscure holdovers of an era when U.S. expansion hardly appeared destined, and many Americans believed that they could found a new nation, just like their forefathers had in 1776. Unlike most Americans, neither Hastings nor Wight could move past that moment, even as their goals changed and diminished in the face of rapidly shifting U.S. and continental politics.

There are other holdovers. When Americans buy Bear Flag or Lone Star paraphernalia at California and Texas airports, respectively, they are inadvertently nodding back to that same era, as are the tourists who visit places like the Alamo in Texas, Sutter's Fort in California, and even the small replica of Champoeg village in Oregon. So too are LDS families who can trace their family roots back to the Mormon "exodus" to the Salt Lake

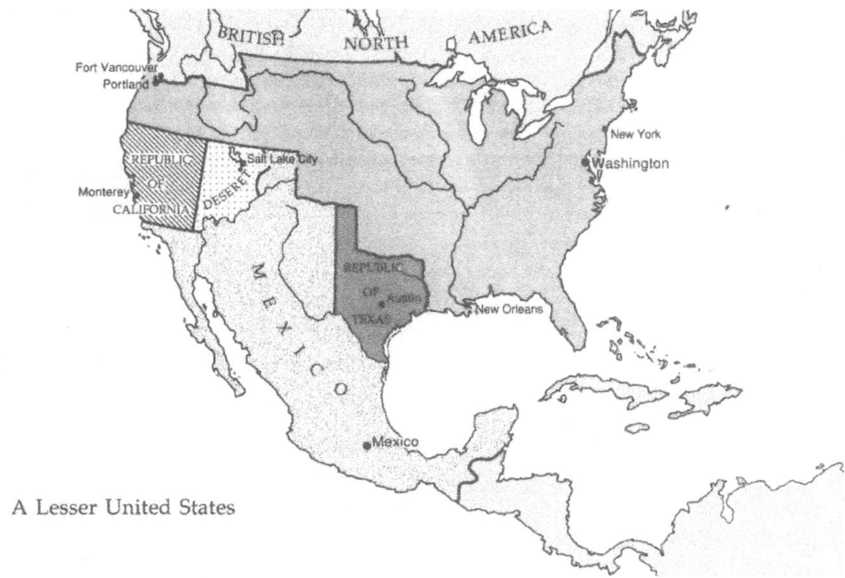

A Lesser United States

Valley in the mid-1840s. Indeed, nineteenth-century LDS history (and its continued resonance in the twentieth and twenty-first centuries) is certainly the most obvious legacy of this period, for unlike nearly all other Americans in the West, the Latter-day Saints kept dreaming of an independent, or at least entirely autonomous, settlement. This dream caused periodic conflicts with the United States, most famously in 1857 during the Utah War. Only in 1896, after LDS leaders agreed to give up polygamy, was Utah made a state. Until then, it was forced into "colonial" status as a U.S. territory governed by a federally appointed governor.

Of course, that airport paraphernalia disguises the fact that an independent California, Texas, and Mormon Deseret were all real possibilities in the early 1840s. In 1993, the renowned American geographer D.W. Meinig published his second (of four) massive tomes on the growth and shape of U.S. borders. In its pages, he imagined what a "lesser United States" would have looked like.[48] The map he drew imagines Mexico maintaining most of its northern territory, but the Republic of Texas, the Republic of California, and Mormon Deseret exist as independent countries. Farther north, U.S. territory reaches the Pacific in Oregon—which makes historical sense, for Oregon settlers were always the most supportive of U.S. annexation. However, the U.S. Pacific Northwest goes no farther north than today's Portland. The British, in Meinig's imagining, gained control of today's state of Washington. Meinig's map may be fictional, but it was a very real possibility in the years before Polk's election and the U.S.-Mexican war. There *were* Americans at the time who saw the United States as a failing country and wanted to found their own countries, and there were *plenty* of Americans in the United States—nearly the entire Whig Party—who were willing to let them. All that was needed was for Henry Clay to win the presidency in 1844 (or, for that matter, a stalemate with Mexico during the war, or a war with Britain—or a host of other contingent possibilities). A few more years without U.S. expansion could have changed everything. What would have happened if California was independent at the time of the 1849 Gold Rush? Would the thousands and thousands of American and foreign prospectors have simply granted the U.S. sovereignty over the rapidly growing republic? Would LDS leaders have backed down in the face of U.S. power if they were not in the middle of U.S. territory, but at its edge? These questions, of course, remain impossible to answer, and few Americans even bothered to ask them, such was the supposed inevitability of U.S. expansion.

But if these questions were not asked, one final question remained, a looming query that had emerged again and again since the time of the American Revolution. It was a question that would come to dominate the politics of the 1850s, and it would take the bloodiest conflict in American history to finally answer it: Could Americans found new nations out of pieces of official U.S. territory? In other words, *could they secede?*

9

Racial Equality, Part II: The Second American Revolution, 1869–77

On July 4, 1859, eighty-three years after the United States declared independence from Great Britain, only a few blocks north from where the Second Continental Congress met, Octavius Catto listened to an address that honored the momentous day. The keynote speaker was William Henry Johnson. A black man born free in Virginia in 1833, Johnson moved to Philadelphia at age twelve, later became a barber and moved to New York, and eventually returned to Philadelphia in 1855. In Philadelphia, he became involved with the Banneker Institute, an African American intellectual and literary society that catered to the city's black elite. There he met Catto, who counted himself among that elite. Catto's father, William, was a prominent Presbyterian minister in Philadelphia, as well as one of the Banneker Institute's founders. A year before Johnson's address, Catto graduated from the prestigious Institute of Colored Youth, after which he was elected the Banneker Institute's recording secretary and then hired as a teacher at his former school. He was only twenty, but he would soon become one of the city's leading black activists.

In 1852, in Rochester, the renowned abolitionist Frederick Douglass had marked the occasion in arguably his most famous speech. "What, to the American slave, is your Fourth of July?" Douglass asked. His answer was provocative: "To him, your celebration is a sham; your boasted liberty, an unholy license; your national greatness, swelling vanity . . . your shouts of liberty and equality, hollow mockery."[1] Seven years later, Johnson had little use for this kind of righteous anger. On the contrary, he was disturbed at the suggestion that abolitionists should repudiate the Fourth of July. "Is not the declaration true?" Johnson asked. "Are not all men born free and equal? Do they not inherit the right to life, liberty, and the pursuit of happiness? And, if this is so, why shall we burn such a declaration?"[2]

Johnson could have stopped there. Since 1776, countless Americans had held up the words of the Declaration of Independence and the general principles of the American Revolution to argue for their right to do . . . well, as we have seen, nearly everything. But Johnson did not just want to defend the Declaration as an idea; he wanted to defend the Revolutionary generation for its real-world actions. "Every proscribed American ought to celebrate [the Declaration]," argued Johnson. Why? "It is because it is true, and its authors meant just what they wrote and said, and *it is not their fault* if we do not enjoy our rights as they would have us do" (italics added).

Johnson took some liberties with his American history, to say the least. As we have seen, the Revolution was hardly an unambiguous antislavery moment. And yet, even if Johnson's interpretation of history was not exactly *true*, his words did contain a larger *truth*. For all its limitations, the Revolution really did spur antislavery thoughts and actions throughout much of the United States. It was thanks to the Revolution—in particular, black Americans' readiness to seize the possibilities of the revolutionary moment—that paved the way for emancipation throughout the North. By 1859, nearly a quarter million free blacks lived in the North, with another quarter million free blacks in the South. In most states outside Upper New England, racist laws deprived black people of many political and civil rights, including the right to vote. Yet black freedom still mattered—as Johnson himself understood. Acknowledging that Pennsylvania had disenfranchised black men in 1838, Johnson nevertheless argued, "We are not deprived of the power to meet and to speak; so far, thank God, we are free. We have our speech, and we will use it to the best advantage, and in doing so place ourselves in a proper position before the world."

According to his idiosyncratic autobiography published forty years later, William Henry Johnson would go on to have a colorful, event-filled life. A few months after his speech, Johnson volunteered to be in John Brown's planned slave insurrection at Harpers Ferry, but Brown rejected him because Johnson and his wife were expecting a child. Johnson then helped a fugitive slave flee slave catchers, for which he was subsequently jailed but somehow escaped, and then fled to New York. He fought in the Civil War, and in the following decades worked to advance civil rights for black New Yorkers, which culminated with New York governor Theodore Roosevelt signing a bill that barred all racial segregation in New York public schools in 1900.[3]

Johnson's life reflected the revolutionary changes wrought by the Civil War, sometimes referred to as the United States' "Second American Revolution" or "Second Founding." So too did the life of Octavius Catto, the twenty-year-old black teacher listening to Johnson on that Independence Day in Philadelphia. Catto's triumphs and failures would thoroughly represent the revolutionary changes of the next decade. Catto never wrote what he thought of Johnson's speech, but, considering he was one of the organizers of the event, he was certainly an ally. Indeed, judging by his later actions, Catto took Johnson's message to heart: The United States had been founded in a moment of revolutionary racial possibility—what historians deem the First Emancipation—but that moment was arrested and turned back in the Upper South and barely touched the Lower South. To realize a Second Emancipation, Catto would seek to create the conditions under which the First Emancipation had been achieved: Once again, black men would need to fight for a country and people that rejected their existence. As Johnson had said in his speech, during the American Revolution "the blood of the black man was spilled for his white brother." Catto understood that to achieve the revolution once again, black Americans would once again need to take up arms—this time, not to realize the freedom of white Americans, but to realize their own.

Unyielding Equilibrium

The United States was hardly the only country in the Americas to rely on racialized chattel slavery as both an economic and ideological system. On the contrary, at the time of the Revolution, slavery could be found in every single colony in the New World. Over the next century, nearly every one of these colonies and countries abolished slavery peacefully. However, many of them, particularly those that heavily relied on slavery—Brazil and Caribbean colonies in particular—refused to couple emancipation with substantial civil and political rights for freed people. Instead, they were placed under an apprentice system akin to indentured servitude, and even when it ended, black people were still treated as second-class citizens.

The one great exception to this trend was, of course, Haiti, where rebel slaves won both emancipation and independence from France in a brutal thirteen-year struggle at the end of the eighteenth century. Other massive slave rebellions erupted in the British Caribbean—Barbados in 1816, Demerara (modern-day Guyana) in 1823, and Jamaica in 1831—and these rebellions helped push Great Britain to become the first European empire to embrace abolition. The complicated internal dynamics and international politics of these rebellions, however, all boiled down to a simple struggle: enslaved versus enslaver, with both sides calling on the intervention of the distant British government.

Not so in the United States—in two ways. First, the Civil War was *about* slavery—but, for the first two years, it was not *between* enslaved and enslaver.[4] On the contrary: At first, Republican leaders like President Lincoln actively tried to prevent enslaved people from participating. Second, the United States did not just stop with the Thirteenth Amendment that ensured emancipation, but followed it with the Fourteenth and Fifteenth Amendments, which respectively guaranteed freed people's civil rights and freed*men*'s political rights. The Civil War's results, at least in the short term, were in every sense a second American Revolution.

From a long-term perspective, these results were thoroughly the product of the *first* American Revolution, for, as we have seen, the Revolution bequeathed what quickly turned out to be wholly incompatible legacies. In the South, the Revolution not only preserved slavery but further empowered slaveholders politically and economically, via the Three-Fifths Compromise and the expansion of slavery westward. In the North, meanwhile, the Revolution paved the way for emancipation via a combination of revolutionary rhetoric, black military service and black activism, individual manumissions, and gradual abolition laws. In the Upper South, and most prominently in Virginia, government officials tried to maintain both legacies at once, but after Gabriel's Rebellion, they realized the two could not go together. In the western, mountainous part of Virginia, where the enslaved population was far smaller, antislavery sentiments lingered much longer, and in the aftermath of Nat Turner's Rebellion in 1831, western Virginians (along with a few newly nervous eastern Virginians) proposed a gradual emancipation act and the colonization of the state's black population in Liberia. Yet, outnumbered by proslavery easterners, the proposal was voted down in the state's General Assembly. It marked the denouement of the Upper South's tepid antislavery trajectory.

For nearly the eighty years following the Revolution, the two sides of the slavery issue were decidedly unequal. Already economically and politically powerful in their own right, Southern slaveholders could also count on most non-slaveholding white Southerners and many white Northerners to support both slavery and white supremacy. Free blacks in the North, by contrast, were only 1 percent of the Northern population and counted few whites as allies, and in most Northern states outside Upper New England they witnessed the erosion of their civil and political rights. By the 1820s, most white Americans had all but abandoned ideas of racial equality, and they only believed in emancipation if it could be coupled with black colonization and a "return" to Africa—if possible, resettlement would be voluntary, and if not, it would happen by force. Black abolitionists (alongside a *very* small number of white allies, Quakers in particular) were now very much alone.

What they lacked in numbers and influence, however, they compensated with persistence. Historians have long been understandably fascinated with the small but impossible-to-ignore radical abolitionist movement of the Jacksonian era, whose members once were deemed dangerous fanatics but have more recently been seen as representing the very best of the long tradition of American radicalism. The conventional story used to begin with William Lloyd Garrison, the white abolitionist who launched his newspaper *The Liberator* in 1831 and founded the American Anti-Slavery Society two years later, but starting the story with Garrison ignores the years of black activism that preceded his emergence. After all, New York's *Freedom's Journal*, the first newspaper published by black Americans, preceded *The Liberator* by four years. The first Colored Convention, in which hundreds of black activists met to demand not only abolition but also political and civil rights, convened in Philadelphia in 1830, three years before the founding of the American Anti-Slavery Society.[5] It was these black abolitionists who birthed a new type of radical abolition, one that was based upon modern print culture, widespread activism, and a refusal to compromise.

Garrison's words in the first issue of *The Liberator* epitomize the uncompromising nature of the movement: "On [the subject of slavery], I do not wish to think, or speak, or write, with moderation. No! no! . . . I am in earnest—I will not equivocate—I will not excuse—I will not retreat a single inch—AND I WILL BE HEARD."[6] At least at first, being heard was what radical abolitionists did best. Through petitions to Congress, antislavery literature mailed into the South, meetings held in Northern cities and towns, and just general agitation, abolitionists could not be ignored—and thus quickly invited backlash. In response, Congress refused to hear antislavery petitions, Southerners refused to receive abolitionist mail, and, most dramatically and violently, anti-abolitionist mobs met abolitionists wherever they went—by one count, there were 175 such riots between 1834 and 1840 alone.[7] Even after such opposition, abolitionists were not dissuaded from their self-proclaimed mission.

For much of the 1830s and 1840s, Garrisonian abolition centered on "moral suasion"—meaning, the attempt to persuade Southerners to emancipate their slaves—and deliberately turned its back on explicit political engagement. Yet the abolitionist movement always intersected with politics, even when radicals like Garrison claimed otherwise. Whether a western territory would become a slave or free state could tip the balance of free and slave states in the U.S. government, while, thanks to the Three-Fifths Clause, every fugitive slave who escaped the South meant less power for slave states and more agitation for a new Fugitive Slave law from those same slave states. Long before most of their white allies, black Northerners understood this, and they acted politically far earlier than is often portrayed. As the historian Sarah Gronningsater has noted, black voting was not simply a "legal abstraction."[8] Wherever black men could vote, they did so, often in numbers significant enough that their support could sway an election. White politicians in most Northern states outside Upper New England responded by eliminating or curbing black suffrage. Many of these same states passed other anti-black laws that restricted black people's civil rights, such as prohibiting blacks from giving legal testimony in court.

None of these repressive measures ended black politics. Instead, black Northerners and their few white allies mobilized against these laws. After 1821 in New York, black men who wanted to vote were required to possess a significant amount of property (comparatively, *all* white men could vote). To get around this law, a wealthy white abolitionist gave away his money to ensure that at least five thousand black men were voting by 1850.[9] In Ohio, abolitionist third parties successfully pushed the state to repeal its anti-black laws. In Upper New England, by far the most racially egalitarian region of the Union, black men even held local political office, such as Wentworth Cheswell of Newmarket, New Hampshire, who was elected to a variety of positions, including justice of the peace from 1805 to his death in 1817.[10]

Alongside radical abolitionism and antislavery politics, the third crucial plank promoting black equality was the work by the enslaved themselves. They could neither vote nor speak publicly, but they could *act*. They could fight, or they could flee. In 1831, the slave minister Nat Turner chose to fight, but his rebellion in southern Virginia never got close to threatening the slave regime. After Turner was caught and executed, slaves seemed to realize that, without powerful allies (as the black rebels in Haiti had, thanks to French revolutionaries' need to fight a world war), outright rebellion was suicide. Therefore, they ran away instead, in greater and greater numbers. By the 1850s, the Underground Railroad was a thoroughly organized (albeit decentralized) national phenomenon, with a plethora of networks that facilitated escape—north to the free states and Canada, south to Mexico, Haiti, and the British Caribbean. Fugitive slaves' precarious freedom was defended by what abolitionists called "Vigilance Committees," which were well-armed and trained Northern paramilitary groups that readily used violence to prevent recapture by equally well-armed slave catchers.

Whether it was abolitionism, black politics, or slave resistance, or, in some cases, a combination of all three, black and white antislavery activists always yoked their struggle to American history—namely, the legacy of the American Revolution. William Henry Johnson may have pushed his version of the Revolution a bit too far in 1859 to make a crucial political point, but he was part of a long line of abolitionists who decried both slaveholding and racism as anti-American. Indeed, it is difficult to find an abolitionist who did not at least invoke the American Founding at some point in his or her rhetoric. A sampling:

- The first Colored Convention, held in Philadelphia in 1830: "Impressed with a firm and settled conviction, and more especially being taught by that inestimable and invaluable instrument, namely, the Declaration of Independence, that all men are born free and equal, and consequently are endowed with unalienable rights, among which are the enjoyments of life, liberty, and the pursuits of happiness. Viewing these as incontrovertible facts, we have been led to the following conclusions; that our forlorn and deplorable situation earnestly and loudly demand of us to devise and pursue all legal means for the speedy elevation of ourselves and brethren to the scale and standing of men."[11]
- Quoted with his memorably unrestrained capitalization and punctuation, David Walker's 1829 *Appeal to the Colored Citizens of the World*: "See your Declaration Americans!!! Do you understand your own language? Hear your language, proclaimed to the world, July 4th, 1776—'We hold these truths to be self evident—that ALL MEN ARE CREATED EQUAL!! that they *are endowed by their Creator with certain unalienable rights;* that among these are life, *liberty*, and the pursuit of happiness!!' Compare your own language above, extracted from your Declaration of Independence, with your cruelties and murders inflicted by your cruel and unmerciful fathers and yourselves on our fathers and on us—men who have never given your fathers or you the least provocation!!!!!!"[12]
- The first issue of Garrison's *The Liberator*, 1831: "Assenting to the 'self-evident truth' . . . that 'all men are created equal' . . . I shall strenuously contend for the immediate enfranchisement of our slave population."[13]
- Henry Highland Garnet's "An Address to the Slaves of the United States," 1843: "The [Declaration of Independence] was a glorious document. Sages admired it, and the patriotic of every nation rev-

erenced the God like sentiments which it contained. When the power of Government returned to their hands, did they emancipate the slaves? No; they rather added new links to our chains."[14]

When it came to tying the American past to racial equality, William Cooper Nell was the most deliberate. Nell was a black Bostonian abolitionist and civil rights activist. In 1851, he petitioned Boston's city government to raise a monument to Crispus Attucks, the black sailor killed at the Boston Massacre and one of the first martyrs of the Revolution, but Nell was rebuffed. Not content with this rejection, he answered by publishing *Services of Colored Americans in the Wars of 1776 and 1812* that same year. In 1855, he added more chapters, retitling this expanded edition *The Colored Patriots of the American Revolution*. In this later version he included introductions by the famed white abolitionists Harriet Beecher Stowe and Wendell Phillips. Nell's use of the adjective "colored" to define black Americans was a half century old by this point, and it was strategic. The term had emerged as part of a strategy to abandon "African," and instead forcefully claim black people's American heritage.[15] This strategy was hardly something new. Americans, as all human beings, have always defined themselves in different ways at different times—for good reason. Words have power, and they make political arguments.

Nell's book was an eclectic summary of countless black contributions to the Revolutionary cause, catalogued exhaustively, state after state after state. Nell included soldiers in the Continental Army, fugitive slaves, activists, slave rebels—really, any black American from the late eighteenth and early nineteenth centuries who embodied the egalitarian potential of the American Revolution. Nell concluded: "The Revolution of 1776, and the subsequent struggles in our nation's history, aided, in honorable proportion, by colored Americans, have (sad, but true, confession) yet left the necessity for a second revolution." Deeming the previous quarter century a period of "anti-slavery war," Nell believed this second revolution would soon arrive.[16]

It is worth asking: privately, did these black abolitionists believe their own rhetoric? After all, there was also evidence that slaveholding revolutionaries supported the Patriot cause to preserve the "peculiar institution."

With regard to Nell, his massive 1855 tome and prodigious research suggest not, but it is impossible to tell what other abolitionists *really* thought about early U.S. history. Their rhetoric was just that—rhetoric, meant to be heard and read in public. In a larger sense, however, it did not matter what black activists like Nell personally believed, for they knew that *white* Americans *did* believe in the meaning of the Revolution. Indeed, it was one of their core identities *as Americans.*

Frederick Douglass intuitively understood this. By the mid-1850s, it was clear that white Northerners were turning against what they deemed "the Slave Power" more than they ever had before. In 1847, Douglass had told Garrison, "I have no patriotism. I have no country." But, by the mid-1850s, this attitude would no longer do—not when there finally existed a growing mass of white Northerners willing to side with Douglass against slavery. And so, Douglass began proclaiming the American Founding to have an antislavery orientation and called the Constitution an antislavery document. "What to the Slave is the Fourth of July?" is rightfully remembered for its righteous anger at American hypocrisy, but even this provocative speech concluded by celebrating the Declaration of Independence and the Constitution. Douglass deemed the latter a "GLORIOUS LIBERTY DOCUMENT"—or, more accurately, it *could* be.[17] He argued that proslavery Americans "slandered" the Founding Fathers by interpreting the Constitution as proslavery. What were needed now, he believed, were antislavery Americans to interpret the Constitution properly, and restore its antislavery foundations.[18]

Here, then, is a second reason why the American Revolution still mattered more than seventy years after it ended. Antislavery rhetoric gained ground in the North because antislavery activists tied their cause to the American Founding. Like the rest of the characters in this book, they maintained: *This is not who we are. This is not what we stand for. This is not what the American Revolution meant. This is not the world it was supposed to make.* In the North, increasing numbers of white Americans, many of whom had for too long shown little care for black people and had long wanted simply to avoid the issue of slavery, finally began to listen.

Abraham Lincoln was one of them. He was, in many ways, exceptional—a brilliant politician, an eloquent writer, a deep thinker. But, in other ways, he was quite typical, which helps explain why he became the Republican Party's presidential candidate in 1860. Like most white Northerners, he was racist—but, like a majority of those same white Northerners, he was deeply disturbed by the existence of slavery in a land of supposed freedom. As he rose to prominence, Lincoln turned to this idea again and again, and it became a sort of mantra. He acknowledged that slavery existed in the South because of historical circumstances, but, like many other Americans, he believed that the Founding Fathers had foreseen an eventual end to slavery. He consistently maintained that blacks were not equal with whites—but he also argued that black inferiority did not justify enslavement. These ideas were encapsulated best in an oft-cited portion of the first of his famous debates with Illinois senator Stephen Douglas, worth quoting in full:

> I have no purpose to introduce political and social equality between the white and the black races. . . . I, as well as Judge Douglas, am in favor of the race to which I belong having the superior position. I have never said anything to the contrary, but I hold that, notwithstanding all this, there is no reason in the world why the negro is not entitled to all the natural rights enumerated in the Declaration of Independence, the right to life, liberty, and the pursuit of happiness. [Loud cheers.] I hold that he is as much entitled to these as the white man. I agree with Judge Douglas he is not my equal in many respects—certainly not in color, perhaps not in moral or intellectual endowment. But in the right to eat the bread, without the leave of anybody else, which his own hand earns, *he is my equal and the equal of Judge Douglas, and the equal of every living man.* [Great applause.][19]

Notice the "loud cheers" and "great applause." Many of Lincoln's fellow Americans felt the same way.

Later in this same debate, in a much less quoted portion, Lincoln returned to the subject of the Founding, particularly Stephen Douglas's statement that the Founders did not mean to include black people in the Declaration of Independence, an assertion recently codified by Chief Justice Roger Taney in the Supreme Court's *Dred Scott* decision. Lincoln countered, "Judge Douglas is going back to the era of our Revolution, and to the extent of his ability, *muzzling the cannon* which thunders its annual joyous return [on the Fourth of July]. When he invites any people, willing to have slavery, to establish it, he is blowing out the moral lights around us. [Cheers.]" (Italics added.) There it was: Douglas and his allies were perverting the memory of the American Founding, and they were denying the ideological power and intent of the Revolution.[20] As Lincoln asked rhetorically of Douglas and his allies in another speech, "Are you really willing that the Declaration shall be thus frittered away?—thus left no more at most, than an interesting memorial of the dead past?"[21]

Denying the Revolution. It would be wrong to boil the Civil War, with its nearly 1 million casualties, into this single pithy phrase, but the sentiment was there. To justify their actions, Southern fire-eaters, as the most vocal secessionists were memorably known, needed to deny their Revolutionary heritage. As Alexander Stephens, the vice president of the Confederacy, argued in his famous "Cornerstone Speech," Thomas Jefferson wrote the Declaration under the flawed presumption that "the enslavement of the African was in violation of the laws of nature," and Stephens acknowledged that "most of the leading statesmen at the time" agreed with him. The Confederacy was now fixing this dangerous flaw. "Its cornerstone rests," Stephens declared, "upon the great truth that the negro is not equal to the white man."[22] Stephens was one of many Southerners who repudiated the Declaration entirely.[23] Secession, therefore, was not a new revolution but, in the words of the historian James McPherson, a "pre-emptive counterrevolution."[24] Secessionists said this themselves. "We are not revolutionists," claimed *DeBow's Review*, the preeminent magazine of the South, "We are resisting revolution."[25] When they considered the consequences of Lincoln's election, they feared the South would mirror the most revolutionary of all revolutions: Haiti.[26]

In contrast, black Americans and their white allies in the North continued to lay claim to the Revolution's heritage. The Republican Party's platform in 1856 made this very clear, maintaining that the party stood in solidarity with "our Republican fathers" in upholding the principles of the Declaration of Independence. The 1860 platform followed suit.[27]

The Political Revolution of 1860

Octavius Catto was part of Philadelphia's small population of black elite. His father, William Catto, had been an enslaved millwright in Charleston, South Carolina, but was able to purchase his freedom. In Charleston, he married Sarah Isabella Cain, a member of the wealthy, mixed-race DeReef family, which had achieved the highest social status possible for non-whites in the city. Together, William and Sarah moved to Philadelphia, where William became a respected minister at the First African Presbyterian Church. He wrote a history of that church, and he also founded the Banneker Institute, the black intellectual and debating society named after Benjamin Banneker, a black polymath who lived in the Revolutionary era. Clearly valuing education, the Cattos sent their son Octavius to several Philadelphia schools founded specifically for black children, as the city's public schools were segregated in the 1850s.

Eventually, Octavius attended the prestigious Institute for Colored Youth (ICY), which was managed by Philadelphia Quakers. Unlike most black schools, the school's day-to-day affairs were left to black instead of white leadership, and these leaders were hardly playing the deferential racial politics that many well-meaning white Quakers expected. The ICY's first principal, Charles Reason, had been born in the United States, but his mother was a refugee from Haiti, one of the thousands of *gens de couleur* (free people of color) who had clashed with the ultimately victorious formerly enslaved population. Before arriving in Philadelphia, Reason was an educator and activist in New York City.[28] ICY's second principal, Ebenezer Bassett, was also a civil rights activist and a friend to Frederick Douglass, and he would go on to become the ambassador to Haiti after the Civil War, making him the first African American ever appointed to an ambassadorship. He also corresponded with radical black abolitionists like Henry Highland Garnet, who famously encouraged slaves to violently rebel.[29] Clearly the young Catto was surrounded by black men unwilling to accept the racial status quo. After graduating from the ICY in 1858, Catto moved to Washington, DC, where he worked as a tutor, but he returned to Philadelphia only a year later to teach at the ICY. Considering that the ICY was *the* elite black school in the city—half of the school's students had to enroll for an extra year to meet the strict graduation requirements—and that Catto was only twenty years old, he clearly had already made a name for himself.[30]

And he knew it. Catto's upbringing was tailor-made to produce a young man self-consciously representative of, and increasingly representing, the city's small but influential black elite. He was educated far more than most Americans, undeniably intelligent, driven, handsome, and, for all these reasons, rightfully self-confident. Judging from letters to friends, he was an impeccable dresser who was obsessed with how the public viewed him.[31] One of his few surviving letters, to his friend and fellow ICY classmate Jacob White, is almost wholly concerned with Catto's mission to obtain a new suit tailored to his exact specifications. Not only was the suit required to have "my famous 'pigeon-tail,'" as Catto wrote, but "it must show the second stud—have *four* buttons close together and be *rounded* at the *lower corners*" (emphasis in original).[32] Catto's obsession with appearances correlated with his method of practicing politics, which was akin to that of his father's generation: While assuming a leadership role among black Philadelphians, he still played respectability politics among white Philadelphians. He hoped to persuade white allies by showing them that his behavior, values, and comportment were impeccable. Yet, while his political *methods* were more conservative, his political ideology—uncompromising insistence on black equality—was thoroughly radical. Perhaps it was this combination of traditional tactics and new demands that made him so effective a spokesman for civil rights at such a young age.

Catto was largely a bystander to the first phase of the Second American Revolution, the political revolution in the North that elected Abraham Lincoln to the presidency in 1860. For nearly the entire history of the United States up to that point, the presidency had been held by either a Southern slaveholder or a Northerner who sympathized with Southern slaveholders, with a few one-term exceptions (both Adamses). Lincoln was not an abolitionist and fervently proclaimed as much, stating again and again that he had no desire to end slavery where it already existed. He did, however, seek to quarantine slavery in the South by preventing its spread into the western territories and Northern states, a policy succinctly stated by Republicans as "freedom national, slavery sectional." For this stance, he was rewarded with nearly 40 percent of the national popular vote in the 1860 election, but more than 50 percent in all but a handful of Northern states, which easily gave him an Electoral College victory against his three opponents (Northern Democrat Stephen Douglas, Southern Democrat John C. Breckinridge, and Constitutional Union candidate John Bell).

Most white Northerners who voted for Lincoln (or Stephen Douglas for that matter) did not yet see that Lincoln's victory was a political revolution. Most of them did not vote for Lincoln to end slavery entirely, let alone to aid black women and men in any fashion, and Lincoln himself never promised to do either of these radical measures. Yet parties with close up, day-to-day connections to slavery certainly saw the election as revolutionary. Certainly, white Southerners did, which explains their counterrevolutionary secessionism. Even more important, as the historian Stephanie McCurry points out, nearly every account we have from enslaved people portrayed Lincoln's election as revolutionary. For the first time in U.S. history, they had an explicit ally in the White House. Slaveholders tried to prevent news from reaching their all-too-human property, but, contrary to proslavery arguments, enslaved black people were not docile and did not behave like property, and they had long cultivated networks of clandestine communication throughout the entire South. They knew the stakes of Lincoln's election.[33]

As an educator and activist, Octavius Catto was doing what he could for a young black man who could not vote. In 1860, at the age of twenty-one, Catto did not carry that much influence beyond the small circle of elite black Philadelphians. For the first two years of the war, life largely went on as usual. Although black men could serve in the U.S. Navy, they were prohibited from joining the army; the prohibition of black enlistees stemmed from the Militia Act of 1792, which explicitly stated that only white citizens were eligible to serve in the army. It was one of the first in a wave of counterrevolutionary anti-black policies that sought to eliminate the integrated army that Washington had commanded during the Revolutionary War.

To Lincoln and most of his fellow white Northerners, this was just as it should be. While most white Southerners and nearly all black people, both enslaved and free, saw Lincoln's election as a political revolution, most white Northerners were not yet ready to embrace the full meaning of his electoral victory. Lincoln himself pleaded for moderation in his First Inaugural Address, in which he famously addressed the South, "We are not enemies, but friends. We must not be enemies."[34] His reasons were both ideological and practical. Ideologically, a majority of white Northerners were willing to fight an antislavery war for union, but they would not fight for slave emancipation. Lincoln, as always acutely attuned to public opinion, was not willing to break so drastically with his constituents. Practically, he could not afford to: He needed to maintain public support among whites, particularly in the four slave states that decided to remain in the Union (Delaware, Maryland, Missouri, and above all Kentucky, whose wealth and population Lincoln desperately needed on his side). Yet Lincoln's First Inaugural also contained a warning: Southerners, he noted, "still have the old Constitution unimpaired," with all its protections for slavery and empowerment of slaveholders. Secession and war, Lincoln warned, could change that.

The Military Revolution of 1863

As soon as the war began, enslaved people proved the Confederacy's bedrock racist ideology to be spectacularly false. For most enslaved people in the South, escape from slavery had long been an impossibility. Most lived very far from free states, and the South's police state ensured that, in most cases, fugitive slaves would be caught and suffer the consequences. Yet as Union armies slowly started to penetrate the South, these armies became accessible islands of freedom for thousands of enslaved people. As they arrived at Union lines in droves, Union generals, spearheaded by General Benjamin Butler, first accepted them and then began to use their labor to aid the Union war effort. In Congress, Republicans responded to this on-the-ground reality by passing the First Confiscation Act in 1861, which justified this policy of using fugitive slaves' labor by deeming fugitive slaves the confiscated property of traitors—which, legally, they were. Of course, as the New York diarist George Templeton Strong memorably wrote, slaves were a unique form of property, "peculiar for possessing a capacity for being invited to go away, and legs to take itself off, and arms wherewith to use such implements as may aid it in doing so."[35]

Even after the First Confiscation Act, which was followed by a more robust Second Confiscation Act a year later, Northern victory was no closer. The Confiscation Acts were only half measures, undermining the Confederacy at its margins but not at its core. It was at this point Lincoln came to believe that the only way to win the war was through mobilizing 4 million enslaved blacks in the South and nearly half a million free blacks in the North and South against the Confederacy. In September 1862, after the Battle of Antietam, Lincoln announced the Emancipation Proclamation, which would fully take effect on New Year's Day, 1863. The document did two momentous things: It freed every slave in every rebellious state and it authorized the raising of black troops.[36] Historians have long debated just how much the Emancipation Proclamation was Lincoln himself taking initiative versus how much fugitive slaves forced Lincoln's hand. Was Lincoln the Great Emancipator (capitalized!), or was he simply a reluctant emancipator (lowercase)? The debate's many details have obscured the truth at the heart of the Emancipation Proclamation: Lincoln and fugitive slaves needed each other. Without thousands of fugitive slaves, there would have been no mountain of letters from Union commanders asking Lincoln what to do about black people arriving at Union lines in the hundreds and thousands, there would have been no Confiscation Acts, and there would have been no impetus for Lincoln to take such a momentous step. Yet, with a more conservative, more risk-averse president, fugitive slaves would have never found the presidential ally that Lincoln eventually became.[37]

In this sense, the Emancipation Proclamation mirrored the Declaration of Independence, in both its lived reality and its distorted posterity. Jefferson's Declaration was not the first declaration of independence in the United States. Indeed, it was late in coming, arriving a year after war had begun and six months after Tom Paine published *Common Sense*. Nevertheless, Jefferson still wrote it, the Second Continental Congress still ratified it, and it thoroughly transformed the nature of the Revolution. Less bold, less radical men may have chosen otherwise. Lincoln's Emancipation

Proclamation was also a response to the reality of the moment, but it too required Lincoln to still take a momentous risk, and it too thoroughly transformed the nature of the conflict. Yet, over time, collective historical memory has attributed authorship of both documents to a single figure, forgetting that both were collaborative efforts involving thousands of their forebears.

Even more important, both the Declaration of Independence and the Emancipation Proclamation defined their respective revolutions, creating circumstances in which now there was no turning back. If the Patriots won the war, Jefferson's Declaration proclaimed, the United States would be fully independent; if the Union won the war, Lincoln's Emancipation portended, then slavery would be destroyed and the Constitution would be transformed. Both envisioned new nations on the world stage. Black Americans did not wait so long, holding celebrations throughout the North on January 1, the day the Emancipation Proclamation became official, to celebrate the revolutionary moment. One black minister proclaimed, "The morning dawns! . . . The Proclamation has gone forth, and God is saying to this constitute nation by its legitimate constitute head, Man must be free."[38] While the name of the United States would not be changed, nearly all Americans, both black and white, now understood that it would nevertheless be a new nation.

The Emancipation Proclamation transformed Octavius Catto's experience of the war. When Confederate general Robert E. Lee's army invaded Pennsylvania in June 1863, the state's governor and the Philadelphia mayor issued a call for new recruits for the state militia. Catto and his friend Jacob White answered, opening a recruiting headquarters in the ICY itself.[39] Throughout the city they put up large posters, with headings like, "MEN OF COLOR, TO ARMS! NOW OR NEVER!" One such poster proclaimed, "This is our Golden Moment. . . . A new era is open to us. For generations, we have suffered under the horrors of slavery, outrage and wrong; our manhood has been denied, our citizenship blotted out, our souls seared and burned, our spirits cowed and crushed, and the hope of the future of our race involved in doubts and darkness. But now the whole aspect of our relations to the white race is changed. Now is our most precious moment. Let us Rush to Arms! **Fail Now and Our Race is Doomed"** (bold in original).[40] At the bottom of the posters, Catto and White printed their names, along with fifty-two other prominent black Philadelphians and the ever-present Frederick Douglass.

In the coming days, Catto and White put together a force of ninety black recruits, a group one young ICY student nicknamed the "Banneker guards" and described in her diary as "nearly all our best young men."[41] With the blessing of Philadelphia's mayor and in the attendance of family and friends, they boarded a train west for Harrisburg, which was in the path of Lee's invasion. Wrote the same ICY student, "To day has bin exciting the most I ever witness."[42] When Catto and his fellow volunteers arrived in the state capital, their services were welcomed by the state's governor, but then Major General Darius Couch, commanding the Department of the Susquehanna, stepped in. Because Congress had authorized the recruitment of black soldiers for "no less than three years," Couch maintained, he could not accept these short-term volunteers. In all likelihood, Couch wanted to exclude black soldiers from his army, and he used this technicality to justify his decision. When Secretary of State Edwin Stanton learned of Couch's decision, he telegraphed him to accept all recruits "without regard to color," but by then it was too late. Catto, White, and the rest had already returned to Philadelphia. The ICY student succinctly captured the mood, writing, "I feel glad and sorry"—glad because her fellow students were out of harm's way, sorry because they were not given the opportunity to prove themselves on the battlefield.[43]

Catto may have failed in his initial bid to serve the Union cause, but his recruitment drive had nevertheless established him as a leader of Philadelphia's black community. For the next two years of the war, he would remain in Philadelphia as a major and inspector in the first division of the Pennsylvania National Guard.[44] Records are scarce, but Catto likely helped recruit and train black troops at Camp William Penn. Situated just beyond the city limits, the camp was the first and largest training ground for black troops during the war. He also continued to teach at the ICY. Most notably, he was elected the corresponding secretary of the Pennsylvania Equal Rights League. This organization was the state branch of the National Equal Rights League, which had been founded in the fall of 1864 in Syracuse by more than a hundred black men, including Frederick Douglass and Henry

Highland Garnet. The organization's demands were simple: full and equal citizenship for African Americans in every state and throughout the Union.

It was no coincidence that the raising of black troops and the founding of the Equal Rights League happened in quick succession. The very existence of black soldiers changed everything. With the arming of black men, both free and enslaved, the revolution's radical phase had begun. Nearly everyone knew it—Northerners and Southerners, conservatives and radicals, men and women, white and black. Octavius Catto himself began to call the Civil War a revolution. Citing the famous French travel writer, he stated, "De Tocqueville prophesied that if ever America underwent Revolution, it would be brought about by the presence of the black race and that it would result from the inequality of their condition. *This has been verified*" (italics added).[45] Catto clearly saw himself as being a key leader in this post-revolutionary world.

For the first time since the Revolutionary War, fully armed and fully trained black men could officially join the U.S. Army.[46] They still suffered the effects of daily discrimination. Not only were they prohibited from becoming commissioned officers, but they were paid less than white soldiers, receiving $7 a month instead of $10. Black soldiers often sent money home to their families, and being deprived of this $3 was a financial hardship. They put up with these day-to-day indignities, for they recognized that their service was revolutionary and that their very presence transformed the Union army into an army of liberation. As one soldier wrote, "Wherever the Federal Army goes, the so-called master dies, and the slaves, once chattels, are transformed into men!"[47] Some black soldiers co-opted the language of the American Revolution itself. "I will close this letter in the language of the immortal [Patrick] Henry, 'Give me liberty or give me death!'" one wrote. A half century before, the enslaved rebel Gabriel had said the same thing.

The Postwar Rights Revolution

Once Robert E. Lee surrendered to Ulysses S. Grant at Appomattox Court House in April 1865, two certainties were firmly established: First, slavery in the United States would not survive for much longer. While the ratification of the Thirteenth Amendment was hardly a political cakewalk, neither Republicans in Congress nor black Americans themselves—whether slave or free, soldiers or not—would countenance the continued existence of slavery after fighting a brutal war over that very subject. Even if the Thirteenth Amendment had not been ratified when it was, in December of 1865, slavery required a police state to thrive, and there's little doubt that Northerners and enslaved people themselves would, by one means or another, prevent that police state from returning to the South. Even Andrew Johnson, Lincoln's vice president and someone who would prove to be one of the most devastating enemies of black equality, supported emancipation.[48]

The second certainty is less obvious in hindsight, but it was not so obvious in the early years of the war: black people would remain in the United States. Before the Emancipation Proclamation, many white Northerners still agreed with an assertion Thomas Jefferson had voiced long ago: After generations of racial slavery, blacks and whites could never live together in peace. For some antislavery Northerners, the solution was the same as it had been during Jefferson's time: black colonization, either forced or voluntary. Among the Northerners who supported colonization was none other than Abraham Lincoln himself, who met with black leaders in the summer of 1862 urging them to voluntarily leave the country, maintaining, "It is better for us both to be separated."[49] Black leaders rebuffed him, and once Lincoln issued the Emancipation Proclamation, he dropped this idea entirely. He could not ask black Americans to voluntarily leave a country—*their* country—once they had fought and died to save it.

Indeed, for black men to be enlisted into the U.S. Army, they needed to be U.S. citizens. As the historian James Oakes has argued, citizenship was not a *reward* for military service, but its *precondition*. In the fall of 1862, Attorney General Edward Bates authorized that black men were U.S. citizens (contrary to Roger Taney's opinion in *Dred Scott*), and their national citizenship took precedence over whether they were citizens of the various states.[50] This made black men not only eligible to serve in the military, but also eligible for conscription.

Yet what did this citizenship actually mean? In the 1860s, it did not necessarily mean the right to vote. After all, white American *women* were U.S. citizens—and not only could they not vote in any state, but most states had not yet abolished coverture, still depriving married women of private property and legal personhood outside their husband's existence. The citizenship of women, as well as children, meant something less than the full citizenship of white men. They had the right to a trial by jury, but they could not serve on juries themselves; they could be protected by their local militia, but they could not serve in the militia.

Lincoln himself seemed to imagine some sort of partial citizenship for black men, never endorsing universal black male suffrage. Instead, in the last speech he gave before his assassination, Lincoln stated that he "preferred" that black suffrage "were now conferred on the very intelligent, and on those who would serve our cause as soldiers."[51]

"Serve our cause as soldiers"—*that* was the key. This line of thinking connected the results of the Civil War—what some historians have deemed the *Second* Emancipation—with the American Revolution and its aftermath, the *First* Emancipation, when Northern blacks gained freedom and suffrage because they had been crucial for Patriot victory. William Cooper Nell understood this, as did Frederick Douglass—and so too did young Octavius Catto. Educated by two black activists at the Institute for Colored Youth, raised in an era of increasing black militarism, Catto had no time for the seeming passivity of the elder generation of black Philadelphians. It was Catto, after all, who, alongside several other young black Philadelphians, had taken the impetus to form a black militia to protect their home state in 1863. Two years later, black soldiers had not only served the United States, but they could argue they had saved the Union itself by doing so. To Catto, blacks deserved both political and civil rights for many reasons, but above all because of this invaluable service. "Prejudice, which is the offspring of ignorance," he said in 1865, "was washed out in the blood of colored men, who sacrificed their lives upon the altar of their native land." (Notice, too, his claim for blacks' Americanness—"*native* land.")[52]

And so, in the years after the war, Catto threw himself into political activism. As one of the secretaries of the Pennsylvania Equal Rights League (once again alongside his friend Jacob White, who was also his teammate on the Philadelphia Pythians, the city's most talented black baseball team), Catto met frequently with other of the state's black leaders, as they strategized how to best force the Pennsylvania state government to guarantee both civil and political equality. Within a year the Equal Rights League was organized in sixteen cities in the state.[53] One general goal was school desegregation, but the specifics divided league members, for school desegregation also implied white teachers for black students, many of whom were hopelessly racist and would not treat black children with respect, let alone equality. Yet, to other league members, endorsing only black teachers for black students seemed to be a step back for racial equality. It was the professional educator Catto who ultimately came up with a compromise resolution. If the qualifications of a black teacher and white teacher were the same, the resolution stated, then the black teacher should be hired, "not because of their complexion, but because they are better qualified by conventional circumstances outside of the school-house." As Catto explained prior to proposing the compromise, "The colored man . . . was the better teacher because he had the welfare of the race more at heart, knowing that they rose and fell together."[54]

Catto's most successful push for civil rights came in his home city of Philadelphia, where the city streetcars remained segregated after the war. For several years, Catto and his allies lobbied Philadelphia authorities and Pennsylvania legislators to end the racist policy, with Catto at one point traveling to Harrisburg to meet with Republican leaders personally. For two years, however, they encountered unrelenting white hostility, particularly in Philadelphia itself. At one point Catto effectively advocated civil disobedience (even if he did not use that term), urging black men to "vindicate their manhood" by no longer tolerating "ruffianly conductors and drivers" throwing "defenseless women and children" off the streetcars. Key to his argument was, once again, black service in the Civil War. These women and children, he argued, were the relatives of "twelve thousand colored soldiers, whose services these very [white] citizens gladly accepted when the nation was in her hour of trouble."[55] Eventually, the campaign bore fruit, with Pennsylvania Republicans passing a bill to end desegregation in a largely party line vote in 1867. To test whether it would be enforced, Catto and his allies sent Caroline LeCount, a woman who, like Catto, was a teacher and a member of the city's black elite. When she was kicked off the streetcar, she went to authorities, and the streetcar company was fined. Catto and LeCount would soon get engaged.

Across the United States, not only in the South but also in the North and West, there were countless other Cattos fighting for civil and voting rights. For them, it was an era of hope and promise, generated by the belief that real racial equality could be achieved. After the war, most white Southerners, their Democratic allies in the North, and President Andrew Johnson planned to cement white supremacy and, in the South, something very close to slavery, but African Americans and their white allies refused to let them. Their struggles were successful. In the face of Southern intransigence, Radical Republicans in Congress implemented what historians now call "Radical Reconstruction," an effort to realize real racial equality throughout the United States. Out of all their efforts, the most important legislation was the passage of the Fourteenth and Fifteenth Amendments. The former guaranteed all black Americans their civil rights, the latter guaranteed black men the right to vote. Together, they marked the culmination of the most revolutionary phase of the Second American Revolution.

The story of how the Fourteenth and Fifteenth Amendments were passed is complicated, and there is no space to tell it here. Yet at the core of the account lies the potent combination of moral justice and political expediency that explains many of the most inspiring moments in U.S. (and world) history. There is no doubt that Radical Republicans in Congress, men like Representative John Bingham and Senator Charles Sumner, both believed in the cause of black equality and were outraged at white Southerners' attempts to reinstall slavery in all but name, via methods such as passing restrictive Black Codes and, through illegal paramilitary organizations like the Ku Klux Klan, waging a war of terror on freed people. Yet Republicans also realized that, as Catto himself noted, blacks were the only "unqualified friends of the Union" in the South.[56] If the Republican Party wanted to keep holding political power in the South once the U.S. Army went home, it needed black votes. This factor, alongside widespread outrage at what was in essence white Southerners' unwillingness to accept defeat, helped sway many of the more moderate Republicans who did not necessarily believe in full racial equality. Just as the Republican Party and black Americans needed each other during the war to achieve victory, they were once again yoked together to maintain Republican power and ensure African American rights.

As many scholars have pointed out, there were obvious loopholes in the text of the Fourteenth and Fifteenth Amendments that would soon be exploited by Southern "Redemptioners." Civil rights activists saw these loopholes at the time. They knew the amendments were imperfect. Furthermore, women were deliberately excluded, and suffragists like Sojourner Truth believed it was now or never. "So I am for keeping the thing going while things are stirring," she urged, "Because if we wait til it is still, it will take a great while to keep it going again."[57]

Yet, like the coalition of revolutionaries from the 1770s, most of those of the 1860s understood that it was only through compromise and coalition that real gains could be achieved. Thaddeus Stevens, long one of Congress's most stalwart supporters of black rights, expressed this pragmatism eloquently, writing, "I will take all I can get in the cause of humanity and leave it to be perfected by better men in better times." Later, when asked why he accepted imperfection, he simply stated, "I answer, because I live among men and not among angels."[58] Catto seems to have taken this stance as well, for he had been a supporter of women's suffrage, but he went silent on the issue by the time of the Fifteenth Amendment's ratification.[59] Supporters of the amendment also knew that time was ticking. Anti-black terrorism in the South, combined with waning support for black equality among white Northerners, meant that the longer it took to secure that equality, the more likely it was that that possibility could vanish entirely. Once again, revolutionary time was perishable.

For all the imperfections of the Reconstruction amendments, however, they were still remarkably, even stunningly, revolutionary. Not only did they go much further toward promoting black equality than any other country in the Americas outside of Haiti, but they committed the United States to equality for all Americans. The first section of the Fourteenth Amendment deserves particular consideration, for it was this section above all that made good on the promises of the Second American Revolution:

> All persons born or naturalized in the United States, and subject to the jurisdiction thereof, are citizens of the United States and of the State wherein they reside. No State shall make or enforce any law which shall abridge the privileges or immunities of citizens of the United States; nor shall any State deprive any

> person of life, liberty, or property, without due process of law; nor deny to any person within its jurisdiction the equal protection of the laws.

The Fourteenth Amendment made three radical changes: First, finally fulfilling the long-dormant wishes of James Madison, it paved the way for the "incorporation" of the Bill of Rights, making it so now states, too, were barred from abridging the rights enshrined in the first ten amendments (although how this "incorporation" worked would take nearly a century to get worked out). Second, it severed citizenship from race and ethnicity, providing for what is now referred to as "birthright citizenship," meaning anyone born on U.S. soil was a U.S. citizen, even if that person had once been enslaved or the child of immigrants (the latter would become increasingly important in the following decades, during the Ellis Island era). Even today, very few countries outside of the Western Hemisphere grant birthright citizenship, and none do in Europe. (At the time of this writing, the Supreme Court has given President Trump more leeway to implement his blatantly unconstitutional attack on birthright citizenship. When all is said and done with this legal chicanery, I still believe the end result will be the preservation of birthright citizenship. I hope I am not wrong.) Finally, as Eric Foner writes, the Fourteenth Amendment elevated "equality to a constitutional right" for the first time. Americans had of course cherished and celebrated, and at times debated and denigrated, the revolutionary principle of equality, ever since the Declaration had declared "all men were created equal." Yet it was only with the Fourteenth Amendment that support for equality appeared in the Constitution itself.[60]

The history of the Reconstruction amendments did not just echo Madison's attempt to ensure states could not violate the rights of their citizens; it also echoed Madison's election to Congress that allowed him to push through the Bill of Rights in the first place. Recall Patrick Henry had tried to gerrymander his rival out of a House seat, but Madison still won by campaigning on the need for a bill of rights. Nearly eighty years later, President Johnson tried to do the opposite: He hoped to gain a congressional majority for his Reconstruction program—which meant, in essence, the restoration of white supremacy in the South—by running against the Radical Republicans and their push for black equality. He failed. Not only did the

Republicans maintain their hold on both the House and the Senate in the 1866 midterm elections, but they expanded their number of seats, aided—justifiably—by the fact that most Southern states had not yet been allowed back into the Union. A majority of American voters, which at the time meant mostly white Northerners, committed themselves to black equality.

Their commitment would not last.

The North, too, experienced its own version of Reconstruction, one that is less well known than the South's Reconstruction. The Fifteenth Amendment gave suffrage not only to freedmen in the South, but also to most blacks in the North, who, outside New England, had long been prohibited from voting in most states thanks to racist suffrage laws passed in the early decades of the century. In Philadelphia, where blacks had lost the right to vote in 1838, ratification of the Fifteenth Amendment was just cause for celebration. In April 1870, black Philadelphians and their white allies held a parade down Broad Street. At the Union League, founded in 1862 to support Lincoln and the war effort, the organization's vice president, Charles Gibbons, delivered a speech that portrayed the Fifteenth Amendment as the culmination of the ideals of the American Revolution.[61] "In this year of our blessed Lord," Gibbons stated, "we realize that divine ideal of human equality . . . [that] was proclaimed from Independence Hall by the representatives of the American colonies."[62]

It was Octavius Catto, still only thirty years old, who was chosen to represent black Philadelphians by providing a response to Gibbons's speech. He did not mince words about future elections and how black voters should use their newly acquired franchise: "The black man knows on which side of the line to vote. He not only reads, but he remembers; and, what is better still—he *thinks*. He knows the party that has throttled slavery; crushed the rebellion; secured us a government; protected the dearly bought institutions of the country. He knows the party that has reconstructed the South on a basis of equality and justice. . . . And so long as it is true to these great problems; so long as it is true to those principles which know no East, no West, no South; no white man's government nor black man's country—but one destiny for all . . . so long will the black man be a voter in and worker for that party."[63]

Catto knew all too well that there was more work to be done, not just in the South but in Philadelphia itself. Since the end of the Civil War, Democrats in this southernmost Northern city had clawed back political power by running on opposition to black equality. As one Democrat newspaper plainly noted before the 1868 elections, the political contest revolved around a single question: "Do you believe there is a difference between the negro and the white man?"[64] In 1868, a Democrat won the mayor's race for the first time since 1858, which was the result of both white opposition to black equality and likely a significant amount of electoral fraud. In response, Republican legislators in Harrisburg decided to respond with their own dirty politics, handing Philadelphia's elections over to a Board of Canvassers stocked with local Republicans.[65] This move, in turn, turned off moderate Republicans in the city who were wary of both black equality and political corruption. For the 1870 elections, this faction, naming themselves Liberal Republicans, joined with the Democrats to contest the majority of Republicans who supported black suffrage and black equality.

This is where Catto filled a crucial role. By 1870, if he was not *the* most important leader of Philadelphia's black community, he had nevertheless firmly established himself as a key spokesman for the community's younger, more uncompromising generation, one that demanded the United States live up to its revolutionary ideals *now* instead of at some point in the distant future. Such was his rising star that he even traveled to Virginia to urge freedmen to vote and to stump for the Fourteenth Amendment, which the state had not yet ratified, even though it was now law of the land (although largely symbolic, states can ratify amendments even after their certification into law).[66] Once he was back in Philadelphia, he and his allies knew that if they could mobilize the city's five thousand black voters to vote Republican, these votes could combine with loyal white Republican voters to overcome the joint Democratic–Liberal Republican ticket.

Hovering around this political drama was the very real threat of election day violence. It had been thirty-two years since black men had voted in Philadelphia, and in 1870 their voting numbers threatened a Democratic Party whose main plank was the preservation of white supremacy. In response, a U.S. marshal based in eastern Pennsylvania sent in a company of marines to maintain order under the terms of the Enforcement Act, which

Congress had initially passed to curb white supremacist violence in the South.[67] Their presence worked: Voting went peacefully, with two separate voting lines for blacks and whites to ease tensions (even though, of course, many whites, like most blacks, were also voting for Republicans). When all votes were counted, Republicans had not won an overwhelming victory, but they still managed to win back a handful of seats in the city and state legislatures that they had lost in prior elections.

And yet, to Pennsylvania governor John White Geary, ostensibly a Radical Republican, there was something unseemly about federal troops being used in Philadelphia to supervise an election. When Daniel Fox, the city's Democratic mayor, wrote Geary to complain about such a precedent, he found a sympathetic ear. Philadelphia, after all, was the North. It did not need reconstructing. It was only in the South where federal troops were really needed. So Governor Geary mandated that Philadelphia would be left to its own devices in the 1871 elections. It would be up to the Democratic mayor and the Democratic-controlled police to supervise the elections, in which the mayor himself was up for reelection against Republican William Stokely.

To absolutely no one's surprise, October 10, 1871, the day of the election, was one of violence and chaos. The violence had started the night before, as gangs allied with the Democrats began attacking black people on the street. The next day riots broke out through the city, mostly targeting black neighborhoods south of Center City. Mayor Fox attempted multiple times to "restore order," but, in reality, this simply meant preventing blacks from getting to the polls. Democratic-allied mobs attacked black voters while the police looked on—or, in some cases, the police simply did the attacking themselves.[68] Indeed, in the words of Catto's friend Jacob White, "all of the trouble . . . was caused by the police."[69]

Catto himself traveled multiple times between the Institute for Colored Youth and his house a block away, as he tried to teach his students while simultaneously mobilizing and protecting black voters. He carried Republican voting tickets to hand out to his political allies, which they in turn would hand in as their votes. At one point he even asked the mayor personally to protect the city's black population, but the mayor said everything was under control. By midafternoon, with anti-black violence showing no signs of slowing down, Catto decided he needed to protect himself and purchased a pistol at a pawnshop. He then walked home.

When Catto was within a half block of his house at 814 South Street, he walked by a man with a bandaged head, who first passed him without recognition. Then, the man, an Irishman named Frank Kelly who was allied with local Democratic politicians, turned and looked—and realized the passerby was Catto. He pulled out a pistol and fired as Catto retreated in the face of the attacker. Catto's last words were reportedly, "What are you doing?" At that point Kelly fired two more times, killing Catto instantaneously. His last act was to fall into the arms of a police officer just arriving on the scene.

Over the next weeks and months, Catto's friends, family, and students mourned his death, among them his longtime friend and baseball teammate Jacob White, his fiancée Caroline LeCount, and his father, for whom his son's murder proved too tragic to overcome. Within seven weeks, William Catto, too, was dead. In the lead-up to the election, one Philadelphia newspaper, anticipating violence, had argued, "To die at the polls in the defense of civil freedom is not a less grand or acceptable sacrifice than death on the field."[70] Whether this writer still endorsed their bold proclamation after Catto's murder remains unknown. If Catto had lived, he surely would have rejoiced that, despite Democratic violence, Republicans had swept the city elections. Surely many of his friends and loved ones now wondered if the victory was worth the dreadful cost.

Thousands of Philadelphians watched Catto's funeral procession down Broad Street, which was attended by a who's who of black activists and Republican politicians. Catto had always yearned for widespread respect, even fame, and the funeral was proof he had achieved it. Of course, this fact only made the events surrounding his murder even more tragic. Catto's life had been cut short just as he began to be recognized as not just a civil rights leader locally but a leader on the national level.

Catto's murder foreshadowed the death of Reconstruction itself. Its death stemmed not just from the virulent white opposition to black rights—*that* had always existed, in both the North and the South. Rather, Reconstruction died because a vast middle swath of white Northerners, individuals like the Pennsylvania governor who had pulled troops out of Philadelphia, had grown disillusioned with Reconstruction's radicalism and believed the time to enforce its policies had come to an end. In 1877, after a contested, controversial presidential election marred by election day violence in several Southern states, Republicans and Democrats made a deal: Republican Rutherford B. Hayes would become president, and in exchange all federal forces would be withdrawn from the South. Over the following decades, white Southerners erected an authoritarian state predicated on racial segregation, the disenfranchisement of black voters, the widespread incarceration of blacks (and some poor whites) based on largely invented crimes, and the rampant use of lynching to ensure black compliance. Things were better for black people in the North. Unlike Southern society, Northern society was not predicated on racial terror—but it was hardly a land of racial equality. Catto's Philadelphia is a case in point. There, black men continued to vote, but few ever held office; schools were legally desegregated in the 1880s, but de facto segregation continued, as did racist policing, hiring practices, and housing policies.

Like the First American Revolution, the Second American Revolution augured radical possibilities that were never fulfilled. Like the First American Revolution, the matter of which story matters more—the valiant attempt or the unsatisfactory result—continues to divide the United States and its people.

Conclusion

A black-and-white photograph has hung in my parents' living room since I was young. It is of a white man in his twenties, sporting a mustache, clear eyes, and a resolute stare, wearing the uniform of a Union army officer. This man is Ezekiel Tomlinson, Union army veteran, Philadelphia native, and my great-great-grandfather.

More than 2 million American men enlisted in the Union army, and another million in the Confederate army, so in itself Tomlinson's service is hardly unique. Unlike most white officers, however, Tomlinson served in a black regiment—and not just in any black regiment, but in the 54th Massachusetts. Immortalized in the film *Glory*, the 54th was the very first black regiment to be formed, and it served as a test for whether black men would fight as well as white men. At Battery Wagner, a fort that protected Charleston Harbor, the answer was a resounding *yes*. The fort was impregnable, but the 54th attempted repeated assaults in the face of unrelenting fire, losing more than a quarter of its force. One newspaper stated that Fort Wagner was "such a name to the colored race as Bunker Hill has been for ninety years to white Yankees."[1] The battle was the catalyst for the Union army's use of black troops for the remainder of the war.

After fighting at Gettysburg with a Pennsylvania regiment, my great-great-grandfather transferred to the 54th later in the summer. This was *his* choice, likely influenced by his Quaker upbringing, and it involved asking his abolitionist brother Reuben to call in a favor from the governor of Massachusetts. For the next nine months, Tomlinson commanded black troops, first helping to rebuild the shattered regiment in the aftermath of Fort Wagner, then taking part in the little-known Union invasion of Florida in early 1864. There, he fought in the small but brutal Battle of Olustee, when the 54th was thrown into the front lines to prevent a Confederate rout. During the battle, he would have heard the black soldiers he commanded raise a battle cry demanding equal pay, for at the time they were paid $3 less per month than white soldiers.[2] The 54th managed to stop the Confederate advance, thereby saving the rest of the Union force, which soon evacuated Florida. During the battle, Tomlinson was shot in the foot. The only two letters that survive in his hand are petitions for an honorable discharge due to the lingering wound, a request that was eventually granted by Secretary of War Edwin Stanton.

Tomlinson married and had several children, but family lore and his ever-shifting employment suggest that the wound never fully healed. The faint archival hints of his later life point to a man utterly exhausted, his best years behind him, his life devastated by the carnage of the Civil War. Until his death in 1885 at the age of forty-five, Tomlinson appears only one more time in the historical record: He signed his name urging Pennsylvanians to vote for his former officer in his Pennsylvania regiment.[3] That officer, Robert Dechert, was a Democrat, which, in the aftermath of the Civil War, was the party dedicated to maintaining white supremacy. Indeed, in 1871, he had been an assistant district attorney for Philadelphia mayor Daniel Fox—the same Daniel Fox who had presided over the disastrous election that culminated in Octavius Catto's murder.

I am fascinated by Ezekiel Tomlinson, not so much by what we know, but by what we don't know. At some point in 1863, Tomlinson decided he was willing to risk his life fighting alongside black men to end slavery and consummate a second American Revolution. It was a small but very real heroic decision. Eventually, however, his commitment waned and he went silent—other than a public endorsement of someone whose politics was anathema to what the 54th Massachusetts fought for. We should not doubt his revolutionary commitment—he nearly died, after all—but at some point, that commitment waned. Why the change? Was Tomlinson simply physically broken and mentally exhausted, and adding his name to the list of supporters for his former comrade was simply a personal favor? Or was he more broadly disillusioned with what Reconstruction had wrought? While his brother Reuben continued to fight for black equality on the South Carolina Sea Islands during Reconstruction, Ezekiel simply moved on.

As we have seen, countless men and women continued to believe that the Revolution had promised more, and they continued the revolutionary struggle—even as others, like my ancestor, made other decisions. That tension—that distinction—is one of our nation's most important internal engines. Two hundred and fifty years later, even as the era of the American Revolution has long passed, its echoes reverberate still.

How, then, should Americans 250 years later remember their founding? As always, it is far easier to poke holes in other approaches. In more recent decades, and particularly during Barack Obama's presidency, a certain strand of conservatism has embraced what was nicknamed "founders' chic"—an acute emphasis on the personalities, decisions, and successes of the Founding Fathers.[4] Some of the scholarship in this vein—namely, David McCullough's *John Adams* and Ron Chernow's *Alexander Hamilton*—has even reached the screen and stage. Countless Americans now think they know John Adams and Alexander Hamilton on an almost personal level. Historians may lament the countless inaccuracies of HBO's *John Adams* and Lin-Manuel Miranda's *Hamilton*, but turning men into myths is something all too human and not necessarily dangerous. Most people, after all, are not historians.

But the Founding Fathers cannot teach us simple lessons. They cannot solve our problems—*even* if they time traveled to the present day. To consider taxes or health care or federalism or DOGE (Department of Government Efficiency, initially helmed by ill-informed government neophyte Elon Musk) by asking "What would George Washington do?" is to place a level of wisdom and expertise on the Founding Fathers that they simply did not possess. If this book has made anything clear, it is that vast numbers of Americans *at the time* did not consider their political leaders perfect, nor did they consider the Constitution a sacrosanct document that contained all the answers. The Founding Fathers themselves agreed. After all, they argued about how to interpret the Constitution and the course the United States should take until their deathbeds. Here is the primary reason the Supreme Court's "originalism" is hollow and disingenuous. There can be no "original" interpretation—because there never was one in the first place.

Just as importantly, no American (or at least no sane American) should actually fantasize about living in the early decades of the United States, no matter how stirring or momentous that era seems. For women, black Americans, and Native people, this is obvious—but even for white men, the world was more often brutal than inspirational. Consider how many times this book has described a parent with a child who has died in childhood, or how many times an adult died in what today is middle age. Even the more mundane was significantly worse: During the Revolution it would take days and weeks to travel places that today only take hours. Nor were early Americans more wise or judicious, even when it came to matters of government for which they have been immortalized. Consider: Alexander Hamilton believed the United States should have an elected monarch who serves for life, the Framers of the Constitution believed that the top two presidential opponents could work together as president and vice president (the Twelfth Amendment changed this in 1804), and, above all, *the Constitution utterly failed to prevent the Civil War, the worst war in all of U.S. history*. To put it another way, the Founding Fathers were often brilliant and fascinating, but they could also be narrow-minded and obtuse. Simply returning to their ideas, even if it were possible, will not restore a fictional golden age.

As the semiquincentennial—July 4, 2026—approaches, President Donald Trump and his MAGA supporters have taken an entirely different tack when it comes to remembering the Revolution. They have imagined something far more ambitious—and it is likely coming to pass in some form as this book hits the shelves. Trump has promised a "most spectacular birthday party."[5] At the time of this writing, nothing more specific has been announced, but whatever is planned will no doubt be a perversion of real history, entirely ahistorical, or a combination of both. This is because, quite simply, Trumpism itself is a twisted perversion of American history. It is not only deeply reactionary—Make America Great *Again*—but it is also based upon a version of America that never really existed in the first place. Indeed, Trump has never defined the exact era of American greatness he would like to return to. On the basis of his celebration of American industry, it would seem to be the post–World War II era, when union membership was robust and marginal tax rates surpassed 90 percent. Trump, of course, has always been hostile to unions and seeks to cut taxes—as well as the federal government, which, in the immediate years after World War II, was large, powerful, and generally trusted.

Trumpism is also predicated on easily disprovable, often dangerous or malicious lies, unbridled demagoguery, and an open embrace of anti-intellectualism—all of which the Founding Fathers abhorred. The Founders were undoubtedly flawed, but they did not lie egregiously, embrace fanaticism, or celebrate stupidity. As Patriots, they were also *patriots.* Trump and his supporters' continued support for the January 6th insurrection may not make them definitively traitors, but at least they bear the stench of treason. If the Founding Fathers were transported to the United States in 2026, they could not fix the various ills of American government—but they would without question be appalled by Donald Trump and his ethos, as well as the Supreme Court's decision to grant Trump immunity in *Trump v. United States*. Most of originalism may be deeply flawed, but there is one thing in which the Founding Fathers were entirely consistent: the fear of a too-powerful executive.

Liberals and progressives have attempted to counter both the flawed traditionally conservative account and the warped MAGA version of the Revolution, but they have frequently failed to find a narrative that sticks with the American public. Reverential biographies of the Founding Fathers have dominated bestseller lists for two decades, whereas more critical accounts of the Revolution consistently fail to make inroads with the wider American public. The focus of these critical accounts (undoubtedly reflected in this book) is usually the many failures of the Revolution—to end slavery, to bring about racial and gender equality, to curb poverty, to realize the better world that Revolutionary-era Americans imagined. This scholarship is immensely valuable, and its production does no discredit to the many brilliant historians doing such work. On the contrary, it is the *job* of academics to poke holes and counter traditional narratives. Universities that uncritically embrace the status quo are intellectual deserts.

Yet a narrative of the American Revolution that only criticizes is a poor replacement for a narrative that only celebrates. At its best, American identity has not been predicated on race or ethnicity or language, but a shared sense of history and values first found in the American Revolution, and then later pushed forward during the Civil War and Reconstruction. That identity breaks down if that history is only portrayed as grim and those values are seen as hypocritical lies. No wonder so many everyday Americans choose celebratory biographies over critical narratives.

For liberals, there is a better way to memorialize the Revolution, one that accounts for its flaws and failings, but still celebrates the American Founding. It is rooted in the contents of this book, in the ways in which early Americans both honored and acclaimed the Revolution—*and* recognized that the Revolution's promises had not yet been realized. Americans in this book had no problem commemorating the "Spirit of 1776." They saw the Revolution as an era of hope and possibility, the beginning of a new era for humanity. The Revolution motivated and inspired, and it helped Americans to make sense of exactly what they were aiming for with their activism and their dreams—whatever those dreams were. That the Revolution did not achieve its lofty, perhaps impossible goals was not a reason to toss the Founding into the dustbin of history. On the contrary, it was a—perhaps *the*—reason to keep fighting for that better world.

Today's liberals should take their cue from these early generations of Americans, commemorating the Revolution neither as a moment when the greatness of America was realized, nor as a moment of singular hypocrisy and disappointment. As this book has shown, the American Revolution propelled ideas of liberty, equality, justice, and harmony. In many cases, these ideas were still quite conservative from the modern perspective, but at the time they represented great strides forward for the cause of humanity. No wonder subsequent generations of Americans continued to latch onto the Revolution to explain their goals and dreams. That these goals and dreams were unfulfilled was not a reason to forget the Revolution, but instead to see it as a starting point—and quite a good one, at that.

So when the Fourth of July comes around every year, liberals and progressives should unfurl flags, set off fireworks, sing patriotic songs, and embrace the hope and possibility of the American Revolution, just like their forebears did. They knew that the promises of the Revolution had not been fulfilled, but these promises still mattered. They still do today.

Realizing the Revolution

In 2026, the American Revolution does not matter just for the American past, but for the American present. In the 250 years since its birth, the United States has never been closer to one-person rule. The specific policies of President Trump are less concerning than his general disdain for the rule of law and any sort of check on his power, including Congress, the courts, the press, and the American people themselves. "Long live the king!" Trump proclaimed only a month after his inauguration, in reference to his attack on congestion pricing in New York City.[6] Trump's attitude was best voiced 250 years ago, by Tom Paine in *Common Sense*, when he encapsulated the attitude of King George III. His "thirst for arbitrary power," Paine wrote, allowed him to proclaim, "*You shall make no laws but what I please*."[7]

Indeed, it is well past time Americans return to *Common Sense*. Months before the United States declared independence, Tom Paine's famous tract spelled out all too clearly the myriad problems with the consolidation of power into a single person. A king deserved "the title of chief of plunderers" who proclaimed "wilful audacious libel against the truth."[8] While the defenders of the British government argued that Britain protected the colonies, Paine argued that, in fact, this protection was only for selfish ends, due to "*interest* not *attachment*." If the colonies end up benefiting too, this was due only to happenstance.

Paine also explained why monarchy had corrupted the unwritten British constitution. Asked Paine, "Why is the constitution of England sickly, but because monarchy hath poisoned the republic, the crown hath engrossed the commons?"[9] Corruption was all too easy when the king could sway powerful people in the government with rewards for their subservience. In one of his most memorable passages, Paine then listed the types of Americans who still favored compromise with the British monarchy: "Interested men, who are not to be trusted; weak men, who *cannot* see; prejudiced men, who *will not* see; and a certain set of moderate men, who think better of the European world than it deserves." This final group, Paine concluded, "will be the cause of more calamities to this continent, than all the other three."[10]

Naked greed, brazen lying, self-interest disguised as magnanimity, the expansion of executive power at the expense of the legislature, and the deliberate or misguided obsequiousness of countless officials who ought to know better—Paine's assessment could describe the United States in 2026 with hardly a word altered.

Neither do Paine's solutions to monarchy require much reinterpretation for today's America. He urged Americans to focus on electing officials to counter the British government, seeing legislatures as more representative of the people—and more honest—than a single person in charge. Crucially, he reminded people that, "in America, THE LAW IS KING."[11] He pressed Americans to "unite in drawing a line" against British depredations.[12] And he warned that urgency was needed. If Americans continued to exhibit "feebleness," they would miss the window for revolution. Wrote Paine, "If something is not done in time, it will be too late to do anything."[13] To put it succinctly: Stopping monarchy required democracy, the rule of law, unity, determination—and the recognition that the crisis has already arrived. There must be action, *now*. Once again, Paine's words resonate.

But Paine's words do not just eerily mirror fears of, and defiance toward, Trump and his acolytes. They also provide a warning for that same defiance. We must also embrace the *common sense* in *Common Sense*. Why, Paine asked, do we have government? Because human beings in a state of nature, living without government, have proven that they do not have the "moral virtue to govern the world." What government provides, therefore, is what everyone in the world wants: "freedom and security."[14]

At some point, those who oppose Trumpism have forgotten these simple truisms. At a time of rapidly rising inequality, increasingly unaffordable housing, the deindustrialization and hollowing out of wide swaths of the country, a lowering standard of living, and the cost of higher education reaching six figures per year, the Democrats have offered unexceptional ideas and stale political platitudes. Slogans and virtue signaling have replaced action, smugness and elitism have replaced understanding and respect for everyday Americans. The Democrats cannot proclaim to be the party of the working class while losing the working class in overwhelming numbers. Yard signs promoting progressive values are all well and good—but they are meaningless, even dishonest, if no one else can move into that neighborhood because housing is unaffordable.[15]

And so it is no wonder that an opportunistic figure like Donald Trump saw a political opening and stepped into the breach to harness the forces of revolution. Certainly, almost none of Trump's solutions will make anything better, and most will make the United States far worse—indeed, his disdain for democracy may end the United States as we know it. Yet of the two parties, Trump's Republicans are the only party offering radical change, at a time when a majority of Americans see their prospects declining. No wonder the working class has embraced Trump, even as so many of these voters know exactly who Donald Trump is. They decided the risk was worth the reward, so they rolled the dice. Meanwhile, Democrats have only added votes in the affluent suburbs, becoming the conservative party of the status quo, at a time when most Americans yearn for change. In a country birthed in revolution, this is and will forever be a path for political failure.

It is about time that Democrats and all those opposed to Trumpism return to the roots of this country, and once again try to realize the possibilities of the American Revolution. I do not offer any concrete political steps or policies to do so. (After all, I am a historian, not a politician or policy expert—and I am always wary of historians who proclaim that their knowledge of the past allows them to understand the present and predict the future better than others.) The lessons in this book are broader: Those who oppose Trump and his minions do not need to embrace the *policies* of the first generations of Americans, but they should embrace their *attitude*. This generation consisted of countless women and men who worked for a better world, who believed in the American Revolution and its many ideas—ideas of hope and possibility, when anything and everything was possible.

Certainly, there are good, practical reasons for liberal staleness, exhaustion, and despair. To have an attitude of acceptance, of lying low, of letting the desire for change once again perish is a natural human reaction. The political forces arrayed against today's liberalism are powerful, and they are seemingly entrenched. Donald Trump is a legitimately elected president who nevertheless harbors deeply authoritarian impulses, and at the time of this writing he commands the allegiance of obsequious Republicans who control both the Senate and the House of Representatives. The Supreme Court is currently composed of a 6–3 conservative majority, and these six justices will likely continue to give Trump incredible leeway to fulfill his ominous agenda. Even if Democrats regain momentum (as is the trend in most midterm elections), that will be stymied by the antidemocratic nature of the Constitution, in which much less populous and much more conservative states share equal power with states like California and New York. And, thanks to the influence of right-wing media, this momentum will likely have a ceiling, for millions of Americans will simply not hear arguments without Trumpian spin—and consequently will never give liberals their votes.

But it is still possible to turn the tide. Trumpism may be rooted in decades of increasingly reactionary, vitriolic politics, but Trump's actual ascendancy has lasted (at the time of this writing) only less than a decade. To assume a quick victory, to expect instant gratification, is to discredit and disrespect the countless revolutionary movements of American history that fought against much longer odds, for much longer periods of time. There is no need for despair: As this book has shown, the political winds can shift rapidly and drastically. Just ask the patriots of the 1760s or the abolitionists of the 1830s. All is still possible. America's future remains open.

Liberals and progressives go too far when they label Donald Trump some sort of uniquely malevolent phenomenon in American history, one that automatically portends the end of the republic and the death of the American experiment. On the contrary: Injustice, inequality, racism, corruption, and decadence are all part of a very long American tradition. Yet so too is the fight against them—a fight that was first inaugurated during the American Revolution, and one that has been repeated over and over and over again by the heirs of that Revolution. For decades and decades, Americans continued to fight for revolutionary ideals, for they imagined that a better world was possible than the one they lived in.

It still is.

Acknowledgments

I began writing this book in the summer of 2019 and over the past seven years a truly remarkable number of people have helped bring it to fruition. While the book's flaws are entirely due to me, its strengths come from the collective efforts of all the people who have supported and advised me over the years.

Acknowledgments must begin with everyone at The New Press who has aided the project in one way or another. My editor Marc Favreau believed in this book from the outset, and his countless comments and suggestions made it significantly better. When I told him that the book was roughly one hundred pages too long, he took the news with remarkable unflappability and then got down to business culling its many excesses. Brian Baughan's copyedits were immensely thorough and flawless, and they improved the book in so many ways. Other people who deserve praise include Maury Botton, Rachel Vega-DeCesario, Gia Gonzales, and a host of other people working behind the scenes.

My agent, Rebecca Friedman, took a chance on me and this book, and I am immensely grateful for her belief in its potential. She gave me brilliantly straightforward suggestions and asked the perfect questions, all of which got me thinking about the project in ways I had never thought of before.

I am immensely grateful that some brilliant historians read chapters, discussed the overall work, or simply offered help and advice. For the first year I was writing this book, I was not really sure what I was writing about—until I realized this was a story about the American Revolution. It was David Waldstreicher who first helped me work through my "Eureka" moment. Sarah Gronningsater, David Thomas, and James Bradley all read chapters and offered vital critiques. Andy Graybill gave me advice about agents, presses, and the big picture. Spencer McBride first introduced me to my agent. Thank you to all.

I workshopped several chapters at various seminars. Thank you to Jessica Roney and the Temple Early American Seminar, Laura Keenan Spero and the McNeil Center for Early American Studies, the readers at the Society for Historians of the Early American Republic's Second Book Workshop, and Madeline Lafuse, Blake McGready, and the CUNY Early American Seminar. Thanks in particular to Maeve Kane, who attended two of these seminars.

All the while I was writing this book, I was working as a history teacher at Springside Chestnut Hill Academy in Philadelphia. I (almost always) love getting up to teach each day, which is a testament to all the faculty, staff, and students at the school. If I did not feel at home a SCH, I would never have had the mental capacity to write nights, weekends, and over the summer. Go Blue Devils.

So many of my friends have offered words of encouragement over these past seven years—though, to be fair, not one of them has read a single chapter. Nevertheless, I could not have done this without them. Alas, there are too many people to be thanked individually, but my gift to all my friends is that, by not naming them, I will feel guilty and they can make me feel bad for at least another decade. Thanks to Shipley friends, Penn friends, rugby friends, SCH friends, weird workout friends, and the many new, irreplaceable friends I have made over the past year. I value you all.

My family has supported this project from the beginning. First, nonhumans: thanks to my dogs Struan (RIP) and Dalton for being open-minded sounding boards for all my ideas. Thanks to the Fifers, Stricklers, and Safnauers, who have always cultivated my love of history. I know that my grandparents continue to be proud of me, and they are looking down at me and smiling. Thanks, too, to my many (many!) in-laws, particularly Deanne and Maryanne, as well as all the rest of the Gosselin and Lawless clans. My brothers, Will and Corey, have always been a source of support. I love you both. My parents, Sandi and Tom, have always been by my side, through thick and thin, for all my forty-two years of history obsession. I could not have done this without them. Thank you, Mom and Dad. I love you.

My kids, Fran, Caleb, and Jo, bring me joy, entertainment, and inspiration (and, every so often, exasperation). When my heart at times feels like it's empty, they always fill it up with their love, warmth, and humor. This book is dedicated to them. I love you guys.

Finally, I cannot write enough about my amazing wife Jill. She is a special person, and I owe her so, so much. Not only does this book not exist without her, but nothing that is good in my life would either. I fell behind—and she waited. Love you to pieces, Jill.

Notes

Introduction

1. For historians, this divide fully came into being after Progressive Era historians challenged the virtue of the Revolution, most famously Charles A. Beard in *An Economic Interpretation of the Constitution of the United States* (Macmillan, 1913). For a summary of the historiographic divide over the past century, see Alfred F. Young and Gregory Nobles, *Whose American Revolution Was It? Historians Interpret the Founding* (NYU Press, 2011); David Waldstreicher, "The Revolutions of Revolution Historiography: Cold War Contradance, Neo-imperial Waltz, or Jazz Standard?" *Reviews in American History*, Vol. 42 (March 2014), 22–35. For an even more recent assessment, see the roundtable discussion in the *Journal of the Early Republic*: T.H. Breen et al., "The Revolution at 250: A Conversation," *Journal of the Early Republic*, Vol. 44, No. 4 (Winter 2024), 514–79. For a helpful and readable update on how the debate has shifted in the past decade, see David Waldstreicher's articles in the *Boston Review*, especially "The Changing Same of U.S. History," November 10, 2021, https://www.bostonreview.net/articles/the-changing-same-of-u-s-history, and "The Hidden Stakes of the 1619 Controversy," January 24, 2020, https://www.bostonreview.net/articles/david-waldstreicher-hidden-stakes-1619-controversy.

2. David Armitage, *The Declaration of Independence: A Global History* (Harvard University Press, 2008); Nathan Perl-Rosenthal, *The Age of Revolution, and the Generations Who Made It* (Basic Books, 2024), 423–25.

3. For those wishing for such a book, see Michael D. Hattem's excellent *The Memory of '76: The Revolution in American History* (Yale University Press, 2024).

4. John Higham, "From Boundlessness to Consolidation: The Transformation of American Culture, 1848–1860," in *Hanging Together: Unity and Diversity in American Culture* (Yale University Press, 2008), chap. 9.

5. Tom Paine, *Common Sense*, Project Gutenberg, https://www.gutenberg.org/files/147/147-h/147-h.htm.

6. On this point, I am persuaded by Sarah L.H. Gronningsater's reasoning in *The Rising Generation: Gradual Abolition, Black Legal Culture, and the Making of National Freedom* (University of Pennsylvania Press, 2024), 27.

7. On the use of "nations" instead of "tribes," see Kathleen Duval, *Native Nations: A Millenium in North America* (Random House, 2024), 22–24.

1. Revolutionary Finale: The Bill of Rights, 1789–91

1. Patrick Henry, "Give Me Liberty or Give Me Death," March 23, 1775, reprinted in *The Avalon Project: Documents in Law, History, and Diplomacy*, Yale Law School, Lillian Goldman Law Library, https://avalon.law.yale.edu/18th_century/patrick.asp. The speech as we read it is a reconstruction. Henry did not keep his original speech, nor did anyone record it verbatim at the time.

2. Patrick Henry, "Speech Delivered at the Virginia Convention Debate of the Ratification of the Constitution," June 7, 1788, *The Documentary History of the Ratification of the Constitution* (hereafter *DHRC*), 48 Vols., ed. John P. Kaminski et al. (The State Historical Society of Wisconsin, 1990), 9: 1044–45. Italics in original.

3. "Brutus," October 18, 1787, reprinted in *The Anti-Federalist Papers and the Constitutional Convention Debates*, ed. Ralph Ketcham (Signet Classics, 1986), 287.

4. "John DeWitt," October 22, 1787, in ibid., 199.

5. Melancton Smith, June 23, 1788, in ibid., 371.

6. Thomas Tredwell, as quoted in Carol Berkin, *The Bill of Rights: The Fight to Secure America's Liberties* (Simon & Schuster, 2015), 29.

7. William Whiting, as quoted in Woody Holton, *Unruly Americans and the Origins of the Constitution* (Hill and Wang, 2007), 105.

8. See Saul Cornell, *The Other Founders: Anti-Federalism and the Dissenting Tradition in America, 1788–1828* (University of North Carolina Press, 1999), chaps. 2 and 3.

9. Henry, "Speech Delivered at the Virginia Convention Debate of the Ratification of the Constitution."

10. Edmund S. Morgan, *Inventing the People: The Rise of Popular Sovereignty in England and America* (W.W. Norton, 1988), 239.

11. Tom Paine, "Common Sense," *The Writings of Thomas Paine, Vol. 1, 1775–1779*, ed. Moncure Daniel Conway (G.G. Putnam and Sons, 1894), 119.

12. John Adams to William Cushing, June 9, 1776, *Founders Online*, https://founders.archives.gov/documents/Adams/06-04-02-0109.

13. Patrick Henry, June 5, 1788, in ibid., 204.

14. "Centinel," No. 3, as quoted in Cornell, *The Other Founders*, 100.

15. Smith, June 23, 1788, in *The Anti-Federalist Papers*, 372–73.

16. James Wilson, December 1, 1787, The Pennsylvania Convention, in *DHRC, Vol. II: Pennsylvania*, 453.

17. James Wilson, December 4, 1787, in ibid., 474.

18. James Wilson, December 11, 1787, in ibid., 559.

19. Michael J. Klarman, *The Framers' Coup: The Making of the United States Constitution* (Oxford University Press, 2016); Holton, *Unruly Americans.*

20. Van Gosse, "In the Woodpile: Negro Electors in the First Reconstruction," in *Revolutions and Reconstructions: Black Politics in the Long Nineteenth Century*, ed. Van Gosse and David Waldstreicher (University of Pennsylvania Press, 2020), 66–83.

21. Pauline Maier, *Ratification: The People Debate the Constitution, 1787–1788* (Simon and Schuster, 2010), 122–24, 248–49.

22. Ibid., 137–38.

23. For a day-by-day description of the Massachusetts convention, see Maier, *Ratification*, 138–213.

24. Massachusetts Convention Debates, January 31, A.M., 1788, *DHRC, Vol. VI: Massachusetts, No. 3,* 1379.

25. Massachusetts Convention Debates, January 31, P.M., 1788, in ibid., 1384.

26. Form of Ratification, Commonwealth of Massachusetts, February 6, 1788, in ibid., 1469.

27. Samuel Nasson to George Thatcher, February 8, 1788, in *DHRC, Vol. VII: Massachusetts, No. 4*, 1649.

28. Todd Estes, "'From the Works of Nature . . . to the Institutions of Man': How Political Moderation Made Possible the Constitution's Ratification," *Journal of the Early Republic*, Vol. 43, No. 3 (Fall 2023), 363–98.

29. James Madison to George Washington, February 15, 1788, in *DHRC, Vol. VII: Massachusetts, No. 4*, 1701.

30. Holton, *Unruly Americans*, 25–26.

31. Madison, as quoted in Andrew Burstein and Nancy Isenberg, *Madison and Jefferson* (Random House, 2013), 78.

32. Martin Oster to Comte de la Luzerne, June 28, 1788, in *DHRC: Ratification by the States, Volume X: Virginia, No. 3*, 1690.

33. James Madison to Richard Peters, August 19, 1789, *The Papers of James Madison, Vol. XII:* , ed. William T. Hutchinson et al. (University of Virginia Press, 1979), 347.

34. As quoted in Jonathan Gienapp, *The Second Creation: Fixing the American Constitution in the Founding Era* (Harvard University Press, 2018), 169.

35. James Madison to George Eve, January 2, 1789, *The Papers of James Madison, Vol. XI*, 405.

36. Thomas Jefferson to James Madison, March 15, 1789, *The Papers of James Madison, Vol. XII*, 14.

37. Gienapp, *The Second Creation*, 175–76.

38. Madison's Notes for Speech in Congress, June 8, 1789, Stagg, *The Papers of James Madison*

39. Richard Beeman, *Plain, Honest Men: The Making of the American Constitution* (Random House, 2010); Catherine Drinker Bowen, *Miracle at Philadelphia: The Story of the Constitutional Convention* (Little, Brown, 1966).

40. Saul Cornell, *A Well-Regulated Militia: The Founding Fathers and the Origins of Gun Control in America* (Oxford University Press, 2006), chaps. 1 and 2.

41. Akhil Reed Amar, *The Bill of Rights: Creation and Reconstruction* (Yale University Press, 1998), 83.

42. Madison Resolution, June 8, 1789, reprinted in Helen E. Veit, Kenneth R. Bowling, and Charlene Bangs Bickford, eds., *Creating the Bill of Rights: The Documentary Record from the First Federal Congress* (Johns Hopkins University Press, 1991), 13.

43. Ibid., 11–12.

44. Aedanus Burke, Speech to the House, August 15, 1787, in ibid., 175.

45. Ibid., 322.

46. James Madison to Thomas Jefferson, March 29, 1789, Stagg, *Papers of James Madison*.

47. Edward Carrington to James Madison, September 29, 1789, in ibid.

48. John Collins to George Washington, September 26, 1789, in *Creating the Bill of Rights*.

49. James Madison to George Washington, January 4, 1790, Stagg, *Papers of James Madison*.

50. Amar, *The Bill of Rights*, chap. 7.

2. The Right to Rebel: The Whiskey Rebellion, 1791–94

1. James Ross, Jasper Yeates, and William Bradford to George Washington, September 24, 1994, *Founders Online*, National Archives, https://founders.archives.gov/documents/Washington/05-16-02-0488.

2. Herman Husband, "An Impartial Relation of the First and Causes of the Recent Differences in Public Affairs Etc," September 14, 1769, reprinted in *History Matters: The U.S. Survey Course on the Web*, http://historymatters.gmu.edu/d/6233/.

3. Much of my understanding of Dickinson is taken from Jane E. Calvert, *Quaker Constitutionalism and the Thought of John Dickinson* (Cambridge University Press, 2009).

4. Dickinson to William Pitt, 1765, as quoted in ibid., 241.

5. As quoted in Laurent Dubois, *Avengers of the New World: The Story of the Haitian Revolution* (The Belknap Press of Harvard University Press, 2015), 59.

6. Thomas Jefferson to William Smith, November 13, 1787, Library of Congress, https://www.loc.gov/exhibits/jefferson/105.html.

7. Terry Bouton, *Taming Democracy: "The People," The Founders, and the Troubled Ending of the American Revolution* (Oxford University Press, 2007), chap. 10.

8. Much of the next two paragraphs are drawn from Bruce E. Stewart, *Redemption from Tyranny: Herman Husband's American Revolution* (University of Virginia Press, 2020).

9. Johann Schoepf, as quoted in ibid., 103.

10. Marjoleine Kars, *Breaking Loose Together: The Regulator Rebellion in Pre-revolutionary North Carolina* (University of North Carolina Press, 2002), 111–15, 135–38.

11. Alexander Hamilton, December 13, 1790, "Final Version: First Report on the Further Provision Necessary for Establishing Public Credit," *Founders Online*, National Archives, https://founders.archives.gov/documents/Hamilton/01-07-02-0227-0003.

12. There is no evidence this is a reason the tax was passed, but it seems likely Hamilton hoped it was at least a beneficial by-product.

13. William Samuel Johnson, as quoted in Richard Beeman, *Plain, Honest Men: The Making of the American Constitution* (Random House, 2009), 169–70; Max Farrand, ed., *The Records of the Federal Convention of 1787*, rev. ed. (Yale University Press, 1937), Vol. 1, Chap. 8, Doc. 10, https://press-pubs.uchicago.edu/founders/documents/v1ch8s10.html.

14. This theory began as early as 1796 in William Findley's account, in which he defended his actions and castigated Hamilton: *History of the Insurrection* . . . (1796), 311–12. Most recently, it has been argued by William Hogeland, *The Whiskey Rebellion: George Washington, Alexander Hamilton, and the Frontier Rebels Who Challenged America's Newfound Sovereignty* (Simon and Schuster, 2006), 124.

15. Hamilton, "Final Version: First Report," *Founders Online*.

16. Neville B. Craig, *The History of Pittsburgh* . . . (Pittsburgh, 1851), 268.

17. Hugh Henry Brackenridge, *Incidents of the Insurrection in the Western Parts of Pennsylvania, in the Year 1794* (Philadelphia, 1795), 122.

18. Thomas P. Slaughter, *The Whiskey Rebellion: Frontier Epilogue to the American Revolution* (Oxford University Press, 1986), 186.

19. Brady J. Crytzer, *The Whiskey Rebellion: A Distilled History of an American Crisis* (Westholme Publishing, 2023), 91.

20. James P. McClure, "'Let Us Be Independent': David Bradford and the Whiskey Insurrection," *Pittsburgh History* (Summer 1991), 74.

21. William Bradford to Edmund Randolph, August 15, 1794, Pennsylvania Whiskey Rebellion Collection, 1792–1796, Library of Congress, Washington, D.C.

22. Alexander Addison to Henry Lee, November 23, 1794, reprinted in Steven R. Boyd, ed., *The Whiskey Rebellion: Past and Present Perspective* (Greenwood Press, 1985), 53–54.

23. Alexander Hamilton to George Washington, August 5, 1794, *Founders Online*, National Archives, https://founders.archives.gov/documents/Washington/05-16-02-0357.

24. James Roger Sharp, "The Whiskey Rebellion and the Question of Representation"; Roland M. Baumann, "Philadelphia's Manufacturers and the Excise Tax of 1794: The Forging of the Jeffersonian Coalition," both in Boyd, *The Whiskey Rebellion*, 119–34 and 135–64.

25. Alexander Hamilton to James McHenry, March 18, 1799, Hamilton Papers, *Founders Online*, https://founders.archives.gov/documents/Hamilton/01-22-02-0344#:~:text=To%20James%20McHenry1&text=Beware%2C%20my%20Dear%20Sir%2C%20of,by%20the%20display%20of%20strength.

26. E.P. Thompson, *The Making of the English Working Class* (Vintage, 1966).

27. Barbara Clark Smith, *The Freedoms We Lost: Consent and Resistance in Revolutionary America* (The New Press, 2010).

28. William Bradford, James Ross, and Jasper Yeates to George Washington, September 24, 1794, *Founders Online*, National Archives, https://founders.archives.gov/documents/Washington/05-16-02-0488.

29. Yeates, Ross, and Bradford to Edmund Randolph, August 30, 1794, Whiskey Rebellion Collection.

30. William Findley, *History of the Insurrection in the Four Western Counties . . .* (Philadelphia, 1796), 129–30.

31. Ibid., 132–37; H.M. Brackenridge, *History of the Western Insurrection in Western Pennsylvania, Commonly Called the Whiskey Rebellion, 1794* (Pittsburgh, 1859), 254–55.

32. William Bradford to George Washington, August 17, 1794, Whiskey Rebellion Collection.

33. David Bradford and committee, September 13, 1794, reprinted in *Report of the Committee Appointed to Examine into the State of the Treasury Department: Made to the House of Representatives of the United States on the 22d day of May, 1794* (Philadelphia, 1794), 36.

34. Elizabeth Bradford to George Washington, December 10, 1794, and January 22, 1795, both in Whiskey Rebellion Collection; McClure, "'Let Us Be Independent,'" 77; Hogeland, *The Whiskey Rebellion*, 242.

35. Philadelphia petitioners to George Washington, June 13, 1795, Whiskey Rebellion Collection.

36. Brackenridge, *Incidents of the Insurrection*, 83.

37. McClure, "'Let Us Be Independent,'" 77

38. Findley, *History of the Insurrection*, 129–30.

39. Ibid., 324–25.

40. Slaughter, *The Whiskey Rebellion*, 226; "Federal Excise Taxes on Alcoholic Beverages: A Summary of Present Law and a Brief History," Congressional Research Report

for Congress, June 15, 1999, Library of Congress, https://www.everycrsreport.com /reports/RL30238.html.

41. Proclamation of Loyalty, September 20, 1794, Whiskey Rebellion Collection.

42. *New Hampshire Sentinel* (Keene), October 6, 1804.

43. For a longer discussion of secession versus revolution, see Daniel A. Farber, *Lincoln's Constitution* (Chicago University Press, 2003), 101–5. See also Manisha Sinha, "Revolution or Counterrevolution? The Political Ideology of Secession in Antebellum South Carolina," *Civil War History*, Vol. 46, No. 3 (September 2000), 205–26.

3. The Rights of Women: New Jersey's Radical Experiment, 1789–1807

1. Bedminster Township Voting Register, 1800, MG 895, New Jersey Historical Society, Newark, NJ. See also "Bedminster Township Voters, 1797–1803," in *Somerset Historical Quarterly*, ed. A. Van Doren Honeyman, Vol. 6 (1917), 268–72 (hereafter *SHQ*).

2. Richard Henry Lee, 1778, as quoted in Joan R. Gundersen, *To Be Useful to the World: Women in Revolutionary America, 1740–1790* (University of North Carolina Press, 2006), 178.

3. Richard P. McCormick, *The History of Voting in New Jersey: A Study of the Development of Election Machinery, 1664–1911* (Rutgers University Press, 1953), 73.

4. Samuel L. Parry, "The Origin of the Name 'Pluckemin,'" *SHQ*, Vol. 1 (1912), 196–205.

5. References to all three women are scattered throughout the eight volumes of the *Somerset Historical Quarterly*. For Hodge's life, see especially Vol. 6 (1917), 104, and Vol. 2 (1913), 154. For Eoff, also see Andrew D. Mellick Jr., *The Story of an Old Farm, or Life in New Jersey in the Eighteenth Century, with a Genealogical Appendix* (Somerville, NJ, 1889), 163.

6. Mark Edward Lender, "The 'Cockpit' Reconsidered: Revolutionary New Jersey as a Military Theater," in *New Jersey in the American Revolution*, ed. Barbara J. Mitnick (Rivergate Books, 2005), 45.

7. Delight W. Dodyk, "'Troublesome Times A-Coming': The American Revolution and New Jersey Women," in Mitnick, *New Jersey in the American Revolution*, 149; Gunderson, *To Be Useful to the World*, 182.

8. See Mark Edward Lender and Garry Wheeler Stone, *Fatal Sunday: George Washington, the Monmouth Campaign, and the Politics of Battle* (Oklahoma University Press, 2016), 326–30.

9. *New Jersey Gazette* (Trenton), July 12, 1780.

10. "General Washington's Reception at Trenton," *Columbian Magazine*, Vol. 5 (Philadelphia, 1789), 288–90.

11. Carl E. Prince, *New Jersey's Jeffersonian Republicans: The Genesis of an Early Party Machine, 1789–1817* (University of North Carolina Press, 1964), 4–6.

12. Rosemarie Zagarri, *Revolutionary Backlash: Women and Politics in the Early American Republic* (University of Pennsylvania Press, 2007), 30–31.

13. Henry Shinn, "An Early New Jersey Poll List," *Pennsylvania Magazine of History and Biography*, Vol. 44, No. 1 (1920), 77–81.

14. Jan Lewis, "Rethinking Women's Suffrage in New Jersey, 1776–1807," *Rutgers Law Review*, Vol. 63, No. 3 (2011), 1020.

15. Zagarri, *Revolutionary Backlash*, 40.

16. Mary Wollstonecraft, *A Vindication of the Rights of Woman, with Strictures on Political and Moral Subjects* (1792), 335.

17. Teresa Anne Murphy, *Citizenship and the Origins of Women's History in the United States* (University of Pennsylvania Press, 2013), 56.

18. Judith Sargent Murray, "On the Equality of the Sexes," *Massachusetts Magazine*, Vol. 2 (Boston, 1790), http://digital.library.upenn.edu/women/murray/equality/equality.html. Most of the information on Murray I draw from Sheila L. Skemp, *First Lady of Letters: Judith Sargent Murray and the Struggle for Female Independence* (University of Pennsylvania Press, 2009).

19. Susan Branson, *These Fiery Frenchified Dames: Women and Political Culture in Early National Philadelphia* (University of Pennsylvania Press, 2001).

20. Elias Boudinot, *An Oration, Delivered at Elizabeth-Town, New Jersey, Agreeable to a Resolution of the State Society of Cincinnati on the Fourth of July* . . . (Elizabeth Town, NJ, 1793), 24.

21. Thomas Cooper, *A Reply to Mr. Burke's Invective Against Mr. Cooper* . . . (1792), 98–99.

22. The endorsement of female suffrage likely went even further. The original suffrage law had mandated that all voters possess £50 "of clear estate," meaning that the £50 property requirement could be easily proven. The 1797 law eliminated this language, making it much more difficult to prove who was eligible to vote. This change would have mostly benefited widows, many of whom controlled their late husband's property but did not legally own it.

23. *Centinel of Freedom* (Newark), November 11, 1800.

24. "When Did Women Get the Right to Vote?," *Human Rights Careers*, 2024, https://www.humanrightscareers.com/issues/when-did-women-get-the-right-to-vote/#:~:text=As%20an%20example%2C%20Sweden%20gave,got%20the%20right%20to%20vote; "Right of Québec women to vote and hold office," *élections Québec*, 2024, https://www.electionsquebec.qc.ca/en/understand/understanding-voting/right-of-quebec-women-to-vote-and-to-stand-for-office/.

25. These are the following poll lists: Bedminster Township Voting Register, Somerset County, October 1800, Manuscript Group 895, New Jersey Historical Society, Newark, NJ; Montgomery Township Poll Book, October 1801, Somerset County, Montgomery Township Municipal Records, New Jersey State Archives, Trenton, NJ; Upper Penns Neck Township, Salem County, for elections in December 1800, October 1801, October 1802, October 1803, December 1803, October 1806, Museum of the American Revolution, https://www.amrevmuseum.org/virtualexhibits/when-women-lost-the-vote-a-revolutionary-story/pages/plg-upper-penns-neck-township-salem-county-new-jersey-poll-lists; Chester Township, Burlington County, for election in October 1807, https://www.amrevmuseum.org/virtualexhibits/when-women-lost-the-vote-a-revolutionary-story/pages/plg-chester-township-burlington-county-new-jersey-october-1807.

26. "Women of the Holton Family," Museum of the American Revolution, https://www.amrevmuseum.org/virtualexhibits/when-women-lost-the-vote-a-revolutionary-story/pages/women-of-the-holton-family; *Centinel of Freedom* (Newark, NJ), February 9, 1807.

27. Sarah King's voting record is found in the Upper Penns Neck Poll Lists, 1800–1806, Salem County, Museum of the American Revolution, https://www.amrevmuseum.org/virtualexhibits/when-women-lost-the-vote-a-revolutionary-story/pages/plg-upper-penns-neck-township-salem-county-new-jersey-poll-lists. For the evidence that Mary Curry, voting after King in 1800, soon married, see "Mary Curry," Museum of the American Revolution, https://www.amrevmuseum.org/virtualexhibits/when-women-lost-the-vote-a-revolutionary-story/pages/mary-curry. For evidence that Susannah Bradaway, two voters after King, married, see Susannah Bradway, Marriage Records, 1804, New Jersey State Archives, Trenton, NJ. It seems almost certain that Susannah Bradaway (as listed in the poll book) and Susannah Bradway (as listed in the New Jersey State Archives) are the same woman.

28. Montgomery Township Poll Book (1801), Montgomery Township Municipal Records, 1797–1921, Control #MMYC001, New Jersey State Archives, Trenton, NJ.

29. David Waldstreicher, *In the Midst of Perpetual Fetes: The Making of American Nationalism, 1776–1820* (University of North Carolina Press, 1997). See 168–69 n97 for gatherings in New Jersey specifically.

30. Prince, *New Jersey's Jeffersonian Republicans*, 134n7.

31. For a different interpretation, see Andrew W. Robertson, "Jeffersonian Parties, Politics, and Participation: The Tortuous Trajectory of American Democracy," in *Practicing Democracy: Popular Politics in the United States from the Constitution to the Civil War*, ed. Daniel Peart and Adam I.P. Smith (University of Virginia Press, 2015), 114.

32. *Centinel of Freedom* (Newark), October 18, 1797.

33. Petition of Inhabitants and Electors of Hunterdon County to the New Jersey General Assembly, October 23, 1802, Papers Related to Women Voting in Hunterdon County, 1802, New Jersey Department of State, AM Papers, Box 17, New Jersey State Archives, Trenton; Prince, *New Jersey's Jeffersonian Republicans*, 84n25.

34. Frederick Frelinghuysen, Report on the Trenton and Maidenhead Election, November 16, 1802, Papers Related to Women Voting in Hunterdon County.

35. *Philadelphia Gazette and Daily Advertiser*, October 20, 1800; *Pittsfield Sun*, December 27, 1802; *City Gazette* (Charleston, SC), January 1, 26, 1803; *Political Repository* (Brookfield, MA), June 15, 1801.

36. *Washington* (DC) *Federalist*, December 2, 1800.

37. Linda K. Kerber, *Women of the Republic: Intellect and Ideology in Revolutionary America* (University of North Carolina Press, 1980). See p. 283 for a definitive statement.

38. Zagarri, *Revolutionary Backlash*, 46–81; Branson, *These Fiery Frenchified Dames*.

39. As quoted in Skemp, *First Lady of Letters*, 303.

40. Abigail Adams to John Adams, March 31–April 5, 1776, *Adams Family Papers: An Electronic Archive*, Massachusetts Historical Society, https://www.masshist.org/digitaladams/archive/doc?id=L17760331aa.

41. John Adams to Abigail Adams, April 14, 1776, *American Social History Project*, City University of New York, https://shec.ashp.cuny.edu/items/show/676.

42. Abigail Adams to Mary Smith Cranch, November 15, 1797, *Founders Online*, National Archives, https://founders.archives.gov/documents/Adams/04-12-02-0166#ADMS-04-12-02-0166-fn-0004-ptr.

43. William Griffith, "Eumenes: Being a Collection of Papers Written for the Purpose of Exhibiting Some of the More Prominent Errors and Omissions of the Constitution of New-Jersey . . ." (Trenton, 1799), 1.

44. Ibid., 33.

45. *Centinel of Freedom* (Newark), November 20, 1804.

46. *Trenton Federalist*, October 15, 1804.

47. David Brion Davis, *The Problem of Slavery in the Age of Revolution, 1770–1823* (Cornell University Press, 1975), 306–26.

48. French Civil Code, Chapter VI, No. 213–215 (1803), reprinted in "The Napoleon Series," *The Waterloo Association*, https://www.napoleon-series.org/research/government/code/book1/c_title05.html#chapter6.

49. As quoted in Sheila Skemp, "America's Mary Wollstonecraft: Judith Sargent Murray's Case for Equal Rights for Women," in *Revolutionary Founders: Rebels, Radicals, and Reformers in the Making of the Nation*, ed. Alfred F. Young, Gary B. Nash, and Ray Raphael (Vintage, 2011), 300.

50. Skemp, *First Lady of Letters*, 305.

51. Zagarri, *Revolutionary Backlash.*

52. Prince, *New Jersey's Jeffersonian Republicans*, 132–34; Judith Apter Klinghoffer and Lois Elkis, "'The Petticoat Electors': Women's Suffrage in New Jersey, 1776–1807," *Journal of the Early Republic*, Vol. 12, No. 2 (Summer 1992), 186–88.

53. *Centinel of Freedom* (Newark), May 26, 1807.

54. William H. Shaw, *History of Essex and Hudson Counties, New Jersey, Vol. 1* (Everts and Peck, 1884), 212–13.

55. New Jersey 1807 Referendum, Essex County, *A New Nation Votes: American Election Returns, 1787–1825*, American Antiquarian Society, 2007, https://elections.lib.tufts.edu/catalog/c247ds363.

56. Klinghoffer and Elkis, "'The Petticoat Electors,'" 187n73.

57. Minutes from November 16, 1807, *Votes and Proceedings of the Thirty-Second General Assembly of the State of New Jersey* (Trenton, 1807), 90; Klinghoffer and Elkis, "'The Petticoat Electors,'" 189.

58. Elizabeth Cady Stanton, "Declaration of Sentiments" (1848).

59. "This Matter of Woman's Voting," *The Lily*, May 1, 1855. The article uses the name "John Q. Adams," but certainly means to refer not to him but his father, John Adams.

60. "Political Non-existence of Women," *The Lily*, November 1, 1850.

61. François Furstenburg, *In the Name of the Father: Washington's Legacy, Slavery, and the Making of the American Nation* (Penguin Books, 2007), chap. 5.

62. Woody Holton, "Equality as Unintended Consequences: The Contracts Clause and the Married Women's Property Acts," *Journal of Southern History*, Vol. 18, Issue 2 (May 2015), 326–39; Melissa J. Homestead, *American Women, American Authors, and Literary Property, 1822–1869* (Cambridge University Press, 2005), 42–43.

63. Lydia A. Jenkins, "Woman-Civil Rights," *The Lily*, February 1, 1850.

64. Elizabeth Cady Stanton, "Justice to Woman: Address of the Women's Rights Convention to the Legislature," *The Una* (April 1854), 251.

65. Susan B. Anthony to William Whitehead, February 14, 1881, William Whitehead Correspondence, MG 177, New Jersey Historical Society, Newark.

66. See, for example, Ellen Carol DuBois, *Suffrage: Women's Long Battle for the Vote* (Simon and Schuster, 2020).

4. Racial Equality, Part I: Gabriel's Revolutionary Plan, 1800

1. Thomas Jefferson to Phillip Mazzei, April 24, 1796, *The Papers of Thomas Jefferson*, Vol. 29 (Princeton University Press, 2002), 81–83.

2. This point was first made by Douglas Egerton in his book *Gabriel's Rebellion: The Virginia Slave Conspiracies of 1800 and 1802* (University of North Carolina Press, 1993).

3. Testimony of Ben Woolfolk, Trial of Gabriel, October 6, 1800, reprinted in *Gabriel's Conspiracy: A Documentary History*, ed. Philip J. Schwarz (University of Virginia Press, 2012), 153.

4. While numbers like these can be found in many works, I have relied particularly upon Douglas R. Egerton, *Death or Liberty: African Americans and Revolutionary America* (Oxford University Press, 2009), chap. 1.

5. David Waldstreicher, *The Odyssey of Phillis Wheatley: A Poet's Journey Through American Slavery and Independence* (Hill and Wang, 2023), 188.

6. "Slave societies" is Ira Berlin's term, from *Many Thousands Gone: The First Two Centuries of Slavery in North America* (Belknap Press of Harvard University Press, 1998), 8.

7. Ibid., 57.

8. Two definitive accounts of this process are Edmund S. Morgan, *American Slavery, American Freedom: The Ordeal of Colonial Virginia* (W.W. Norton, 1975), and Kathleen Brown, *Good Wives, Nasty Wenches, and Anxious Patriarchs: Gender, Race, and Power in Colonial Virginia* (North Carolina University Press, 1996).

9. Through a complicated series of events, Cushing's ruling was based upon and related to a similar ruling in *Brom and Bett v. Ashley*, which awarded the freedom of an enslaved woman named Mum Bett. Mum Bett's case never went beyond *her* personal freedom, however.

10. William Cushing, "Instructions to the Jury in the Quock Walker Case, *Commonwealth of Massachusetts v. Nathaniel Jennison* (1783)," reprinted in National Constitution Center, https://constitutioncenter.org/the-constitution/historic-document-library/detail/william-cushing-instructions-to-the-jury-in-the-quock-walker-case-commonwealth-of-massachusetts-v-nathaniel-jennison-1783. Importantly, Cushing's ruling did not free every slave at once, for each enslaved person needed to sue for their freedom individually. However, enslavers knew they would lose in court, so many quickly contracted with slaves to free them in return for many years of service. In other cases, some of the more vengeful slave owners sold their slaves outside the state. See Egerton, *Death or Liberty*, 108–9.

11. "An Act for the Gradual Abolition of Slavery," March 1, 1780, Pennsylvania Historical and Museum Commission, http://www.phmc.state.pa.us/portal/communities/documents/1776-1865/abolition-slavery.html.

12. Edward Countryman, *Enjoy the Same Liberty: Black Americans and the Revolutionary Era* (Roman and Littlefield, 2014), x.

13. James Otis, "The Rights of the British Colonies Asserted and Proved," 29, reprinted in *Evans Early American Imprint Collection*, University of Michigan, https://quod.lib.umich.edu/e/evans/n07655.0001.001/29?page=root;size=100;view=text.

14. Technically, they were not manumitted until the death of Martha Washington, in 1802.

15. Manisha Sinha, *The Slave's Cause: A History of Abolition* (Yale University Press, 2016), 42.

16. *Virginia Gazette*, September 20, 1800, in Schwarz, *Gabriel's Conspiracy*, 49.

17. Egerton, *Gabriel's Rebellion*, 29.

18. Waldstreicher, *The Odyssey of Phillis Wheatley*, 12.

19. Washington, as quoted in Robert G. Parkinson, *The Common Cause: Creating Race and Nation in the American Revolution* (University of North Carolina Press, 2016), 175.

20. Benjamin Quarles, "The American Revolution as a Black Declaration of Independence," in *Slavery and Freedom in the Age of the American Revolution*, ed. Ira Berlin and Ronald Hoffman (University of Virginia Press, 1983), 289.

21. Egerton, *Death or Liberty*, 77.

22. Karen Cook Bell, *Running from Bondage: Enslaved Women and Their Remarkable Fight for Freedom in Revolutionary America* (Cambridge University Press, 2021), 9.

23. Waldstreicher, *The Odyssey of Phillis Wheatley*, chap. 16. The details of how Wheatley became free remain contested, but this broader point holds true.

24. Jacqueline Beatty, *In Dependence: Women and the Patriarchal State in Revolutionary America* (New York University Press, 2023), 164.

25. Thomas J. Davis, "Emancipation Rhetoric, Natural Rights, and Revolutionary New England: A Note on Four Black Petitions in Massachusetts, 1773–1777," *New England Quarterly*, Vol. 62, No. 2 (June 1989), 255.

26. Lemuel Haynes, "Liberty Further Extended," reprinted in Richard S. Newman, ed., *Black Preacher to White America: The Collected Writings of Lemuel Haynes, 1774–1883* (Carlson Publishing, 1990), 19; Chernoh M. Sesay Jr. "The Revolutionary Black Roots of Slavery's Abolition in Massachusetts," *New England Quarterly*, Vol. 87, No. 1 (March, 2014), 99–131.

27. Eric Slauter, "Life, Liberty, and Happiness," July 3, 2011, *Boston Globe*, http://archive.boston.com/news/politics/articles/2011/07/03/life_liberty_and_the_pursuit_of_happiness/?page=full.

28. St. George Tucker, "Letter to a Member of the General Assembly of Virginia, on the Subject of the Late Conspiracy of Slaves" (Baltimore, 1801), 7.

29. Parkinson, *Common Cause*.

30. *Somerset* against *Stewart*, May 14, 1772, p. 510, http://www.commonlii.org/int/cases/EngR/1772/57.pdf.

31. Parkinson, *Common Cause*, 639.

32. Alexander Tsesis, *For Liberty and Equality: The Life and Times of the Declaration of Independence* (Oxford University Press, 2012), 145.

33. Kate Masur, *Until Justice Be Done: America's First Civil Rights Movement, from the Revolution to Reconstruction* (W.W. Norton, 2021), 5.

34. My interpretation is drawn from David Waldstreicher, *Slavery's Constitution: From Revolution to Ratification* (Hill & Wing, 2009). I largely reject Sean Wilentz's formulation that the Constitution was an antislavery document: Wilentz, *No Property in Man: Slavery and Antislavery at the Nation's Founding* (Harvard University Press, 2018).

35. Paul J. Polgar, *Standard-Bearers of Equality: America's First Abolition Movement* (University of North Carolina Press, 2019); Nicholas P. Wood, "'A Class of Citizens': The Earliest Black Petitioners to Congress and Their Quaker Allies," *William and Mary Quarterly*, Vol. 74, No. 1 (January 2017), 109–44.

36. Winthrop D. Jordan, *White over Black: American Attitudes Toward the Negro, 1550–1812* (University of North Carolina Press, 1968), 391.

37. Egerton, *Death or Liberty*, 136–38.

38. Robert Carter's Deed of Gift, August 1, 1791, *Encyclopedia Virginia*, https://encyclopediavirginia.org/entries/robert-carter-iiis-deed-of-gift-august-1-1791/.

39. James Sidbury, *Ploughshares into Swords: Race, Rebellion, and Identity in Gabriel's Virginia, 1730–1810* (Cambridge University Press, 1997), 210–11.

40. Daniel Bard, as quoted in Jordan, *White over Black*, 388.

41. Monroe, as quoted in Egerton, *Gabriel's Rebellion*, 49.

42. Egerton, *Gabriel's Rebellion*, 103–4.

43. James Monroe to the Speakers of the General Assembly, December 5, 1800, in Schwarz, *Gabriel's Conspiracy*, 196.

44. Egerton, *Gabriel's Rebellion*, 70–77; Michael L. Nicholls, *Whispers of Rebellion: Narrating Gabriel's Conspiracy* (University of Virginia Press, 2013), 69.

45. James Callender to Thomas Jefferson, September 18, 1800, in Schwarz, *Gabriel's Conspiracy*, 83.

46. Egerton, *Gabriel's Rebellion*, 105–9.

47. Thomas Newton to Monroe, September 24, 1800, in Schwarz, *Gabriel's Conspiracy*, 102.

48. Egerton, *Gabriel's Rebellion*, 105.

49. This assertion is based upon the testimonies of participants. See Egerton, *Gabriel's Rebellion*, 58–63.

50. See, for example, *Epitome of the* (Norfolk) *Times*, September 25, 1800, in ibid., 111.

51. Compare Egerton's *Gabriel's Rebellion* to Nicholls's *Whispers of Rebellion*.

52. Egerton, *Gabriel's Rebellion*, 55. For this radical Atlantic world more generally, see Peter Linebaugh and Marcus Rediker, *The Many-Headed Hydra: Sailors, Slaves, and Commoners and the Hidden History of the Revolutionary Atlantic* (Beacon Press, 2001).

53. Confession of Solomon, September 11, 1800, in Schwarz, *Gabriel's Conspiracy*, 37.

54. Sidbury, *Ploughshares into Swords*, 74–79.

55. Trial of James, September 30, 1800, in Schwarz, *Gabriel's Conspiracy*, 129.

56. Trial of Jack Bowler, October 29, 1800, in ibid., 182.

57. John Randolph to Joseph Nicholson, September 26, 1800, in ibid., 112.

58. Observations of Robert Sutcliff, September 25, 1804, in ibid., 238.

59. This is Egerton's argument in *Gabriel's Rebellion*.

60. See Eugene D. Genovese, *From Rebellion to Revolution: Afro-American Slave Revolts in the Making of the Modern World* (University of Louisiana Press, 1979), 3–4.

61. As quoted in Egerton, *Gabriel's Rebellion*, 163.

62. Monroe to Speakers of the General Assembly, December 3, 1800, in Schwarz, *Gabriel's Conspiracy*, 199.

63. Ibid., 200.

64. Thomas Wentworth Higginson, "Gabriel's Defeat," *The Atlantic*, September 1862.

65. As quoted in Sinha, *The Slave's Cause*, 58.

5. Political Harmony: The End and Beginning of the Two-Party System, 1816–24

1. Andrew Jackson to James Monroe, November 12, 1816, in *National Intelligencer* (Washington, DC), May 12, 1824, as quoted in Thomas M. Coens, "The Formation of the Jackson Party, 1822–1825" (PhD diss, Harvard University, 2004), 42.

2. Ibid.

3. Tom Paine, *Common Sense*, full text found at https://americainclass.org/wp-content/uploads/2023/08/Common-Sense-Full-Text.pdf, 29.

4. For the "disaffected," see Aaron Sullivan, *The Disaffected: Britain's Occupation of Philadelphia during the American Revolution* (University of Pennsylvania Press, 2019).

5. These quotes are taken from Jeffrey L. Pasley, "The Two National 'Gazettes': Newspapers and the Embodiment of American Political Parties," *Early American Literature*, Vol. 35, No. 1 (2000), 69–71.

6. This is Pasley's argument, in ibid.

7. David Waldstreicher, *In the Midst of Perpetual Fetes: The Making of American Nationalism, 1776–1820* (University of North Carolina Press, 1997), 201, 203–7.

8. Charles Royster, *A Revolutionary People at War: The Continental Army and American Character, 1775–1783* (University of North Carolina Press, 1979), chap. 1.

9. Billy Coleman, *Harnessing Harmony: Music, Power, and Politics in the United States, 1788–1865* (University of North Carolina Press, 2020), chap. 2.

10. George Dangerfield, *The Era of Good Feelings* (Elephant Paperbacks, 1952; repr., I.R. Dee, 1989), 99.

11. *Eastern Argus* (Portland, ME), March 18, 1817.

12. *American Mercury* (Hartford, CT), July 29, 1817.

13. Charles Bulfinch to James Monroe, July 2, 1817, *The Papers of James Monroe*, University of Mary Washington, Fredericksburg, VA.

14. Monroe to Mr. Bartlett, July 5, 1817, *Papers of James Monroe*.

15. For example, Sean Wilentz titles his chapter on the subject "The Era of Bad Feelings" in *The Rise of American Democracy: Jefferson to Lincoln* (W.W. Norton, 2005), 181.

16. *Dedham* (MA) *Gazette*, July 11, 1817.

17. Andrew H. Browning, *The Panic of 1819: The First Great Depression* (University of Missouri Press, 2019), 8.

18. Thomas Astley, as quoted in ibid., 184.

19. Robert Pierce Forbes, *The Missouri Compromise and Its Aftermath: Slavery and the Meaning of America* (University of North Carolina Press, 2007), 39.

20. Speech of James Tallmadge, *Annals of Congress, Fifteenth Congress, Second Session, Vol. 1* (Governmental Printing Office, 1855), 1205.

21. For contrasting arguments about Monroe's influence on the Missouri Compromise, see Forbes, *The Missouri Compromise*, 64, 83, 89–90, 173–74; John Craig Hammond, "President, Planter, Politician: James Monroe, the Missouri Crisis, and the Politics of Slavery," *Journal of American History*, Vol. 105, No. 4 (March 2019), 843–67.

22. John Quincy Adams, May 22, 1820, *John Quincy Adams: Diaries, Vol. 1, 1779–1821*, ed. David Waldstreicher (Library of America, 2017), 560.

23. Adams, February 3, 1819, *John Quincy Adams: Diaries, Vol. 1*, 470.

24. Adams, February 25, 1821, *John Quincy Adams: Diaries, Vol. 2, 1821–1848*, ed. David Waldstreicher (Library of America, 2017), 594–95.

25. "Jackson's Description of His Experiences During and Immediately Following the Revolutionary War," n.d., *The Papers of Andrew Jackson, Main Series, Vol. 1, 1770–1803*, ed. Michael E. Woods (University of Virginia Press, 2015), 5.

26. John Easton, *The Letters of Wyoming* (1824), 11.

27. Ibid., 5.

28. Ibid., 36.

29. Ibid., 103.

30. James M. Bradley, *Martin Van Buren: America's First Politician* (Oxford University Press, 2024), 4.

31. See Richard Hofstadter, *The Idea of a Party System: The Rise of Legitimate Opposition in the United States, 1780–1840* (University of California, Press, 1970), chap. 4.

32. Martin Van Buren, *Inquiry into the Origin and Course of Political Parties in the United States* (New York, 1867), 3.

33. Martin Van Buren to Thomas Ritchie, January 13, 1827, *The Papers of Martin Van Buren*, Cumberland University, Lebanon, TN.

34. Van Buren, *Political Parties*, 4.

35. Donald Ratcliffe, *The One-Party Presidential Contest: Adams, Jackson, and 1824's Five-Horse Race* (University Press of Kansas, 2015), 154.

36. As quoted in Robert V. Remini, *Henry Clay: Statesman for the Union* (W.W. Norton and Co., 1991), 279.

37. Jackson, as quoted in Lynn Hudson Parsons, *The Birth of Modern Politics: Andrew Jackson, John Quincy Adams, and the Election of 1828* (Oxford University Press, 2011), 106.

38. Sarah J. Purcell, *Sealed with Blood: War, Sacrifice, and Memory in Revolutionary America* (University of Pennsylvania Press, 2002), 179–80.

39. Wheaton, as quoted in Ratcliffe, *One-Party Presidential Contest*, 227.

40. Bradley, *Martin Van Buren*, 159.

41. Coens, "The Formation of the Jackson Party," 241–46.

42. Martin Van Buren to Thomas Ritchie, January 13, 1827, *Papers of Martin Van Buren*.

43. Bradley, *Martin Van Buren*, 186.

44. The term itself, "Democratic Party," would not be used widely until the 1830s.

45. Jackson to John Coffee, as quoted in Robert V. Remini, *Andrew Jackson, Vol. 2, The Course of American Freedom, 1822–1832* (Johns Hopkins University Press, 1981), 138.

46. Remini, *Andrew Jackson, Vol. 2*, 109.

47. John Quincy Adams, First Annual Message, December 6, 1825, reproduced by the Miller Center, University of Virginia, 2022, https://millercenter.org/the-presidency/presidential-speeches/december-6-1825-first-annual-message.

48. As quoted in Remini, *Andrew Jackson, Vol. 2*, 154–55.

6. Economic Equality: The Relief War in Kentucky, 1818–28

1. As quoted in Matthew G. Schoenbachler, *Murder and Madness: The Myth of the Kentucky Tragedy* (University of Kentucky Press, 2009), 110.

2. Ibid., 39–40.

3. Daniel R. Mandell, *The Lost Tradition of Economic Equality in America, 1600–1870* (Johns Hopkins University Press, 2020), 57.

4. James L. Huston, *Securing the Fruits of Labor: The American Concept of Wealth Distribution, 1765–1900* (Louisiana State University Press, 2015), 7.

5. Ibid., 7–19.

6. Richard D. Brown, *Self Evident-Truths: Contesting Equal Rights from the Revolution to the Civil War* (Yale University Press, 2017), 298.

7. Ibid., 19.

8. E.P. Thompson, *The Making of the English Working Class* (Vintage, 1966).

9. Vermont Constitution, Chapter 1, Section II, 1777, reprinted in Vermont State Archives and Records Administration, https://sos.vermont.gov/vsara/learn/constitution/1777-constitution/.

10. J. Hector St. John Crèvecour, *Letters from an American Farmer* (London, 1792), in Project Gutenberg, https://www.gutenberg.org/cache/epub/4666/pg4666-images.html.

11. Noah Webster, "A Citizen of America: An Examination of the Leading Principles of the Federal Constitution" (1787), reprinted in *Teaching American History*, https://teachingamericanhistory.org/document/a-citizen-of-america-an-examination-into-the-leading-principles-of-america/.

12. Constitution of the United States, Article I, Section 10, Clause 1.

13. Steven R. Boyd, "The Contract Clause and the Evolution of American Federalism, 1789–1815," *William and Mary Quarterly*, Vol. 44, No. 3 (July 1987), 529–48.

14. Huston, *Securing the Fruits of Labor*, 83; James L. Bronstein, *Two Nations, Indivisible: A History of Inequality in America* (Praeger, 2016), 3.

15. Bronstein, *Two Nations, Indivisible*, 14.

16. Mandell, *The Lost Tradition of Economic Equality in America*, 50.

17. See Gordon S. Wood, *The Radicalism of the American Revolution* (Vintage Books, 1993), Part 3, for a broad overview.

18. Webster, "A Citizen of America."

19. Mandell, *The Lost Tradition of Economic Equality in America*, 96.

20. John Lauritz Larson, *The Market Revolution in America: Liberty, Ambition, and the Eclipse of the Common Good* (Cambridge University Press, 2010), 40.

21. Andrew H. Browning, *The Panic of 1819: The Nation's First Great Depression* (University of Missouri Press, 2019), 185.

22. Ibid.

23. Ibid., 47.

24. Larson, *The Market Revolution in America*, 41.

25. *Argus of Western America* (Frankfort, KY), March 26, 1819, as quoted in Sandra F. VanBurkleo, "'The Paws of Banks': The Origins and Significance of Kentucky's Decision to Tax Federal Bankers, 1818–1820," *Journal of the Early Republic*, Vol. 9, No. 4 (Winter 1989), 471.

26. Stephen Aron, *How the West Was Lost: The Transformation of Kentucky from Daniel Boone to Henry Clay* (Johns Hopkins University Press, 1996).

27. Theodore W. Ruger, "'A Question Which Convulses a Nation': The Early Republic's Greatest Debate About the Judicial Review Power," *Harvard Law Review*, Vol. 117, No. 3 (January 2004), 841–42.

28. Amos Kendall, *Autobiography of Amos Kendall*, ed. William Stickney (Boston, 1872), 113.

29. Ibid., 126.

30. Ibid., 147.

31. Daniel B. Cole, *A Jackson Man: Amos Kendall and the Rise of American Democracy* (Louisiana State University Press, 2004), 61.

32. *Kentucky Gazette*, May 31, 1819, quoted in William Elsey Connelly and E.M. Coulter, *History of Kentucky, Vol. 2* (American Historical Society, 1922), 607.

33. Sandra Frances VanBurkleo, "'That Our Pure Republican Principles Might Not Wither': Kentucky's Relief Crisis and the Pursuit of 'Moral Justice' 1818–1826" (PhD diss., University of Minnesota, 1988), 121–22. This dissertation has been absolutely critical for this chapter, and I think VanBurkleo for her exceptional work.

34. Kendall, *Autobiography*, 245, quoting from the *Argus*, July 5, 1821.

35. Frank F. Mathias, "The Relief and Court Struggle: Half-Way House to Populism," *Register of the Kentucky Historical Society*, Vol. 71, No. 2 (April 1973), 158.

36. *Argus of Western America*, October 22, 1823, quoted in Billie J. Hardin, "Amos Kendall and the 1824 Relief Controversy," *Register of the Kentucky Historical Society*, Vol. 64, No. 3 (July 1966), 198.

37. Cole, *A Jackson Man*, 85.

38. Ibid., 178.

39. Ibid., 182.

40. See Appendix B in VanBurkleo, "'That Our Pure Republican Principles Might Not Wither.'"

41. *Argus of Western America*, August 21, 1821, quoted in VanBurkleo, "'That Our Pure Republican Principles Might Not Wither,'" 243. Kendall was responding to the lower court decision that preceded the Court of Appeals' decision, but the sentiment was the same.

42. Lewis Tarascon, quoted in VanBurkleo, "'That Our Pure Republican Principles Might Not Wither,'" 313.

43. Ruger, "'A Question Which Convulses a Nation,'" 850.

44. *Louisville Public Advertiser*, January 1, 1825, quoted in Schoenbachler, *Murder and Madness*, 108.

45. Robert Henry Pryor et al. to Andrew Jackson, February 22, 1825, *The Papers of Andrew Jackson, Main Series, Vol. 6, 1825–1828*, 39.

46. Schoenbachler, *Murder and Madness*, 116–17.

47. Ruger, "'A Question Which Convulses a Nation,'" 863.

48. William Barry, as quoted in VanBurkleo, "'That Our Pure Republican Principles Might Not Wither,'" 181.

49. Ruger, "'A Question Which Convulses a Nation,'" 863.

50. Ibid., 871–72.

51. Ruger, "'A Question Which Convulses a Nation,'" 873.

52. *The Patriot* was published anonymously, but all signs point to Kendall as the author. See VanBurkleo, "'That Our Pure Republican Principles Might Not Wither,'" 315.

53. *Argus*, December 17, 1823; *Argus*, February 11, 18, 25, 1824, as quoted in Cole, *A Jackson Man*, 83.

54. Ruger, "'A Question Which Convulses a Nation,'" 854.

55. *The Patriot*, as quoted in VanBurkleo, "'That Our Pure Republican Principles Might Not Wither,'" 321.

56. I borrow this helpful term from Seth Rockman, "What Makes the History of Capitalism Newsworthy?," *Journal of the Early Republic*, Vol. 34, No. 3 (Fall 2014), 447.

57. *Argus*, October 20, 1824, quoted in Hardin, "Amos Kendall," 205.

58. Schoenbachler, *Murder and Madness*, 112–13.

59. Jereboam O. Beauchamp, "The Confession of Jereboam O. Beauchamp," in *The Kentucky Tragedy: A Problem in Romantic Attitudes*, ed. Loren J. Kallsen (Bobbs-Merrill Co., 1963), 5.

60. *Argus*, November 30, 1825, as quoted in Schoenbachler, *Murder and Madness*, 147.

61. Schoenbachler, *Murder and Madness*, 49.

62. This argument is made by both Schoenbachler, *Murder and Madness*, and Dickson D. Bruce Jr., *The Kentucky Tragedy: A Story of Conflict and Change in Antebellum America* (Louisiana State University Press, 2006).

63. Quoted in Clifford F. Thies, "Murder and Inflation in Kentucky," *Quarterly Journal of Austrian Economics*, Vol. 12, No. 4 (2009), 79.

64. J.M. Opal, *Avenging the People: Andrew Jackson, the Rule of Law, and the American Nation* (Oxford University Press, 2017), 178–87.

65. Cole, *A Jackson Man*, 101.

66. Thomas Skidmore, "The Rights of Man to Property!" (New York, 1829), cover page.

67. Cassius M. Clay, "Kentucky's New Deal of the 1820's," *Kentucky State Bar Journal*, December 1939. Presumably this Cassius Clay is a descendant of the abolitionist Cassius Clay, although his name makes him difficult to track (because he was neither the original Cassius Clay nor the Cassius Clay who became Muhammad Ali).

68. Browning, *The Panic of 1819*, 276.

7. Indigenous Rights: The Cherokees' Fight to Remain, 1830–1838

1. Ross to Samuel Cooper, April 17, 1838, *The Papers of Chief John Ross*, Vol. 1, ed. Gary E. Moulton (Oklahoma University Press, 1985), 632.

2. Ross to Job Tyson, January 19, 1838, *Papers of Chief John Ross*, Vol. 1, 583.

3. Akhil Reed Amar, *America's Constitution: A Biography* (Random House, 2005), 107–8.

4. Samantha Seeley, *Race, Removal, and the Right to Remain: Migration and the Making of the United States* (University of North Carolina Press, 2021), 59.

5. Maggie Blackhawk, "The Constitution of American Colonialism," *Harvard Law Review*, Vol. 137, No. 1 (November 2023), 230.

6. Ibid., 205.

7. As quoted in Gregory Ablavsky and W. Tanner Allread, "We the (Native) People: How Indigenous Peoples Debated the U.S. Constitution," *Columbia Law Review*, Vol. 123, No. 2 (March 2023), 275. This paragraph is drawn from this article.

8. Blackhawk, "Constitution of American Colonialism," 226.

9. "Indians Must Have Teachers of Their Own Coular or Nation," November 1791, in *The Collected Writings of Samson Occom: Leadership and Literature in Eighteenth-Century Native America*, ed. Joanna Brooks (Oxford University Press, 2006), 133–34.

10. William Apess, *Experience of Five Christian Indians of the Pequod Tribe* (Boston, 1837), 4.

11. Robert G. Parkinson, *Common Cause: Creating Race and Nation in the American Revolution* (University of North Carolina Press, 2016), 432. See also Peter Silver, *Our Savage Neighbors: How Indian War Transformed Early America* (W.W. Norton, 2009); Patrick Griffin, *American Leviathan: Empire, Nation, and Revolutionary Frontier* (Hill & Wang, 2009); Richard Slotkin, *Regeneration Through Violence: The Mythology of the American Frontier* (Oxford University Press, 2000).

12. Nicholas Guyatt, *Bind Us Apart: How Enlightened Americans Invented Racial Segregation* (Basic Books, 2016), chap. 6.

13. Thomas Jefferson, as quoted in ibid., 144–45.

14. U.S. Treaty with the Cherokee, 1791, *The Avalon Project: Documents in Law, History, and Diplomacy*, Yale Law School, https://avalon.law.yale.edu/18th_century/chr1791.asp.

15. Guyatt, *Bind Us Apart*.

16. See Eric Hinderaker, *Elusive Empires: Constructing Colonialism in the Ohio Valley, 1673–1800* (Cambridge University Press, 2010), Part II.

17. Cody Lynn Berry, "Quatie Ross, 1791–1839," in *Encyclopedia of Arkansas*, last updated September 2022, https://encyclopediaofarkansas.net/entries/quatie-ross-12527/.

18. William G. McLoughlin, *Cherokee Renascence in the New Republic* (Princeton University Press, 1992).

19. Cherokee delegation to James Monroe, March 5, 1819, *Papers of Chief John Ross*, Vol. 1, 35.

20. Constitution of the Cherokee Nation, 1827, p. 1, https://tsla.tnsosfiles.com/digital/teva/transcripts/33638.pdf.

21. Ibid., 2.

22. Memorial of the Cherokee Legislature to the House of Representatives, reprinted in *Cherokee Phoenix*, April 14, 1830.

23. Theda Perdue, "Rising from the Ashes: The Cherokee Phoenix as an Ethnohistorical Source," *Ethnohistory*, Vol. 24, No. 3 (Summer 1977), 213.

24. As quoted in ibid., 211.

25. The scholarship on Indian removal is vast and ever expanding. For a succinct summary, see Christina Snyder, "Many Removals: Re-evaluating the Arc of Indigenous Dispossession," *Journal of the Early Republic*, Vol. 41, No. 4 (Winter 2021), 623–50.

26. Ross et al. to the U.S. Senate and House of Representatives, April 15, 1824, in *Ross Papers*, 1: 78.

27. Mary Hershberger, "Mobilizing Women, Anticipating Abolition: The Struggle Against Indian Removal in the 1830s," *Journal of American History*, Vol. 86, No. 1 (June 1999), 22–23.

28. Jeremiah Evarts, "Essay XXII," reprinted in *Cherokee Removal: The "William Penn" Essays and Other Writings*, ed. Francis Paul Prucha (University of Tennessee, 1981), 177–78.

29. Robert Hare, "A Vindication of the Cherokee Claims, Addressed to the Town Meeting in Philadelphia, on the 11th of January, 1830" (Philadelphia, 1830), https://babel.hathitrust.org/cgi/pt?id=mdp.69015000003810&view=1up&seq=9&skin=2021.

30. Hershberger, "Mobilizing Women, Anticipating Abolition," 18.

31. Martin Van Buren, *The Autobiography of Martin Van Buren, Vol. 2*, ed. John C. Fitzpatrick, reprinted in *Annual Report of the American Historical Association for the Year 1918* (Government Printing Office, 1920), 288.

32. On Northern Indian Removal, see John P. Bowes, *Land Too Good for Indians: Northern Indian Removal* (University of Oklahoma Press, 2016); Claudio Saunt, *Unworthy Republic: The Dispossession of Native Americans and the Road to Indian Territory* (W.W. Norton, 2020).

33. "Remarks of the Honorable David Crockett," *Congressional Record*, Vol. 158, No. 10 (Government Publishing Office, 2012), https://www.govinfo.gov/content/pkg/CREC-2012-01-24/html/CREC-2012-01-24-pt1-PgE63-3.htm.

34. Some historians have used the word "genocide" to describe removal, which I reject for several reasons, but above all for the fact that debates over its use return again and again to semantics and the precise meaning of "genocide" as defined by the United Nations.

35. Jeremiah Evarts, "Draft of a Protest Against the Principles and Policies of the Indian Bill of May, 1830," in *Cherokee Removal*, 249.

36. *Cherokee Nation v. Georgia*, 30 U.S. 1 (1831).

37. *Worcester v. Georgia* 31 U.S. 515 (1832).

38. Ross to Cherokee Delegates, March 30, 1832, *Papers of Chief John Ross*, Vol. 1, 241.

39. Constance Owl, "*Tsalagi Tsulehisanvhi*: Uncovering Cherokee Languages Articles from the *Cherokee Phoenix* Newspaper" (master's thesis, Western Carolina University, 2020), 70–71.

40. This quotation was reported by Horace Greeley in *The American Conflict: A History of the Great Rebellion in the United States of America, 1860–1864* (Hartford, CT, 1865),

106, but Jackson scholars do not believe he said it (although he wrote something with the same meaning).

41. Treaty of New Echota, 1835, in *Indian Affairs: Laws and Treaties, Vol. 2* (Government Printing Office, 1904), 443.

42. Saunt, *Unworthy Republic*, 266.

43. Evarts, "Present State of the Indian Question, to the Editors of the *National Intelligencer*," November 27, 1830, reprinted in *Cherokee Removal*, 280.

44. See especially Saunt, *Unworthy Republic*, 275–81.

45. Lewis Ross to John Ross, March 5, 1838, *Papers of Chief John Ross*, Vol. 1, 605.

46. As listed on the National Congress of American Indians website, https://www.ncai.org/about-tribes.

47. See especially David Treuer, *The Heartbeat of Wounded Knee: Native America from 1890 to the Present* (Riverhead Books, 2019); Kathleen Duval, *Native Nations: A Millennium in North America* (Random House, 2024), Afterword: Sovereignty Today.

48. Saunt, *Unworthy Republic;* Jeffrey Ostler, *Surviving Genocide: Native Nations and the United States from the American Revolution to Bleeding Kansas* (Yale University Press, 2019).

49. For the Trail of Tears National Historic Trail, see "Trail of Tears National Historic Trail," *National Park Service*, last updated April 23, 2025, https://www.nps.gov/trte/index.htm. For Cherokee population figures, see Ana I. Sánchez-Rivera, Paul Jacobs, and Cody Spence, "Detailed Data for Hundreds of American Indian and Alaskan Native Tribes, *U.S. Census Bureau*" (2023), https://www.census.gov/library/stories/2023/10/2020-census-dhc-a-aian-population.html. For an example of the inclusion of the Trail of Tears in textbooks, see the conservative-leaning Thomas A. Bailey and David M. Kennedy, *The American Pageant*, tenth edition (Lexington, MA, 1994), 285. Historians have been documenting the Trail of Tears since the 1930s, beginning with Grant Foreman in *Indian Removal: The Emigration of the Five Civilized Tribes* (University of Oklahoma Press, 1932).

8. Declarations of Independence: The Right to Found a New Nation, 1835–48

1. Organic Laws of Oregon, 1843, reprinted in W.H. Gray, *A History of Oregon: Drawn from Observation and Authentic Information* (Portland, OR: Harris & Holman, 1870), 353.

2. Texas Declaration of Independence, November 7, 1835, reprinted in Texas State Library and Archives Commission, https://www.tsl.texas.gov/exhibits/texas175/declaracion.html.

3. William B. Ide, "Bear Flag Declaration," June 15, 1846, reprinted in Simeon Ide, *A Biographical Sketch of the Life of William B. Ide* (1880), 139–40.

4. April 11, 1844, *The Joseph Smith Papers: Administrative Records: Council of Fifty, Minutes, March 1844–January 1846*, ed. Matthew J. Grow et al. (Church Historian's Press, 2016), 110–14.

5. Jessica Choppin Roney, "An Expansion of the Same Society: Republican Government and Empire in the Early Republic," *Journal of American History*, Vol. 111, No. 1 (June 2024), 15–38, Monroe quotation on p. 31.

6. See Pekka Hämäläinen, *The Comanche Empire* (Yale University Press, 2009) and *Lakota America: A New History of Indigenous Power* (Yale University Press, 2019).

7. Moses Austin, as quoted in Sarah K.M. Rodriguez, "'The Greatest Nation on Earth': The Politics and Patriotism of the First Anglo American Immigrants to Mexican Texas, 1820–1824," *Pacific Historical Review*, Vol. 86, No. 1 (February 2017), 62.

8. Sarah K.M. Rodriguez, *One National Family: Texas, Mexico, and the Making of the United States, 1820–1867* (Baltimore, 2024); Eric R. Schlereth, *Quitting the Nation: Emigrant Rights in North America* (University of North Carolina Press, 2024), chap. 6.

9. Austin, quoted in Rodriguez, "'The Greatest Nation on Earth,'" 82.

10. All quotations are taken from Mirabeau Lamar, "The Inaugural Address of Mirabeau Lamar," in *The Papers of Mirabeau Lamar*, ed. Charles Adam Gulick Jr. (Texas State Library, 1922), 316–27.

11. Lamar, "Notes on the Annexation of Texas," December 10[?], 1838, in *Papers of Mirabeau Lamar*, 324.

12. Thomas Richards Jr., *Breakaway Americas: The Unmanifest Future of the Jacksonian United States* (Johns Hopkins University Press, 2020), 33.

13. Ibid., 150–53.

14. Ibid., 184–86.

15. Much of the following pages is drawn from my essay on Hastings: Thomas Richards Jr., "The Lansford Hastings Imaginary," in *Inventing Destiny: Cultural Explorations of US Expansion*, ed. Jimmy L. Bryan Jr. (University Press of Kansas, 2019), 181–204.

16. Lansford W. Hastings, *The Emigrants' Guide to Oregon and California . . .* (Cincinnati, 1845), 5–7.

17. Ibid., 9.

18. Oregon Organic Laws, May 1844, in "The Oregon Archives, 1841–1843," ed. David C. Duniway and Neil R. Riggs, *Oregon Historical Quarterly*, Vol. 60, No. 2 (June 1959), 273.

19. For details on Champoeg, including the various versions, see Richards, *Breakaway Americas*, 198–200.

20. Ibid., 153–54.

21. John D. Unruh Jr., *The Plains Across: The Overland Emigrants and the Trans-Mississippi West, 1840–1860* (University of Illinois Press, 1979), 119.

22. Thomas J. Farnham to John Marsh, July 6, 1845, Marsh Family Papers, Bancroft Library, University of California Berkeley, Berkeley, CA.

23. John Corrill, as quoted in Melvin C. Johnson, *Polygamy on the Pedernales: Lyman Wight's Mormon Village in Antebellum Texas* (Utah State University Press, 2006), 16.

24. Ibid., 19.

25. Ibid., 47–48.

26. Lyman Wight et al. to the Quorum of the Twelve, February 15, 1844, in, *The Joseph Smith Papers: Administrative Records: Council of Fifty Minutes, March 1844–January 1846*, ed. Ronald K. Esplin et al. (Salt Lake City, 2016), 31 (hereafter *CFM*).

27. All these discussions can be found in Part I, March–June 1844, in *CFM*. For a general summary, see Richards, *Breakaway Americas*, 92–98.

28. Richards, *Breakaway Americas*, 95.

29. Lucien Woodworth statement, *CFM*, 143.

30. Joseph Smith, *Views of the Powers and Policy of the Government of the United States* (1844; repr., Salt Lake City, UT, 1886), 8, 15.

31. Wight, as quoted in Johnson, *Polygamy on the Pedernales*, 30.

32. Ibid., 224–25.

33. John O'Sullivan, "Annexation," *United States Magazine and Democratic Review*, Vol. 17, No. 1 (July–August 1845), 5–10. There was no author listed in the original article, but O'Sullivan was the editor of the magazine and so he was the logical suspect. However, there is some evidence that the actual author was Jane Cazneau. See Linda S. Hudson, *Mistress of Manifest Destiny: A Biography of Jane McManus Storm Cazneau, 1807–1878* (Texas A&M University Press, 2001).

34. "Polk's First Annual Message," December 2, 1845, in *A Compilation of the Messages and Papers of the Presidents*, comp. James D. Richardson (1902), https://gutenberg.org/files/12463/12463.txt.

35. Quotes in Richards, *Breakaway Americas*, 217.

36. Peter Daniel to James K. Polk, March 22, 1845, in *Correspondence of James Polk, Vol. 9*, ed. Wayne Cutler (University of Tennessee Press, 1996), 223.

37. "Polk's Third Annual Message," December 7, 1847, in Richardson, *Compilation*.

38. Richards, *Breakaway Americas*, 239.

39. Ide, "Bear Flag Declaration," 140.

40. Simeon Ide, *A Biographical Sketch of the Life of Sketch of William B. Ide*, 162–63.

41. *CFM*, 336.

42. Richards, *Breakaway Americas*, 114, 234.

43. Little, as quoted in ibid., 234–35.

44. Polk, as quoted in ibid., 235.

45. Joseph Fielding, as quoted in Johnson, *Polygamy on the Pedernales*, 44.

46. Young, as quoted in Richards, *Breakaway Americas*, 100.

47. Wight, quoted in Johnson, *Polygamy on the Pedernales*, 51.

48. D.W. Meinig, *The Shaping of America: A Geographical Perspective on 500 Years of History, Vol. 2, Continental America, 1800–1867* (Yale University Press, 1993).

9. Racial Equality, Part II: The Second American Revolution, 1861–77

1. Frederick Douglass, "What to the Slave is the Fourth of July?" July 4, 1852, reproduced in Blackpast, https://www.blackpast.org/african-american-history/speeches-african-american-history/1852-frederick-douglass-what-slave-fourth-july/.

2. William H. Johnson, *The Celebration of the Eighty-Third Anniversary of the Declaration of American Independence, by the Banneker Institute. Philadelphia, July 4th, 1859* (Philadelphia, 1859), 13–14. All subsequent quotes in this paragraph and the next are taken from this source.

3. William Johnson, *Autobiography of Dr. William Henry Johnson* (The Argus Co., 1900).

4. In the historian Patrick Rael's words, "The United States stands alone as the only society in which controversies over slavery initiated the complete breakdown of national politics, and thus an incredibly bloody civil war that wound up destroying slavery." See Patrick Rael, *Eighty-Eight Years: The Long Death of Slavery in the United States, 1777–1865* (University of Georgia Press, 2015), 240.

5. P. Gabrielle Foreman, "Black Organizing, Print Advocacy, and Collective Authorship: The Long History of the Colored Conventions Movement," in *The Colored Conventions Movement: Black Organizing in the Nineteenth Century*, ed. P. Gabrielle Foreman, Jim Casey, and Sarah Lynn Patterson (University of Pennsylvania, 2021), 28; Manisha Sinha, *The Slave's Cause: A History of Abolition* (Yale University Press, 2016), 216–17.

6. *The Liberator* (Boston), January 1, 1831.

7. John L. Brooke, *"There Is a North": Fugitive Slaves, Political Crisis, and Cultural Transformation in the Coming of the Civil War* (University of Massachusetts Press, 2019), 37.

8. Sarah L. H. Gronningsater, "'Expressly Recognized by Our Election Laws': Certificates of Freedom and the Multiple Fates of Black Citizenship in the Early Republic," *William and Mary Quarterly*, Vol. 75, No. 3 (July 2018), 505. This paragraph is also drawn from Van Gosse, *The First Reconstruction: Black Politics in America from the Revolution to the Civil War* (University of North Carolina Press, 2021); Kate Masur, *Until Justice Be Done: America's First Civil Rights Movement, from the Revolution to Reconstruction* (W.W. Norton and Co., 2021).

9. Van Gosse, *The First Reconstruction*, 448.

10. Ibid., 179–80.

11. "Constitution of the American Society of Free Persons of Colour, for improving their condition in the United States; for purchasing lands; and for the establishment of a settlement in upper Canada, also, The Proceedings of the Convention with their Ad-

dress to Free Persons of Colour in the United States" (Philadelphia, 1830), Colored Conventions Project, Digital Records, accessed February 10, 2024, https://omeka.coloredconventions.org/items/show/70.

12. David Walker, *Walker's Appeal in Four Articles; Together with a Preamble, to the Coloured Citizens of the World, but in Particular, and Very Expressly, to Those of the United States of America* (Boston, 1829), 83, reprinted in *Documenting the American South*, https://docsouth.unc.edu/nc/walker/walker.html.

13. *The Liberator*, January 1, 1831.

14. Henry Highland Garnet, "An Address to the Slaves of the United States" (1843), Blackpast, https://www.blackpast.org/african-american-history/1843-henry-highland-garnet-address-slaves-united-states/.

15. Van Gosse, *The First Reconstruction*, 48.

16. William Cooper Nell, *The Colored Patriots of the American Revolution, with Sketches of Several Distinguished Colored Persons* (Boston, 1855), 380.

17. Douglass, "What to the Slave is the Fourth of July?"

18. Sinha, *The Slave's Cause*, 492–95.

19. Abraham Lincoln, First Lincoln-Douglas Debate, August 21, 1858, Ottawa, Illinois, reprinted in "Lincoln Home," National Park Service, https://www.nps.gov/liho/learn/historyculture/debate1.htm.

20. On Lincoln's view of the Founding, see Lucas E. Morel, *Lincoln and the American Founding* (Southern Illinois University Press, 2020).

21. Abraham Lincoln, "Reply to the Dred Scott Decision," June 26, 1857, Teaching American History, https://teachingamericanhistory.org/document/reply-to-the-dred-scott-decision/.

22. Alexander Stephens, "Cornerstone Speech," March 21, 1861, reprinted in "American Battlefield Trust," https://www.battlefields.org/learn/primary-sources/cornerstone-speech.

23. Michael D. Hattem, *The Memory of '76: The Revolution in American History* (Yale University Press, 2024), 91.

24. James M. McPherson, *Battle Cry of Freedom: The Civil War Era* (Oxford University Press, 1988), 245.

25. As quoted in Rael, *Eighty-Eight Years*, 244. To be sure, many Southerners invoked the Revolution in some way to defend secession, but in ways that defined the American Revolution as a conservative defense of Americans' rights against British aggression, not a revolutionary change (which, of course, was also a legacy of the American Revolution, as we have seen). See Jason Phillips, *Looming Civil War: How Nineteenth-Century Americans Imagined the Future* (Oxford University Press, 2019), 132–35.

26. Phillips, *Looming Civil War*, 141–43.

27. "Republican Party Platform," June 18, 1856, The American Presidency Project, https://www.presidency.ucsb.edu/documents/republican-party-platform-1856.

28. Daniel R. Biddle and Murray Dubin, *Tasting Freedom: Octavius Catto and the Battle for Equality in Civil War America* (Temple University Press, 2010), 156–58.

29. Henry Highland Garnet to Octavius Catto, March 14, 1860, Leon Gardiner Collection, Historical Society of Pennsylvania (HSP), Philadelphia.

30. Harry C. Silcox, "Nineteenth Century Philadelphia Black Militant: Octavius V. Catto (1839–1871)," *Pennsylvania History*, Vol. 44, No. 1 (January 1977), 55–57.

31. Octavius Catto to Jacob White, October 10, 1870, Leon Gardiner Collection, HSP.

32. Ibid.

33. Stephanie McCurry, *Confederate Reckoning: Power and Politics in the Civil War South* (Harvard University Press), 226–33.

34. Abraham Lincoln, First Inaugural Address, March 4, 1861, *The Avalon Project*, Yale Law School, https://avalon.law.yale.edu/19th_century/lincoln1.asp.

35. George Templeton Strong, diary entry for April 18, 1861, in Allan Nevins and Milton Halsey Thomas, eds., *Diary of George Templeton Strong, Vol. 3, 1860–1865* (Macmillan, 1952), 124.

36. Critics of the Emancipation Proclamation, most famously Richard Hofstadter, point out that an order freeing slaves in Confederate territory not controlled by the Union meant that no slaves were actually freed at the time it was issued. I find this position trivial. The proclamation fundamentally transformed the nature of the war, and everyone at the time—white and black, Northerner and Southerner—knew it.

37. On this point, see especially William W. Freehling, *The South vs. the South: How Anti-Confederate Southerners Shaped the Course of the Civil War* (Oxford University Press, 2001).

38. Jonathan C. Gibbs, as quoted in Daniel R. Biddle and Murray Dubin, "'God Is Setteling the Account': African American Reaction to Lincoln's Emancipation Proclamation," *Pennsylvania Magazine of History and Biography*, Vol. 137, No. 1 (January 2013), 73.

39. Silcox, "Nineteenth Century Philadelphia Black Militant," 59.

40. Black Volunteers recruiting poster, n.d., Leon Gardiner Collection, HSP.

41. Memoranda, 1863, reprinted in *Memorable Days: The Emilie Davis Diaries*, Falvey Library, Villanova University, Villanova, PA, https://davisdiaries.villanova.edu/memoranda-1863-2/.

42. Ibid., June 18–20, https://davisdiaries.villanova.edu/june_18-20_1863/.

43. Ibid.

44. Silcox, "Nineteenth Century Philadelphia Black Militant," 61.

45. *Christian Recorder* (Philadelphia), April 22, 1865.

46. Blacks did serve in the War of 1812, but not as soldiers in the U.S. Army. They either served in the navy or were raised as part of emergency forces, e.g., Andrew Jackson's army at the Battle of New Orleans.

47. William Johnson, March 9, 1862, in Edwin S. Redkey, ed., *A Grand Army of Black Men: Letters from African-American Soldiers in the Union Army, 1861–1865* (Cambridge University Press, 1992), 18.

48. Eric Foner, *The Second Founding: How the Civil War and Reconstruction Remade the Union* (W.W. Norton, 2019), 38.

49. James Oakes, *Freedom National: The Destruction of Slavery in the United States, 1861–1865* (W.W. Norton, 2014), 309.

50. Ibid., 361–62.

51. Abraham Lincoln, April 11, 1865, Last Public Address, *The American Presidency Project*, ed. John Woolley and Gerhard Peters, https://www.presidency.ucsb.edu/documents/the-presidents-last-public-address.

52. *Philadelphia Press*, December 5, 1865.

53. Andrew Diemer, "Reconstructing Philadelphia: African Americans and Politics in the Post–Civil War North," *Pennsylvania Magazine of History and Biography*, Vol. 133, No. 1 (January 2009), 36.

54. *Proceedings of the States Equal Rights' Convention of the Colored People of Pennsylvania, Held in the City of Harrisburg, February 8th, 9th, and 10th, 1865* . . . (1865), reprinted in HathiTrust, https://babel.hathitrust.org/cgi/pt?id=mdp.39015027011892&seq=7&q1=Catto.

55. *Christian Recorder* (Philadelphia), June 30, 1866.

56. *Christian Recorder* (Philadelphia), April 22, 1865.

57. Sojourner Truth, May 9, 1867, Address to the First Annual Meeting of the American Equal Rights Association, reprinted in Society for the Study of American Women Writers, https://www.lehigh.edu/~dek7/SSAWW/writTruthAddress.htm.

58. As quoted in Foner, *The Second Founding*, 86–87. See these pages for the pragmatism of Radical Republicans more generally.

59. *National Anti-Slavery Standard* (New York), February 2, 1867.

60. Foner, *The Second Founding*, 77.

61. *Chronicle of the Union League, 1862–1902* (William Fell and Co., 1902), 462.

62. *Public Ledger* (Philadelphia), April 27, 1870.

63. Ibid.

64. *The Age* (Philadelphia), October 13, 1868, quoted in Diemer, "Reconstructing Philadelphia," 48.

65. Diemer, "Reconstructing Philadelphia," 50–51.

66. Biddle and Dubin, *Tasting Freedom*, 413.

67. Diemer, "Reconstructing Philadelphia," 53.

68. For the most detailed description of the day, see Biddle and Dubin, *Tasting Freedom*, 421–30.

69. As quoted in ibid., 432.

70. *Philadelphia Press*, October 12, 1870, as quoted in Diemer, "Reconstructing Philadelphia," 53.

Conclusion

1. *New York Tribune*, as quoted in ibid., 87.

2. Noah Andre Trudeau, *Like Men of War: Black Troops in the Civil War, 1862-1865* (Little, Brown, and Co., 1998), 146. Although we do not have evidence that Tomlinson himself heard it, it seems impossible he would *not* have, since the cry was considerable.

3. *Lancaster* (PA) *Daily Intelligencer*, October 28, 1880.

4. The original phrase comes from Evan Thomas, "Founders Chic: Live from Philadelphia," *Newsweek*, July 8, 2001, https://www.newsweek.com/founders-chic-live-philadelphia-154791.

5. Beverly Gage, "America Is Suffering an Identity Crisis," *The Atlantic*, October 14, 2014, https://www.theatlantic.com/ideas/archive/2024/10/america-birthday-national-story/680248/.

6. Donald Trump, "CONGESTION PRICING IS DEAD. Manhattan, and all of New York, is SAVED. LONG LIVE THE KING!," @TheWhiteHouse, February 19, 2025, *X*.

7. Thomas Paine, *Common Sense* (Dover Publications, 1997), 27.

8. Ibid., 13, 45.

9. Ibid., 17.

10. Ibid., 23.

11. Ibid., 30–31.

12. Ibid., 52.

13. Ibid., 40.

14. Ibid., 5.

15. I am hardly the only person to make this point. See, for example, Yoni Applebaum, "How Progressives Froze the American Dream," *The Atlantic*, March 2025.

Index

About the Author

Thomas Richards Jr. teaches history at Springside Chestnut Hill Academy in Philadelphia and holds a PhD in History from Temple University. The author of *Breakaway Americas: The Unmanifest Future of the Jacksonian United States*, he lives in Gulph Mills, Pennsylvania, where George Washington and his army once camped.

Publishing in the Public Interest

Thank you for reading this book published by The New Press; we hope you enjoyed it. New Press books and authors play a crucial role in sparking conversations about the key political and social issues of our day.

We hope that you will stay in touch with us. To keep up to date with our books, events, and the issues we cover, follow us on social media and sign up for our newsletter at thenewpress.org.

Please consider buying New Press books not only for yourself, but also for friends and family and to donate to schools, libraries, community centers, prison libraries, and other organizations involved with the issues our authors write about.

The New Press is a 501(c)(3) nonprofit organization; if you wish to support our work with a tax-deductible gift please visit https://thenewpress.org/donate/ or use the QR code below.